W9-ADY-950

PAUL BÉNICHOU is Professor of Romance Languages and Literature at Harvard University where he teaches during the Spring Term. He is the author of *L'Écrivain et Ses Travaux.*

Man and Ethics

Studies in French Classicism

PAUL BÉNICHOU

Translated by Elizabeth Hughes

Anchor Books
Doubleday & Company, Inc.
Garden City, New York
1971

Morales du Grand Siècle published by Editions Gallimard

Anchor Books edition: 1971

Library of Congress Catalog Card Number 69-20104

Printed in the United States of America

Table of Contents

Introduction

This study grew out of a desire to bring to light some of the relationships that bound together the social and moral conditions of life during a famous century. We have used as our point of departure the common-sense principle, indispensable to all criticism, that moral thought, whether explicit or only obscurely present, has its natural roots and sphere of action in men's lives and interrelationships, especially when such thought emerges in widely read literary works. We have tried to discern the many forms this relationship assumed in one of the best known of literary epochs.

This attitude does not derive from indifference or disdain for value problems, but rather from the desire to pose these problems in their proper terms. We do not cease to judge ideas when we describe their meaning and their source. Such an approach can stem from more than a love of the concrete or a desire to consider ideas as facts, which, from one angle, they undoubtedly are; for when we bring to light the variable conditions in which certain judgments on man or ideas of the good have originated we also make possible a sounder appraisal of these judgments or these ideas. How else can we assess, in the moral values of the past, that which transcends particular circumstances and bears a relation to the human condition in our own times, or even to those elements in the human condition that are presumably the least subject to change? Constructive thought has nothing to gain from an excess of confidence; illusion is the most common cause of its frailty.

Specialists who deal with the literature and thought of the seventeenth century, in fact, often allow considerations of social history to enter into their general judgments. Modern French criticism, from its beginnings with Sainte-Beuve, or even Victor Cousin, seems to be permeated by a concern to relate seventeenth-century ideas on man to social conditions.

This concern was later intensified by an increasing awareness of the conflict of ideas, the moral variations, and the clash of various currents that beneath a semblance of majestic unity form the basis of classic French literature.

Nothing could better reinforce the sense of what is real and what is relative than an awareness of the diversity and contradictions at the heart of things. It is not enough to distinguish an epoch, a milieu, a social environment; every period is a battleground of diverse forces and contrary ideas. The relationship of literature and society is not that of two homogeneous spheres made on each other's likeness. Each is governed by the laws of diversity and contradiction, and it is from this point of view that we can best perceive their interdependence. Ideas seem all the more closely bound to society the more we conceive of them as the elements of a debate that accompanies and stimulates the real conflicts of history.

At the end of the last century and the beginning of our own, no one disputed the theory that there were two different seventeenth-century literatures: that of the sublime, the brilliant, the romanesque, and that of nature and truth. This view, systematized with a good deal of exaggeration by Brunetière, ultimately replaced, though not without difficulty, the traditional idea held by an enlightened reading public that the seventeenth century was an age of serene uniformity. We do violence to truth when we try to make these two contrasting frames of mind coincide with two different periods, divided approximately by the year 1660. The two trends have long coexisted intertwined with one another, alternately blending and struggling against one another, and in the tangle it is not easy to discern either sudden changes of fortune or decisive dates. But even simplification opens up certain suggestive views. It helps us to perceive in the literary evolution of the seventeenth century, sketched in such bold contrasts, and in the profound moral evolution it reflects, the real contours of its political history. In this reconstruction the period of noble sentiments, of romances, of heroic poems, and brilliant poetry is the period of aristocratic restlessness; the triumph of reason and of nature is that of the already bourgeois reign of Louis XIV. The notion of such a division is frequently found, with more or less solid support, among the writers of the nineteenth century. After thorough study one might be tempted to describe the seventeenth century as the last battlefield between the ethics of feudalism and those of the modern world.

But the conflict thus established between two fundamental tendencies at the heart of the seventeenth century tends to take on a noticeably different aspect when we attempt to describe it on a moral rather than a literary plane. Henceforth, the terms no longer oppose imagination that turns to lofty themes and common sense in search of truth, nor even the cult of the ideal and that of the real. The debate becomes a more impassioned and more immediate one, on the excellence or the mediocrity of human nature. All conflicts in seventeenth century thought, as soon as they attain some gravity and some breadth, have for their final object the evaluation of humanity. The writers of this period are distinguished not so much by their preference for the beautiful or for the true as by the stronger or weaker case they make for human virtue, understood in the general sense of valor, strength, and magnanimity. And on these grounds, the only proper ones, the debate is not merely confined to the conflict of two opposing factors, or two clearly conflicting camps, one that exalts humanity and another that depreciates it. Reaching out in all directions, jointly influencing ethics and psychology, both of which provide weapons for the conflict, drawing in even religious thought in order to divide it, the argument on man defies facile formulas and summary interpretations. The seventeenth century knew several different moralities which were in alliance or opposition in various ways according to circumstances. He who would simplify must distinguish at least three centers of interest: a heroic ethics, which opens the way for nature to rise to greatness and defines the conditions thereof; a rigorous Christian ethics, which attaches no value at all to human nature; and finally a worldly ethics, lacking both illusions and anguish, which denies us greatness without stripping us of confidence. The problem of social influences thus grows more difficult, and the usual contrast between feudal France and modern France appears inadequate for the forces involved are more detailed and more complex. Yet a happy accident, or better still the very nature of things, determined that the three fundamental conceptions just defined would be found in an almost pure state in the three greatest moralists of this century, Corneille, Pascal, Molière. And this makes it possible for this essay on the moral trends of the seventeenth century to retain the traditional form of a series of studies on the most important classical authors.

As a result of all this, we have deliberately neglected the purely esthetic or literary discussions pursued throughout the seventeenth century, and those elements in the classical works that could be related to such discussions, so as to consider only the ethical aspect of the authors' creations. The interpenetration of esthetic and moral values, as close in the literature of the seventeenth century as in any other, imposes further analysis and ultimately a whole new task on anyone attempting to define their relationship. Consequently we have limited ourselves to considering the classic writers from the point of view of ethics, dealing with that aspect of their works which claims to be concerned with the basic problems of life and human conduct. We see literature above all as the crucible in which our direct experience of life and society is elaborated philosophically, but without loss of immediacy. French literature, more than any other, fits this definition. There is no other literature that reveals in such a striking manner how the problems of life are bound up with those of the mind. That is precisely what is meant when we call it the literature of moralists.

In trying to define the complex relationships between social life and thought, however, one may jeopardize the individuality of great writers by trying to integrate them into an impersonal whole that transcends them. Thus, in pursuing a hazardous systematization, one runs the risk of distorting those idiosyncratic realities–so privileged within our human patrimony–that we call great men and great works. The contradiction between the individual and the social can, however, be rather easily solved when approached without preconceptions. More important, I have tried to keep in view at all times the relationship of the writer's individual attitudes to the more general social debate in which they occur. In the pages that follow I have attempted to show the connection between writer and milieu in its most natural, obvious aspect, as it always appears once we are familiarized with a particular historical period. In doing this I hope to escape from the reproach so often leveled at this method, that it destroys realities by substituting abstractions for them, a reproach often accompanied by its contrary, that universal human values have taken second place to the contingencies of social history. For it is precisely between the writer's concrete reality and the general phenomenon of man that society is to be found, in that vast milieu where changes transcend the individual while maintaining the continuity of the species. But it is also from this vantage point that one can see in their true light both the individual significance of a given thinker and the universal import of his thought. If we must consider as an illusion the thinker's conviction that he has come face to face with the human condition, and that his ideas are only faithful reflections of what his eyes see, this is no offense to thought. Whatever protests reason might offer, one must admit that thought, like everything else, is relative to circumstances. Nor is there any conflict here with the spirit or the methods of science which, when it studies the emergence of ethical values, cannot be better defined than by its obligation to criticize vigorously the illusions of the individual mind. The essential thing is to perform this duty with prudence, with the sole purpose of giving the work under study all the meaning and all the richness that it truly contains, independently of the consciousness of its author. The essays that follow are meant to serve no other purpose.

Man and Ethics

The Hero in Corneille

Few great writers have been so hastily judged as Corneille. There are many reasons for this, the most powerful of which is probably the aversion most of us feel for moralizing literature, a category to which our schoolday recollections have consigned the tragedies of Corneille. A fairly widespread revival of interest in Corneille over the last several years has hardly influenced the general public. For the average reader of our times Corneille remains a kind of exaggerated classic, in whose works the literary proprieties common to an entire school are reinforced by a dehumanized moral propriety. So we have continued to deny him the sympathy which we accord to Racine or Molière for the boldness of their genius.

But in fact, we had to go a long way–and distance does not necessarily help one to see clearly–to succeed in making Corneille's name a symbol of hostility to the natural forces of life. Rightly or wrongly, his contemporaries admired him for his fire, his dash, and his ardor. Saint-Évremond, for example, writes that Corneille "elevates the soul," and concedes to Racine the feeble advantage of "winning over the mind."[1] Similarly, Mme. de Sévigné admires in Corneille "those tirades . . . that make one shiver."[2] Corneille himself, in his *Examen,* of *Le Cid,* (a critical study written almost thirty years after his tragedy) remembered having observed during its first performances that when Rodrigue came to Chimène's house after the duel, "at the moment this unhappy lover appeared in her presence a certain stirring could be heard in the audience, which betrayed a marvelous expectation . . ." The memory of this Corneille was still alive among the Romantics, in France

[1] Saint-Évremond, *Jugement sur quelques auteurs français,* in Vol. V of the *Oeuvres mêlées,* Amsterdam edition (1706).

[2] Letter of March 16, 1672.

and abroad, who willingly exempted him from their attacks against the coldness and vapidity of the classical style. Enthusiasm was certainly the natural medium of Corneille's tragedy; those nineteenth-century critics who strove to rediscover the atmosphere of his public felt this, even when they yielded in other respects to prevailing ideas on Corneille. Sainte-Beuve conjures up the excited audience of *Le Cid;*[3] Guizot links the admiration aroused in the audience by Corneille's tragedies to a "heightened awareness of our own existence."[4]

Yet already in the seventeenth century other voices were making themselves heard. Without denying altogether Corneille's power to sweep one along, some felt that this power acted only on the higher faculties, and they were tempted to dismiss as cold an author who inflamed only one's intelligence and moral sensibility. La Bruyère, and occasionally Boileau, incline to this judgment, which obviously implies all kinds of reservations in their admiration. In Longpierre's *Parallèle de M. Corneille et de M. Racine* (1686) we read, "The first injects intelligence, that is to say, brilliance and ideas, everywhere. . . . The heart grows cold, while the mind is excited." In this comparison, only Racine speaks to the heart; it is the opposite, point for point, of what Saint-Évremond said. Thus in Corneille's own century, he is at one point praised to the skies for his power to ignite emotions, and at another denied both heat and passion.

This is in reality a contradiction between two successive but related moments in French society. Passion in Corneille was entirely steeped in the atmosphere of aristocratic pride, glory, nobility, and romance that pervaded France during the reign of Louis XIII, and permeated the entire literature of that epoch. Under Louis XIV, the sublime as Corneille had envisioned it already seemed a bit archaic, and when Mme. de Sévigné wrote in 1672, "Long live our old friend Corneille," she was doubtless thinking not only of the age of his works but of the even greater age of their inspiration. A

[3] Sainte-Beuve, *Nouveaux lundis,* Vol. VII, articles on Corneille, 1864.

[4] Guizot, *Corneille et son temps,* 1852.

half-century after *Le Cid* the old themes of greatness that had regained popularity in Corneille's time began to appear less exciting. Why should we be surprised then, that at the end of the nineteenth century, at a distance of almost three centuries, readers often had difficulty in appreciating the inspiration that animates Corneille's work? Deprived of its natural life and movement, Corneille's concept of the sublime ultimately drew itself up above the passions in frigid splendor. The *bien pensant* bourgeoisie of the nineteenth century was attracted to the notion of an almost puritanical Corneille, sublime in a bourgeois fashion by the value he placed on self-constraint and effort.

Nevertheless it was very difficult to explain the irregularities of sentiment and behavior in Corneille's heroes solely in terms of duty.[5] To obviate the difficulty Brunetière introduced a subtle distinction between duty, which is often ill-treated in the theater of Corneille, and will, which always prevails. It cannot be said that everything turns out in favor of sound morals in Corneille's plays, "but what is truer, what is even absolutely true, is that the theater of Corneille is the glorification or the apotheosis of the will."[6] If we can still profit morally from Corneille's theater it is thanks to this distinction, since the striving of the will, even when it is badly directed, is in essence laudable. In Corneille, even the morally irregular teaches us the value of energy. It is up to us to put it to better use than did his heroes. Jules Lemaître,[7] more careful in his distinctions and also more contradictory, discovers behind the renowned will of Corneille an inordinate pride, an "inflated ambition," that at certain moments seems to scandalize him; nevertheless, he concludes, for the indispensable edification of his readers, that "Corneille remains our great master of energy," without further concern for either the nature or the source of that energy. Adhering more closely to Brunetière's

[5] Chimène marries her father's murderer, Horace kills his sister, Cinna conspires against his benefactor, etc.

[6] Brunetière, *Études critiques,* 6th series.

[7] J. Lemaître, *Corneille,* in Petit de Julleville's *Histoire de la langue et de la littérature française.*

view and carrying it ever further, Lanson[8] completely rules out the world of emotions as an active ingredient in the theater of Corneille. "Tension, the power of the will," he writes, "this is the whole perspective from which Corneille looks at the human soul." And he specifies that this will, in every move it makes, carries out a decision dictated by reason. What is left of the old image of Corneille in such a judgment? Are we to believe that his first admirers understood him so poorly?

Corneille's idea of the sublime is not peculiar to him; it permeates the tragic theater of his time. Extraordinary figures of noble character people the tragedies of Rotrou, Mairet, Tristan, Du Ryer. And what first strikes one in these authors, as in Corneille, is the lofty tone, the proud stance of the heroes they hold up to the audience as models. Neither restraint nor muted desire seems to characterize the *grandes âmes* as they were then conceived; in all of them we find the sublime in the same glorious and ostentatious form, the same showy display of the powers of the ego, the same glorification of pride and of love. In this respect Corneille and his contemporaries were echoing a tradition of fairly distant origin. At first glance it may seem anachronistic to apply the term *feudal* to Corneille's inspiration. But there is no other word to designate what persists, in the psychology of the well-born gentleman of the seventeenth century, of the old ideas of heroism and bravado, magnanimity, devotion to duty, and ideal love, all opposed to the aristocracy's more modern tendencies toward simple moral elegance or *honnêteté*. The ideas, the sentiments, and the behavior that formed a part of feudal life were still alive long after the decline of feudalism. No violent revolution had struck down the old institutions; they had changed gradually, and the spirit of adventure, the noble individualism, the taste for unattainable extremes and dramatic sublimations had never completely disappeared. In fact, in the modern period it is during the age of Corneille that the older moral themes of the aristocracy came to life again with the greatest intensity.

[8] Lanson, *Corneille,* 1898.

We cannot retrace here the history and vicissitudes of aristocratic idealism from the Middle Ages to Corneille. But there exists an uninterrupted current of thought which the Renaissance modified, and in a sense reinforced, rather than reversed. The prestige of heroic chivalry was revived when contact was established once more with the rediscovered heroes of antiquity, as seen through the eyes of Plutarch or Seneca. Similarly, the ideal of love inherited from the Middle Ages drew new strength from the rediscovery of Plato. Thus the heroic ideal of the feudal centuries and the theory of courtly love were continuously refurbished and enriched up to the time of *Le Cid,* when favorable social conditions, the renewed prestige of the nobility, and political unrest created the conditions for their most dazzling development. It is in this sense that Corneille's feudal inspiration can be considered both a strong and distant influence. In discovering this influence we strip off the mask that has concealed Corneille's true features; we see in his moral view something other than the repression of nature; and we understand that a certain kind of passion, inseparable from the aristocratic tradition, inspires all of his heroes.

Aristocratic society never considered the condemnation of the passions a prerequisite of human worth. They were hardly able to imagine what we call the moral imperative, that abstract obligation imposed on us from without. The yoke that moral law usually imposes on our desires is the same that society imposes on individuals. Now it is characteristic of feudalism that the social yoke does not weigh too heavily on the nobles. For them virtue cannot lie in deprivation, in the painful restraint that duty imposes on the ego's desires. On the contrary, every virtue is of necessity rooted in their own nature. Their only duty is to be worthy of themselves, to raise their sights high enough, and to give lesser men sufficiently edifying examples of their greatness. They owe it to themselves to disdain paltry ambitions, to despise all things that common people can reach as well as they. Consequently pride seconds, judges, and approves all their desires. This simple and forceful moral mechanism, in which the self is constantly exalted, does not at all imply a real condemnation of nature; on the contrary, it portrays nature so favorably that from the Middle Ages on it is consistently denounced by Christian moralists. As universal disciplinary power the Church fulfilled its function by censuring aristocratic pride; lay society nonetheless continued to live and think as it pleased. The advent of modern times did not appreciably change this situation. Rather, the Renaissance and the return to the sources of antiquity reawakened the audacity of the aristocratic ego, endowed the old appetite for success and glory with the prestige of philosophic thought, and once again confronted the Church, this time more directly, with the problem of adapting a Christian doctrine to the aristocratic ethic. In a sense, the contact with pagan antiquity led to a newly bold affirmation of modernized aristocratic values, to a glorification of human power as embodied in the aristocrat. Without cutting itself off from its origins, the old noble ethic emerges in a new light, closer to our own, in which its own peculiar physiognomy is sometimes overlooked. Yet it is scarcely altered, and with only a little effort we can perceive once more its real contours beneath the already modern form of Corneille's tragedies.

It is difficult to imagine drama that has no strong emotional impact. And in point of fact, emotions permeate all of Corneille's theater. They form the first, but always visible thread of the complicated fabric that would unravel if ambition, love, and family interests did not hold all the parts together. It is true that the way in which the emotions behave in Corneille's characters is enough to bewilder modern readers. Today, because of our naturalistic tradition, common sense sees passion as above all a violent seizure, alien to every sentiment of dignity, and more apt to result in the obliteration of the ego than in its exaltation. The tragic aspect of the passions is inseparable from moral catastrophes or personal disaster. All of naturalistic literature from Racine to the present has been based on this concept. It is this view that falsifies the eternal parallel of Corneille and Racine: since Corneille is not the poet of perdition, he is considered, in contrast to his successor, an enemy of the passions. But in the tradition from which he draws his inspiration it is quite the reverse: desires, however impetuous they may be, are linked to the glorifications of pride. And it is precisely in this way that the idea of virtue finds its way into the life of great men and corrects the derangement of instinct. Corneille's sublime springs less from the austerity of duty than from the impulses of a proud nature.

Of course there is in the very nature of pride itself, a principle of restraint with respect to the spontaneous impulses of nature. This is so true that common sense, adopting the reciprocal proposition a bit too rapidly, is apt to discover hidden pride at the root of all moral severity. It is nonetheless true that an ethics which is truly rigorous toward the passions normally condemns pride, and that the puritan cannot be accused of pride without at the same time being accused of hypocrisy. In the feudal character, in which this kind of hypocrisy is the least of faults, pride is asserted with as much ingenuity as insolence. Glory and the desires are constantly interwoven, more often sustaining than contradicting one another. If pride demands a preliminary concession from desire, that concession is amply rewarded by a resounding success which is much more evident, as in the case of a Rodrigue, than is the tragic aspect of sacrifice. We cannot emphasize too strongly the profound optimism of this idea, in which the demands of virtue are always less costly than the ultimate rewards, in which virtue is based less on effort than on a permanent bias in favor of the satisfactions of glory as opposed to those of pure and simple pleasure, when ill fortune forces us to choose between them.

We are by no means always forced to make such a choice. Far from being mutually exclusive, glory and the satisfaction of desire are more often identical. Their unity is the first datum of Corneille's theater, the basis for his complicated elaborations of heroism. The rough framework of this system is clearly visible in the many scenes in which noble sentiment springs from a rivalry of ambition that to us may appear trivial. For instance, when Don Gormas is denied an important office he vents his wrath in the presence of Don Diègue, who has been entrusted with that office and rejoices in it. A scene such as this seemed in its own way great. From the outset, a conflict of interests appears with all the trappings of a rivalry for glory. Every passion–hatred, desire, resentment–is turbulently chained into pride, and all discourse ends in defiance. In this way Corneille transcends the simple dramatic interest of the scene; sympathy, earnestly evoked, becomes a passion. On this level such sympathy is still quite naïve, as naïve and elementary as the impulses that awaken it. The identification of triumphant ambition with glory, the ingenuous display of the ego, the struggle between wounding pride and wounded pride–we have here the whole archaic aspect of Corneille's dramas. Nevertheless, right up to our own times this Corneille has continued to move audiences; one can imagine the effect he must have had on his first audiences, with whom he had everything in common. In what still survived of feudal society at that time, the supreme values were ambition, daring, and success. The weight of the sword and boldness in one's desire and speech constituted excellence; evil consisted in weakness or timidity, in the paucity of desire and daring, and in sustaining an offense without inflicting one in return–these were enough to exclude one from the ranks of the great and consign one to the common herd.

An inflated love of greatness and a tendency to glorify oneself mark almost indistinguishably all of Corneille's characters: the notion of "glory" stamps them all with a family resemblance. Nicomède is often cited, for example, singing the praises of his own merit in every key and making of a whole tragedy a hymn to his own heroism; and yet Nicomède does not differ essentially from the others. Rodrigue may suffer more intensely, but he thinks no less highly of himself. Horace, brought before the king and accused of the murder of his sister, does not lose sight of his own worth–

> I will not boast of what my arm has wrought;
> Your Majesty, Sire, witnessed my three combats:
> It would be hard for another to match them . . .
> So that in order to leave an illustrious memory
> Only death today can preserve my glory.[9]

[9] *Horace,* V, 2.

To be thorough one would have to summon as witnesses all of Corneille's heroes; for any of them, self-doubt would constitute a demission from heroism.

For Corneille's women, glory consists in the conquest of a powerful husband, especially a royal husband–witness those princesses who are prey to a real obsession with the throne, from *Rodogune* on. One is Princess Aglatide, who is loath to wed the prince who has been chosen for her and cries out guilelessly,

> He is not a king, I tell you, and that is a
> great shortcoming.[10]

More impressive still is Domitie in *Tite et Bérénice,* who first falls in love with Domitian, the Emperor Titus' brother, and accounts for her feelings with the following words–

> I saw him and loved him. Condemn not my passion:
> Nothing greater than he then dazzled my soul.

She loves him as long as Titus is far from her and as long as she believes the emperor is in love with Bérénice; but, she says,

> No sooner did I see him without mistress and
> without wife,
> Than pride turned my whole soul to him;
> And as he won my sweetest attentions,
> His brother began to please me somewhat less.[11]

The emperor's brother is, of course, not so great as the emperor himself. In the same way Sophonisbe, in the tragedy of that name, boasts of preferring the conqueror Massinissa to her husband Syphax, who has been defeated and is in chains. It is to Syphax himself that she says, without shame,

> My glory lies in avoiding the chains you bear.[12]

A relentless drive carries the noble individual from desire to pride, and from inner pride to the display of pride, or

[10] *Agésilas,* I, 1.
[11] *Tite et Bérénice,* I, 1.
[12] *Sophonisbe,* III, 6.

in other words to glory. Understood in this sense, glory is but the halo of success, the flying spray raised by the impact of force, the admiration that follows in the wake of every triumph. Drunken power, in the one who wields it and in those who see it wielded, awakens joys, terrors, and hopes that go beyond their immediate cause and foster an elemental emotion, the primitive, quite barbarous poetry of grandeur. Success is felt and proclaimed to be superhuman; it sings its own praises, and the hymn impresses the crowd as much as does the success itself. Confidence, self-assertion, and majestic tone are not simply the ornaments of power; they are, in the eyes of the audience, the mark of a character born to wield power, and to wield it rightfully. Guizot, trying to explain the *vertu parleuse* of Corneille's heroes, observes that in Corneille's time "the need to defend one's social standing demanded the proclamation of one's work almost as a duty to be accomplished, or at least as a practice marking the man of courage." Voltaire can no longer understand this point. In his *Commentaire sur Corneille* he writes, "We have often been deceived on this score; more than once we have mistaken the speech of a *matamore* for that of a hero." Such a remark gives an idea of the distance separating Voltaire, and us even more, from the old Corneille. In any case, his audience in no way felt deceived; the line of demarcation between heroes and *matamores* shifted only later.

The public attending a performance of one of Corneille's tragedies find themselves, in fact, in a rather complex role. The spectators at *Cinna* or *Nicomède* are not simply spectators in a theater; they are also comrades of the heroes and witnesses to their glory. They are the indispensable audience for these beings, who are made to be admired and whose life would have no meaning if it could not successfully pass the test of public judgment. The people of Rome or Bithynie, whom our heroes have supposedly taken as their judges, do not appear on stage; rather they are in the audience. It is there, at least, that indignation or applause is expressed. In short, it is there that judgment is passed on the genius of the author and on his characters' greatness of soul, without distinguishing too carefully between them.

Corneille's tragedy, then, is a twofold spectacle, because the grandeur it portrays is already a spectacle in life before it becomes one on the stage. The audience takes part in two celebrations, one social, the other literary. The first, doubtless the least apparent, is not the least important. Into the emotional exchanges between the audience and the protagonists of the tragedy is compressed the whole system of psychological relationships which define society. In the theater as in society the mainspring is admiration, but not an unconditional admiration. In both instances, the public judges the virtue of the heroes, because society is directly concerned with seeing that the great are worthy of their rank and that they are able to sweep the common man along, to protect him, and to dazzle him. The heroic theater and the society of which it is the expression presuppose the uncontested power of public opinion. The very idea of glory is inseparable from it. Contests of valor between great men before the public tribunal–a public made up of peers, of inferiors, or more often of both–are the moral institution most in keeping with the spirit of this society, and the most useful for its functioning and its preservation. In such contests each man forms himself with a view to what he must be, according to his station. So one should not be surprised by the part that rivalries and challenges play in Corneille's dramas. We have seen examples of this in his heroes. In the same way, we will see princesses enter the lists for the conquest of kings or great men–in Corneille female jealousy involves a tournament of pride in which the weapons are malicious banter and bravado. Scenes of this type between two heroines abound; the audience must have been especially fond of them.[13]

Corneille laid particular stress on the social significance of his theater by constantly intermingling personal ambition and pride of ancestry in his heroes. The choice of princely or royal characters is not simply a theatrical convention; it is a condition of the drama itself, without which everything would collapse since the bearing and the speech consonant with

[13] Cf. especially the scenes of rivalry in *Sophonisbe* between Eryxe and Sophonisbe (I, 3; II, 3; III, 3; V, 4).

This sudden transmutation of unattainable victory into certain glory through the metamorphosis of passion, thrilled the audience. All the sublime quality of the famous *qu'il mourût*[18] that Corneille repeats a hundred times in different forms, lies in this transformation. It was the idea, taken up again and again, of a dramatic death or glorious martyrdom—

> If there are souls so base as to betray me
> My courage at least will not prove false;
> You will see it, shining at the brink of precipices,
> Crown itself with glory by braving tortures,
> Make Auguste jealous of the blood he will spill,
> And make him tremble as he destroys me.[19]

Virtue in Corneille, far from resulting in the submission of the ego to any discipline whatever, consists of a new glorification of the self which protects it against the blows of fate.

Corneille's sublime, then, springs from a particular impulse through which human motivation, without repudiating or condemning itself, rises above necessity. It is an impulse that springs directly from nature but transcends it. It is nature by virtue of a driving ambition without restraint, and more than nature because of the strength that enables the ego to escape from all bondage. In Corneille virtue is to be found at the point where the natural outburst of pride encounters the sublime quality of liberty. The *grande âme* is precisely the one in which this encounter takes place.

The point is worth stressing. In our day the understanding of Corneille's psychology has often been distorted by an erroneous use of the concepts of will and reason. In a famous article,[20] Lanson thought he could infer a close parallel between Corneille's theater and Descartes' *Traite des passions,* since in both *magnanimity* is defined by the triumph of the will and reason over the passions. But this conclusion is possible only through a misunderstanding of the ideas borrowed

[18] "Would that he had died" (*Tr. note*).
[19] *Cinna,* I, 4.
[20] *Revue d'histoire littéraire,* 1894.

from Descartes, which could not help us define Corneille's concept of magnanimity unless they were themselves defined. Lanson, and with him most critics, attribute to the word "will" the meaning it has in modern speech, naturally influenced by the moral attitudes of the conservative bourgeoisie. By "will" they mean the power to repress oneself, to silence one's desires. It would be difficult to find the word employed in this way in Descartes, who sometimes uses it to indicate desire itself insofar as it leads to action, and at other times to indicate the faculty of translating into action one desire rather than another, the free ordering of desires, or freedom of choice. And moral perfection seems to consist precisely in a harmony between desire and freedom. This harmony is achieved in noble souls by the fact that desire, always tending toward objects worthy of it, does not surrender the freedom of the ego, which is but another name for one's dignity. The whole *Traité des passions* is a search not for a means to crush desire by an effort of the will, but much rather a search for the conditions of harmony between the impulse of desire and the good. Harmony is achieved within that nature that is more beautiful than nature, the nature proper to a noble soul. We must not lose sight of the fact that the dominant inspiration of this ethics is the wish to give the ego its full value and its full sovereignty, and that this sovereignty would be just as compromised by an outburst of desire as by its stifling. Virtue treads a path between the two, giving a valid object to desire and a glorious motive to restraint: it consists in loving and desiring all things the love and desire of which affirm and strengthen freedom. Descartes is completely concerned with the prestige of noble passions, benevolent love, devotedness of men of honor, love for the true good, and justified self-esteem. A reading of the *Traité des passions* no more leaves one with an impression of the tense and rigid restraint alleged as the basis of merit common to Corneille and Descartes than does a reading of *Le Cid* or of *Cinna*.

In the concept they do indeed have in common, the role of intelligence is to tell us if our passions are well or ill-founded; that is to say, ultimately, whether or not they lead us to love liberty and flee servitude. Judgment is simply the handmaiden and explain this form of the sublime by the sum of energy invested in such dubious conduct. In the case of Cléopâtre it cannot be said that strength of will, with no regard for good and evil, engenders the sublime; it is rather the contempt for good and evil that is sublime, insofar as ambition, pride, and hatred of mediocrity and dependence underlie this contempt. On these terms the horror stirred by the spectacle is mixed with admiration. If we want to rediscover the true atmosphere of *Rodogune* or *Attila* (Saint-Évremond recommends *Attila* to lovers of the "savage and bloody theater"[22]) we have little to gain by invoking the abstract implementation of pure will. It would be better to think back to the bloody origins of the feudal world, to barbaric heroism, and to the whole violent and unrestrained aspect of aristocratic life up to the beginning of modern times.

However, very few examples such as this are found in Corneille's tragedies. Truly heroic pride is loath to destroy the moral law. What it seeks is an accord in which pride itself sanctions the law, an accord in which the interests of glory coincide with the limitations that society, as poorly disciplined as it may be, renders indispensable. This is certainly the mainspring of magnanimity in Corneille when it accompanies and moderates, in one who practices it, the superiority of physical force. Indeed, in an excessively close attachment to force there is a constantly dangerous compromising of the ego which might rue the day it placed its glory in a good that it was not sure to be able to hold on to. Intemperance too often ends in disaster and shame. Nature already teaches us that; society, by the rivalry of our ambitions with those of other men, shows us at still closer range the limits beyond which we cannot venture without madness. Consequently we can speak of a wisdom in pride, a certain bent toward impartiality or fairness by which the ego shields itself in advance from the humiliating disappointments of fate. Never to claim too much so as never to be forced to retract, to refrain from transgressing a command when we are not likely to have the last

[22] In one of his letters to the Count of Lionne (*Oeuvres mêlées*, Vol. II).

word because the nature of things sanctions that command, such is the law of ordinary prudence. Such is the law also of heroic prudence, except that it is inspired by the consideration of glory or shame rather than by that of happiness or misfortune. Thus Cléopâtre, mad in the ordinary sense of the word, is no less so if one judges her according to the measure of heroes. She has flung before the world a challenge that she could hardly keep. One who aspires to run counter to the order of things can succeed only under exceptional circumstances. Moreover, such a victory, if by chance it is won, cannot have the value of a moral example; and what is not exemplary is worthless in ethics.

Pride, then, must be wise in its own way so as not to be destroyed. But reason, which makes it wiser, does not leave it without sustenance. On the contrary, it delights pride with new enticements, it exalts and transfigures it. It shows pride the whole range of material grandeurs and teaches it that nothing, not even the throne, merits total homage; it teaches it to overcome all by the virtue of detachment, and to find indeed the true good, the supreme good, in a glorious self-confidence. In restraining itself pride does not exactly yield to necessity; rather it frees itself of necessity and gloriously resolves in advance the problem of its relations with the world. What Cléopâtre lacks, then, along with true lucidity, is pride in the highest degree. The throne is her master; it takes her measure, and there is nothing in her that can take its measure and transcend it; that is her profound and crucial weakness. The lesson that Corneille embodied in her is that the passion of greatness degenerates into servitude as soon as the consideration of the coveted end, however marvelous in itself, takes precedence over the impulse of ambition, as soon as the ego is fixed on a prey instead of remaining faithful to itself, and searching for the secret of true greatness by transcending every covetous desire.

Thus respect for the rights of others, moderation, and justice are injected into heroic ethics through a critique of immoderation and greed based on the idea of pure glory. If we now wish to define on the plane of concrete social relations the nature of this justice, whose law coincides with that of glory, and if we bring closer to one another the two heroic attitudes thus far described, defiance of force and moderation in the use of force, we cannot help but evoke the spirit of the feudal contract, the diffused memory of which dominated the common notion of justice for centuries. The feudal compact determines the point up to which rule is legitimate and revolt criminal and beyond which rule is unwarranted and revolt heroic. We are dealing here not so much with the political institution as with the form taken, in keeping with this institution, by the relations between the stronger and the weaker parties, a relationship ideally governed by chivalric loyalty, by what was called faith. Just as the pact between a lord and his vassal remains a definite man-to-man agreement, the faith that guarantees the part is confined to the level of the emotions and susceptibilities of the ego, which it elaborates and moralizes without condemning. Pride, shame, and the wounds of self-love will remain the natural forces by which chivalric faith sustains itself and makes itself felt, much more than the idea of an abstract discipline. A man will pride himself on serving the one to whom he has given himself because he would be breaking his word if he should fail to do so; if he feels oppressed by his lord he will for the same reason defy him in the presence of everyone, oppose pride to force, and seek to shame him. Cinna, Émilie and all like them do just this. The heroic defiance of the victim leads the victor's pride into an ideal direction. To punish too harshly would be to lower himself to the level of those he is punishing; from the role of the victor he would pass to that of the rival. On the contrary, by despising the triumph after having shattered all obstacles he adds to the prestige of conquest the prestige of rising above his own victory. The magnanimous disinterestedness of the victor, on a higher and more serene note, corresponds to the stoic defiance of the vanquished. The code of magnanimity that regulates the relations of Cinna and Auguste according to the likeness of the old relations, ideally conceived, between vassal and suzerain, formulates in moral terms the natural workings of self-love. One scarcely needs to transpose anything to pass from the spontaneous impulses of *la belle nature* to the highest idea of the good.

Nietzsche, in "Magnanimity and allied Qualities," writes, "In magnanimity there is the same amount of egoism as in revenge, but a different quality of egoism."[23] Corneille, instead, would have said, "There is in generosity the same passion to conquer that we find in vengeance, but it is of a higher, more exalted quality." In any case, he would not have said what some have ascribed to him, "In generosity the passions are completely silenced." From the start he shows us in Auguste a man glutted with power and, as it were, wearied by its very repletion. It is at this point that he is counseled to renounce the throne and show himself greater than the very glories over which he holds sway–

> Make them yield to you, not be your master,
> In short, proclaim loudly for all to hear
> That you are above all that they can give you. . . .
> In scorning the empire you redouble your glory.[24]

The famous scene of clemency at the end of the play effects such a redoubling of triumph. This clemency is certainly not without calculation, but it is a calculation of glory not of politics. It would be still more correct to say that it is a burst of glory that suddenly disarms the thirst for vengeance at the very moment when it reaches a fever pitch in the face of treacheries revealed in rapid succession. The unexpected announcement of the faithlessness of Maxime provokes suddenly, and contrary to all expectations, a burst of generosity surging up in defiance of fate and the temptation to punish, and dedicated at once to future ages as to a great assembly of witnesses–

> Is this enough, oh Heavens? And will fate, to do
> me injury,
> Turn against me still others I called my own?
> Let the powers of hell assist its efforts:

[23] F. Nietzsche, *Le Gai savoir,* I, 49.
[24] *Cinna,* II, 1.

I am master of myself as of the universe;
Such I am and such I will to be. Oh time to come,
oh memory,
Keep ever fresh my final victory![25]

It was at this line that tears of rapture were shed. Lanson, who explains Corneille in terms of the triumph of will and reason, has difficulty explaining this lyrical outburst. He says the will, when it has come to the highest point of its strength, "sings its own praises." But Corneille's heroes sing their own praises from start to finish because noble virtue cannot at any moment dispense with either exaltation or publicity.

Nor can it any more easily do without a partner. The contest of two or of several persons vying with each other in magnanimity heightens the feeling of the sublime by adding to simple admiration the dramatic interest of competitive bidding. Rivalry in heroism is found throughout Corneille, but it has its strongest impact in the final scenes: magnanimity, calling forth magnanimity in return, culminates as it were in a final burst of fireworks with which the author seems to try and satiate the audience. It is a duel of this type that Auguste proposes to Cinna–

As my enemy, I gave you life,
And despite the fury of your base design,
I give it to you again as my assassin.
Let us begin a contest whose outcome will show
Which of us will prove the better, as giver or receiver.

There is an obvious kinship between this rivalry for greatness of soul and the tournaments of the age of chivalry. Auguste's pardon, like a brilliant passage of arms, wipes out the hatred of the conspirators. After the pardon is granted, such hatred would simply be unjust obstinacy; through a new maneuver that answers the first, it is immediately transformed into noble devotion, the only possible response to the generous clemency of Auguste. So it is with Émilie–

[25] Ibid., V, 3.

My hatred, which I thought deathless, is dying;
It is dead, and this heart becomes a loyal subject;
Henceforth I hold this hate in horror
And in place of its fury dwells a passion to serve you.[26]

Cinna and Maxime, laying down their arms after her, complete the picture. Almost all the tragedies of Corneille end this way, in a general apotheosis in which every glory is assuaged and finds its proper place.

The ending of *Cinna* indicates that in Corneille's thought the ambition of the ego is not condemned in its essence. It purifies itself, detaches itself from tangible interests, and takes the form of an ideal assertion of dignity or superiority; it is sublimated, not repressed.[27] The Church proceeded, at least in principle, to a radical condemnation of pride, of the ego, to which she opposed Christian humility. But this was not the direction taken by worldly ethics. Worldly ethics did not argue that it was necessary to deny oneself in order to be saved. Humility was neither in fact nor in principle the virtue of the great. Thus Corneille's hero is never humble. The Hôtel de Rambouillet did not like *Polyeucte,* if we are to believe Fontenelle, precisely because of its Christian spirit,[28] and Saint-Évremond goes so far as to say that the Christian virtues of the martyrs depicted in *Polyeucte* all but stripped Corneille of his reputation.[29] If for Christianity pride is the

[26] Ibid., V, 3.

[27] Ordinarily the word "sublimation" is used whenever a desire is satisfied under another guise that is deemed morally superior. Here it is used in a more specific sense, and for want of a better term refers to those cases in which the transfigured desire is not repudiated but persists *consciously,* with greater vigor, under its ideal form. The transformation allows guilt to be relieved, and the desire to be sublimated without having to be repudiated. This is a crucial distinction in an ethics avowedly based on egoistic impulses but claiming to reconcile them with a conscious idea of the good. Otherwise there would be repression, not sublimation. Our whole discussion centers on this difference.

[28] Fontenelle, *Vie de Corneille.*

[29] Saint-Évremond, *De la tragédie ancienne et moderne* (*Oeuvres mêlées,* Vol. III)—"The spirit of our religion is directly

very root of sin, it is characteristic of aristocratic ethics, on the contrary, that pride and the sublime are almost indistinguishable. Aristocratic ethics is both a natural and an ideal ethics, because it postulates the existence of beings placed by nature above nature herself—of men who by nature of their pride and because of their pride are superior to the common man.

In the world of the aristocracy the creation of heroic values went hand in hand with a very special elaboration of the amorous instinct. There is a general tendency in the spirit of chivalry to make love a spur to greatness. Amorous conquest, with its rivalries, its difficulties, and its glory, imitated military conquest and could demand the same virtues. The woman herself could challenge her suitors and, like Brünhild in the *Niebelungen,* give herself only to the man who could subdue her. Love then becomes the direct reward for strength and valor. But the amorous conquest ordinarily prefers to take other paths; a triumph of pure force over a woman in real life would scarcely please lovers of exemplary prowess and would be offensive to pride, which takes much greater satisfaction in gaining the consent of the loved one. Hence the primitive combat is replaced by a symbolic struggle in which the woman, before she yields to man, requires that he cover himself with glory. Examples in which the man must seek glory to obtain the desired consent of the one he loves abound in Corneille. Thus in *Attila,* Princess Honorie, the rejected fiancée of the king of the Huns, refuses to give herself in marriage to King Valamir, though she loves him, because he let Attila reduce him to a state of humiliating subjection. To win her consent he must brave Attila, he must snatch her

---

opposed to that of tragedy. The humility and patience of our saints are too opposed to the virtues of the heroes that the theater demands. What zeal, what force does Heaven not grant to Néarque and Polyeucte . . . ? Nonetheless, what might have been a fine sermon would have made a wretched tragedy if the scenes between Pauline and Sévère, who are quickened by other sentiments and other passions, had not salvaged for their author a reputation which the Christian virtues of our martyrs might have taken from him."

boldly from the Hun's hands, and even refuse, should the occasion arise, to take her with the consent of the tyrant—

> If you love me at all, my Lord, you must believe
> That I do not cherish anything so much as my glory.
> Reign like Attila, and I prefer you to him;
> But I'll have no husband who does not dare to
> scorn his support,
> No husband who will reduce me to the level of
> his subjects.
> In short, I want a king: see if you are such.[30]

Contrary to the historical sense that his contemporaries ascribed to him, on this score Corneille attributes the customs of chivalry to all nations and all periods: if César has conquered many lands and wants to conquer still others, it is to win the right to Cléopâtre's attentions.[31] Séleucus and Antiochus, princes of Syria, both desire the throne to set the Parthian princess Rodogune upon it;[32] Héraclius, legitimate heir to the Eastern Empire, aspires to this glorious inheritance only to share it with his beloved Eudoxe.[33]

Thus in the world of chivalry woman wields an influence quite opposed to that of her primitive condition; from a simple object of conquest she becomes a demanding and overbearing "mistress." The social supremacy of man persists, but sentimentally and morally it is accompanied by a kind of vassalage in relation to woman. Man casts aside his physical superiority before her and in a voluntary act of worship renounces his right to be her master in order to be her servant, or, as they said in the seventeenth century, her prisoner, weighed down by the chains or irons she imposes on him with his blessing. The lady's service becomes the very symbol, and as it were the innermost source, of the renunciation of brutal force. The lady, jealous of her new advantages, tends to encourage in her suitor not only the love of greatness but

[30] *Attila,* II, 2.
[31] *Pompée,* IV, 3.
[32] *Rodogune,* I, 3.
[33] *Héraclius,* II, 2.

also a sublimation of instinct from which she is the first to benefit. The high value accorded to woman is then spiritualized and identified with the esteem accorded to virtue itself:

> He who worships you alone worships virtue,

says one of Corneille's heroes to his loved one.[34] An act of love, then, confirms all moral excellence, and creates one more connection between the impulses of the ego and those of virtue. If ideal love occupied such a place in aristocratic thought since the Middle Ages, it is because the feudal world made use of every path leading from desire to the ideal good that required only simple sublimation, and that did not repress the *élan* of the aristocrat, who was always impatient with severe restraints. Sublimated love took its place beside sublimated ambition or pride, each engendering and sustaining the other.[35]

[34] *Pertharite,* II, 5.

[35] We can only deal with the phenomenon in broad outline here, disregarding the difficulties that accompany it of which something will be said further on. The main point is to grasp the relation of the courtly love to aristocratic individualism. The fact that from the Middle Ages on woman prevails in literature, although her real condition is so inferior, has not ceased to surprise and puzzle us. Perhaps we lack the necessary data to form a sound judgment on medieval customs. Let us observe, however, that society is the realm of real man, and literature the realm of ideal man, and that one does not and cannot completely overlap the other; and this rule applies even more to the Middle Ages than to other times. One might be just as shocked at the small rapport that exists at that time between Christian sentiments and real conduct. It is true that there must be a point of contact between what is imagined and what is real. Why should this point be more difficult to find in the case of courtly lyricism than elsewhere? For example, could one not discern in this worship of woman a deep-seated tendency in feudal man to place what he loves on the plane of the rare, the precious, and the unique? The deification of woman, even her rigorousness, flatter a certain ambition in the lover: he comes into contact with something marvelous. The vocabulary of the troubadours, which bases worship on the "prize," is to be understood in

This idea in which love strengthe
the feudal world during the twelft
it permeates the chivalric romanc
sists, taking on new vigor in the
influence of Platonism and the
lectual life; and appears still intac
when its strength and prestige
generally believed. Courtly love
poetry and in the romances, its time-hon
L'Astrée, the famous pastoral romance which appeared be-tween 1607 and 1627 and was widely read throughout the seventeenth century, develops all the aspects of the courtly doctrine with an unbelievable richness and variety of argu-ments and situations. The *précieux* romances that followed express with similar nuances the same ideas as *L'Astrée.* For example, we read in *L'Astrée,* "Love has the power to add perfection to our souls,"[36] and in Madeleine de Scudéry's *Grand Cyrus,* "This beautiful passion is the noblest cause of all heroic deeds."[37] The romances published in the course of the seventeenth century in which the characters, being real princes and princesses and not imaginary shepherds, are closer to social reality than *L'Astrée* and are also closer to Corneille in the glorious and grandiloquent form they give to the religion of love.

Indeed, we must not disregard the influence exercised by the tradition of the romances on Corneille's work. First of all,

---

this sense. Far from being astonished that the Middle Ages con-ceived courtly love, one would have to be even more astonished had it conceived of love in terms that did not offer idealization as a flattering solution for one's amour-propre. One can argue about the intellectual origins of courtly love and about precise influences that gave rise to it; but none of these would have been strong enough to make the ideal of courtly love triumph without the aristocrat's predisposition to reconcile his desires with his idea of the good.

[36] *L'Astrée,* Part II, Book I, ed. Vaganay, p. 18.

[37] *Le Grand Cyrus,* Part I, Book 2, ed. in-12, p. 333. Cf. ibid., p. 784, with respect to love: "How glorious this weakness is! and what a great soul one must have to be capable of it!"

knights from whom they are descended, Cor- affect a perfect submission to their lady; they it base to win the one they love without first mak- selves pleasing to her. Even though the Cid, accord- the rules laid down by the king, had won Chimène by nphing over Don Sanche, he throws himself at her feet ter the duel and submits once again to her will—

> I do not come to demand my prize:
> I come once more to offer you my life,
> Madam; my love will turn to my profit
> Neither the law of combat nor the will of the king.[38]

In the same way Sévère, although the favorite of the emperor, trembles the moment he sees Pauline again—

> For I would rather die than draw unfair advantage
> From the Emperor's permission that I may marry her.[39]

Moreover, in Corneille as in the romances, the ladies exercise the absolute power at their disposal to make their lovers virtuous. Eurydice, seeing that her suitor is going to commit murder, asks,

> Would I be able, after that, to preserve my fidelity to you?
> As if you were still worthy of me?[40]

In many passages Corneille makes the virtue of his heroes stem from their submission to their lady and from their love, accepting in that respect the essential point of courtly morality and also the one most contested by the strict moralists, to whose ranks he allegedly belongs. *Le Cid* owed a good part of its success—we have read the testimony of Corneille himself on this point—to the famous Scene 4 in Act III, in which Rodrigue explains to Chimène that he was forced to avenge his honor precisely out of consideration for his love, and not at its expense. He came very close to choosing love he says,

[38] *Le Cid,* V, 7.
[39] *Polyeucte,* II, 1.
[40] *Suréna,* IV, 3.

But vying with your strongest charms
Was the knowledge that a man without honour could not deserve you,
And that in spite of the place I held in your heart,
One who loved me noble would detest me base. . . .[41]

It was in order to preserve love untarnished that he chose duty.

If the idea that love can produce virtue, even the most austere virtue, always appeared improper to the champions of a strict ethics, it certainly had the approval of Corneille's contemporaries. It is expressed in this period in every literary genre, novel, theater, and poetry, and it can even be found in the epic compositions, scoffed at by Boileau and forgotten today, of people like Chapelain, Scudéry, Desmarets de Saint-Sorlin. The latter gives us one of its most striking formulations in his epic *Clovis* (1657), in which Lisois, the ancestor of Montmorency, answers the beautiful Yoland, whom he loves and who wants to persuade him to betray his king, that he would no longer possess the heart of a true lover in serving her if his honor were sullied–

Would you want me to possess one without the other,
If honor and the heart are one and the same?[42]

Corneille, too, reconciles honor and love more than he opposes them, and in his work the dramatic movement progresses from a momentary division of the soul toward a rediscovered consciousness of its unity–a unity that is not the fruit of constraint but the law of *grandes âmes* and the very condition of their happiness.[43]

It is this aspect of his inspiration more than any other that

[41] *Le Cid,* III, 4.

[42] Desmarets, *Clovis,* Book XVIII. The author plays on the double meaning of the word "heart," which suggests both grandeur of soul and love, and this double meaning itself is very significant.

[43] Notice, for example, the way Émilie in *Cinna* (I, 1) resolves her doubts:

Love, be subservient to duty, and struggle no more against it:
To yield to it is your glory, to vanquish it your shame.

closely links Corneille with what we call *précieuse* literature. Accepting the testimony of those who despised and fought against the aristocratic sublime in the seventeenth century, above all Boileau, we too often forget that ideals of glory and courtesy permeated a good part of literature up to the time of Louis XIV. We reduce *préciosité* to a bizarre and fleeting state of soul and we lament finding traces of it (which we consider superficial, furthermore) in the great writers of the century. In fact the huge success of the romances, which were appreciated not only by a restricted circle but by all members of cultured society who continually quote from them and comment on them in their letters and conversations, reveals what was, for the most part, the spirit and the taste of the public. The austere Corneille of traditional criticism seems very far from the *carte de Tendre*[44] and from the romantic affectations that, more than anything else, characterize *précieuse* literature for us today. But in spite of its affectation the romance is full of heroic or magnanimous sentiments and acts, and Corneillian grandeur of soul is constantly linked there with tenderness in keeping with the conventions of chivalric literature. In the romances love turns into the sublime as often as the sublime in Corneille turns into gallantry. One is rarely found without the other.

Why should one be surprised, then, that the very people who loved the romances also admired Corneille? Mme. de Sévigné is among them–she loudly proclaims the superiority of Corneille over all his rivals and writes, "I am mad about Corneille, everyone must bow to his genius."[45] On the other hand, she also confesses her passion for Mlle. de Scudéry and for La Calprenède, and says of the latter's *Cléopâtre* that its sentiments are "of a perfection that fulfills *her* idea of noble souls."[46] Similarly, in Perrault's, *Parallèles des anciens et des modernes* (1688–97), a panegyric of Corneille is followed by a defense of purified and idealized gallantry,[47]

[44] The *carte de Tendre* is a famous map of the ways of love in a novel of Madeleine de Scudéry (*Tr. note*).

[45] Letter of March 9, 1672.

[46] Letter of July 15, 1671.

[47] Perrault, *Parallèles,* Part II, p. 31 ff.

and then by a defense of *L'Astrée, Cyrus,* and other tales. The same author had previously praised Corneille to the skies in his poem on *Le Siècle de Louis-le-Grand* (1687) and was later, in his *Apologie des femmes,* to defend the talents of Mlle. de Scudéry[48] and the honor of the female sex against Boileau. Finally there is Pradon who, in his *Nouvelles Remarques sur les oeuvres du sieur D.*[49] which appeared in 1685, argues at the same time the superiority of Corneille over Racine and the excellence of *Cyrus* and *Clélie.*

One hundred years later, Voltaire would again link Corneille's work with the literature of the romances, but to criticize both; one can scarcely read a page of his *Commentaires sur Corneille* without seeing this author's tragedies compared with the "wretched novels of his times." In *Cinna* he criticizes the expression, too reminiscent of the romances for his taste, of the *veritable amant,*[50] and judges it more worthy of *L'Astrée* than of a tragedy.[51] He judges Polyeucte's gallant ways harshly: "This imitation of the heroes of chivalry infected our theater from its very beginnings."[52] One by one all the courtly themes are given a taste of his sarcasm: the austerity of the women, the dedication of the heroes, the total amorous devotion of the conquerors. According to Voltaire,[53] it is Corneille who particularly merits Boileau's reproach to Mlle. de Scudéry, of

Portraying Cato as a *galant* and
Brutus as a ladies' man.[54]

"Anyone," he writes further, "who says that Racine sacrificed everything to love, and that Corneille's heroes always rose above that passion, has not studied these two authors

48 Perrault, *Apologie des femmes,* Preface.
49 That is to say, Sieur Despreaux.
50 "True lover" (*Tr. note*).
51 Voltaire, *Commentaire sur Cinna.*
52 *Commentaire sur Polyeucte.*
53 *Commentaire sur Pompée.*
54 Boileau, *Art Poétique,* verse 115.

closely." This leads to the following contemptuous reflection, "Reading is very common, fruitful reading is very rare."[55] Lanson was far wide of the mark when, after observing that purified love contributes to virtue in Corneille's characters, he wrote that this love is "quite different from the desire that is born of attraction, which is the ordinary love of the romances."[56] Ideal love, the courtly tradition, and the spirit of the romances are not different, and are found together in Corneille.

The harmony established by the courtly spirit between love and the social virtues, valor, honor, and greatness of soul, raises serious problems that merit particular attention inasmuch as they constitute the most delicate point in Corneille's ethics. In the relation of virtue to love, all the courtly conciliations have trouble effacing one profound contradiction, which sometimes seems to threaten an open break.

In aristocratic society, as in all societies known up to the present, the nature of things requires that what one adds to love one subtracts from virtue. Society and its ethics always teach us in one way or another to look for and reach out to something beyond us, but love knows only self-abandon. It follows from this that society condemns love as the very principle and symbol of moral dissolution. Aristocratic ethics seeks in vain to take up the defense of pure impulse; for there is a point past which impulse, scorning all other considerations, endangers all ethics. This point, no doubt, is more easily reached in love than elsewhere, to judge by the particularly strong misgivings that this passion arouses in moralists. The partisans of the romances set out precisely to lessen these misgivings, to make all of love enter completely into the sphere of virtue. Alongside of public opinion, and in accord

[55] *Commentaire sur Rodogune.*

[56] In the article already referred to on Corneille and Descartes. Elsewhere, however, Lanson writes, "Through the chivalric and pastoral romances, the elegies, and the tragedies, the concept of the troubadours will be all-pervasive and will flower until it assumes its definitive formulation, philosophical in Descartes, poetic in Corneille . . ." (*Histoire illustrée de la littérature française,* Vol. I, p. 68.

with it, they introduce the opinion of the woman loved, and thus claim to make the impulses of love coincide with the demands of social law. But their endeavor inspires only a feeble trust. "Chivalry," writes Saint-Marc Girardin in his *Cours de littérature dramatique,* "attempted, but never succeeded, as often as it tried, to make use of the human passions, and particularly love, to lead man to virtue."[57] Virtue, then, must be the enemy of love. This certainly does not flatter virtue or encourage it. Like all such attempts to reconcile love and the good, the courtly attempt is the mark of a higher civilization. When in advance of its time, such an attempt naturally provokes suspicion. Against it are invoked habits and values of the past, before love won its pernicious prestige. Opposed to the idea of the romances is an older, more archaic idea which the romances never destroyed, that love runs the

[57] Vol. II, Chapter 35. The difficulties encountered by the courtly concept in its attempts to reconcile morality and instinct will also be apparent in inner contradictions, easily recognizable even in the seventeenth-century philosophy of love. On one hand, love is always supposed to be directed toward merit, but on the other it must be irresistible and instinctive. We find this contradiction in Corneille, too. Despite previous criticism on the subject of love based on esteem in Corneille, nothing prevents the choice of the beloved from being based on instinct. For the choice cannot be wholly and consciously justified without reducing the affective value of the object of love, which supposedly defies all judgment. All the romances before and after Corneille confirm and develop endlessly Rodogune's phrase concerning "that *je ne sais quoi* that can't be explained." (I, 5) It is part of the perfection of love that it is answerable neither to morality nor to reason nor to justice, even though they are the norms of perfection. And there is another, more immediate and more embarrassing contradiction—that attitude which presents the joy of loving as the supreme good and is at the same time loath to consummate that love. It is an almost impossible balance in which desire becomes suffering in order to justify itself; an equilibrium in which one becomes slave and martyr to a woman as a punishment for having become her worshiper. According to one's perspective, the Middle Ages, with its creation of courtly love, brought into being either a source of life and of beauty or a neurosis.

risk of dishonoring those it subdues, that it turns them away from great deeds, debases their thoughts, and breeds indolence and evil doing. In its primitive purity the ideal of the valiant knight was rather strongly opposed to love and to women; heroic behavior was accompanied by one cult only, that of virility. The dying Roland thinks of his conquests, of the "men of his lineage," of Charles, his lord, and nothing else. This anti-love tradition is often embodied in Corneille by the old people, particularly the fathers, the natural custodians of the healthy misogyny of earlier times–Don Diegue and the aged Horace. It is they who teach contempt for woman, relegating love to the background, valuing only the glory of arms and the approval of men. It remains to be seen to what degree their preaching permeates his whole work, and whether Corneille, while pointing out the question that it is the function of such characters to raise, does not offer an interpretation different from theirs.

Confronted with a condemnation of love, courtly literature frequently tends to break with conventional morality and place love above all law, identifying it with virtue and divinity itself. This is the quality of the courtly spirit as formulated in the poetry of the South of France. The defense of love can take the drastic form of a rebellion against social values, whether feudal, familial, or conjugal. In such instances morality is the loser. Of course this does not always happen. The more extreme forms of the cult of love should not blind us to the fact that the value of love was generally accepted by society as it became more civilized. However, the fact remains that the early romances are full of unedifying examples. Not only does courtly love tend to consider itself incompatible with marriage, but it makes one forget social standing: Aucassin does not want to bear arms as long as he is refused Nicolette; Chrétien de Troyes' Lancelot allows himself to be carried in the cart of dishonor to be closer to his lady. Love commands him to do so while reason tries to dissuade him. But love must and does triumph. Courtly love in this form is no longer distinguishable in the eyes of society from pure and simple derangement; it differs from it only in its idealized "devotion" and adoration of the beloved. The religion of love, then, becomes a religion alien to society and contrary to its laws.[58]

If the Cid had been Lancelot, he would undoubtedly have forsaken his father and his glory rather than grieve Chimène. But we must admit that Corneille invariably resolved such cases in a different way, not by freeing courtly love from all constraints, but by stretching its moral resources even further and crowning all the sacrifices inspired by love with the sacrifice of love itself. For him perfect love is not simply the most complete love but the one most capable, if need be, of renouncing itself. From this point of view Rodrigue is as different as can be from Lancelot. In his own explanation of his conduct, when he declares that he was forced to renounce Chimène's love to be truly deserving of that love, which means more to him than anything else, the tension of his dialectic is such that one might almost say that the heart has lost its rights in the face of tyrannical duty. We feel this even more strongly with the female characters–Pauline explicitly admits to Sévère that her reason tyrannizes her heart, and many other heroines constantly proclaim the harsh supremacy of duty over passion. In these cases reason seems clearly the direct enemy of instinct, drawn up against it and destined to prevail over it. The general opinion of Corneille rests above all on this aspect of his theater, and seems to be confirmed by Corneille himself when he writes, "Up to now I thought that love was a passion too weighted down with weakness to be the dominant passion in a heroic play."[59] Nevertheless, it would be a mistake to see in this a formal condemnation of the

[58] Note that to the degree that it breaks openly with society and with reason, courtly love turns into tragedy and can scarcely be conceived of as other than misfortune. The circumstances that surround it, then, are such that rebellion and punishment are almost one, as in *Tristan and Iseut*. On the contrary, when a balance is maintained between the law of society and love, love is happy and the story ends well, as is most frequently the case with Chrétien de Troyes, as well as in the seventeenth-century romances and in Corneille.

[59] Corneille, Letter to Saint-Évremond (in thanks for his praise in *Dissertation sur l'Alexandre*).

ethics of the romances. One must consider the fact that these words were written at the time of Racine's *Alexandre,* and that they were directed against the "tender" tragedy which was successfully vying for public favor with Corneille, who was then approaching the end of his career. It is natural that Corneille, attempting to distinguish himself from his rivals, should imagine a radical opposition between them and himself. In reality the difference is only a question of degree. And in any case, what does he say? That love should not take precedence over all else, and should not be the compelling force in a tragedy. He does not say that this passion should be eliminated or appear on the scene only to be suppressed. The formula he employs is very significant: *"Grandes âmes* should yield to love *only to the extent that love is compatible with nobler sentiments."* He establishes hierarchy but desires a harmony. It is quite obvious that in his eyes love is not the highest virtue; nor do all other virtues spring from love. Love tends to assume this role only in the romances and Corneille did not write romances. Still, it remains true that when properly understood, love may be compatible with these nobler sentiments that the great interests of honor, war, or the nation produce. In Corneille there is no absolute opposition between love and that greatness which is the very stuff of the tragic theater. In all his works he tried to reconcile the two, rather than set them against one another.

In fact, even when Corneille strains the ties that bind duty to love, he is loath to break them. In his work the sentimental dialectic never abandons the idea of reconciling love and duty, and never leaves them, so to speak, confronting one another like two enemies. One must also note that the alleged devaluation of love in his theater does not reflect a low opinion of woman. Female supremacy and the idealization of woman constitute the true foundation of the whole notion of courtly love. Love as such is not condemned so long as woman retains her place of honor. To make the system collapse, she must be thrown down from her pedestal. This is why the true enemies of the courtly spirit, from the Middle Ages on, attacked woman; intransigent clerics or cynical bourgeois, they denounced woman as the embodiment of weakness and her deification as a crime or a folly. Boileau acts no differently in the period which interests us. But Corneille, on the contrary, is so bound to the courtly tradition that even when he observed the weaknesses of love he absolved from them the character of woman, and at all times embodied the demand for virtue in the woman loved. One is more likely to find protestations of love in the mouths of his heroes. In Corneille's dramas it is by means of the woman's authority that virtue triumphs: however austere it may be, virtue continues to be identified with an ideal image of woman. And this was, with few exceptions, the general tendency of his century.

In Corneille, then, couples are more frequently than not composed of a heroine of strict virtue and a pining knight-suitor who alone laments the harshness of duty. In *Polyeucte* Pauline and Sévère are such a couple. Othon is likewise reluctant to comply with the duty that enjoins him to renounce Pauline; it is Pauline who urges him to control his desires and to raise his love "above the senses," and it is he who will object

> What courage such purification demands![60]

In Corneille's time this situation had become an almost intangible literary and moral convention. One finds it in all the romances of the period. Everywhere heroines of austere virtue guarantee the respect of strict morality, assailed by tenderhearted heroes.

Such a combination preserved the heritage of the romances while emphasizing as much as possible its austere elements; it reconciled the prestige of love with the demands of society. We have seen that originally courtly love often placed itself outside of and in opposition to the rules of society. In the romances of the Middle Ages the love of knights and ladies often rebels against obligations imposed by birth, parental authority, or the laws of marriage. In Corneille's tragedies, as in all the serious literature of his times, we generally find neither the social disgrace of heroes and heroines, nor rebellion

[60] Othon, 1, 4.

against the authority of the family,[61] nor faithlessness in marriage. In the world of Corneille, society regulates love. The courtly ideal has made itself socially acceptable. It is interesting to note in this legitimization of love the influence of a rather modern idea of social discipline, as well as the influence of the most archaic traditions of the feudal world.

The spirit of absolute monarchy tended to impose a certain orderliness in all spheres of life. But the primitive brutality of family power in the Middle Ages had in fact coexisted with numerous disorders that often enjoyed public support and literary approval. Contradictions abounded in that society without causing undue concern. But the clash of law and of opinion, of rule and of events, was more painfully felt in the large state shaped under the rule of the monarchy. This new society needed a synthesis that would permit both the right of lovers and the reinforced authority of social imperatives. It is this almost official synthesis of restraint and sentiment that we find in Corneille.

The fact remains that Corneille constantly made personal pride, the most forthright and impressive form of pride, measure up to harsh sacrifices. In his tragedies the social group in whose name the heroic act is performed is never larger than the family, since the state is the family for a hero or heroine of royal lineage.[62] The authority that calls for sacrifice, then, is close at hand and tangible. It barely transcends the individual. The aristocratic family does not compel the hero to sacrifice himself in the name of either reason or abstract duty. The family is not so much a disciplined social entity as a community sustained by pride. The honor of the

[61] Camille, in *Horace,* is a notable exception, and the only one if one disregards the involuntary weakness of Chimène, which nevertheless created a scandal and constituted one of the principal themes in the dispute over *Le Cid.*

[62] Early Rome, as depicted in *Horace,* hardly represents a wider horizon than the family. Besides, the heroes speak of the honor of Rome as the gentlemen in Corneille's audience spoke of the honor of their line, not as they spoke of the honor of France. Roman local color consisted precisely in the personal quality attributed to patriotic interest in ancient Rome.

group is barely distinguishable from that of any of its members, and great questions of state or family directly concern the individual's honor.[63]

> . . . To die without being revenged!
> To seek a death so fatal to my name,
> To let Spain ascribe to my memory the shame
> of having failed to uphold the honor of my line![64]

So Rodrigue cries out, spontaneously identifying the glory of his family with his own. In the same way the painful sacrifice of princesses married against the dictates of their heart would scarcely be possible for them were it not sustained by the pride of their social standing and by the fear of proving unworthy of the name they bear by marrying poorly in the eyes of society. As she renounces Rodrigue, Chimène cries out,

> My glory is at stake, I must avenge myself,[65]

revealing thereby the true source of her heroism. In the tragedy *Don Sanche,* Queen Isabelle, urged to choose a husband according to the dictates of her heart, answers,

> Madam, I am queen, and must govern myself.
> The station that we hold jealous of our glory,
> Often in such a choice forbids us to yield to our feelings,
> Sets an imperious yoke on our desires
> And scorns the counsel of both heart and eyes.[66]

In *Pompée* Cléopâtre goes even further—

> Princes have this from their high birth:
> In their blood their soul assumes certain powers
> That order their passions beneath their virtue.[67]

[63] When there is a conflict individual honor may win out, as in the case of Camille in *Horace*; this is the cult of unrestrained love, sanctioned by an ego that finds all its pride in itself.

[64] *Le Cid,* I, 6.

[65] Ibid., III, 3.

[66] *Don Sanche,* I, 2.

[67] *Pompée,* II, 1.

A proud consciousness of superiority is clearly the indispensable handmaiden of moral rigor in Corneille. The harshest constraint in this ethics, which has no support but the individual himself and no profound resources other than those of the ego, must ultimately appeal to the interest of personal glory.

The many different elements that account for Corneille's inspiration often give a disjointed or inconsistent air to his characters, who are drawn more for dramatic impact than for verisimilitude, and who derive this dramatic impact at times from the excess of their arrogance, and at times from the delicacy of their virtue. Voltaire, censuring the "mixture of naïve tenderness and horrible atrocities in *Rodogune,*"[68] censures, in fact, behind the inconsistencies of Corneille's works, that of a moral philosopher and a society in which cruelty and virtue engender each other and constantly intermingle. Presumably the role of reason would be to better harmonize us with ourselves. But reason understood as a moderator and peacemaker between the warring forces within us cannot easily solve the problems posed by Corneille's characters. Inner harmony is not natural to *grandes âmes,* always at odds with themselves because they are at odds with the world. When the ego aspires only to conform completely the way things are, when it attempts to dissolve all dramatic tension between itself and the world, the reason that guides it is the very image of that total restful harmony it seeks. But in Corneille the ego has a different goal. It aspires to prove itself superior to fate, to win liberty by sheer force. If it feels the need to know the limits of what is possible, it is so that its *élan* will not be blind; but it always demands that this *élan* seek the highest goal. In Corneille the sublime lives on valiant deeds, it thrives on the rare and the original. It springs up in unusual situations like a brilliant solution to problems beyond the understanding of ordinary men. The reason that illuminates it bears the mark of rarity, difficulty, and paradox. The inner conflicts and problems of the struggle for greatness

[68] Voltaire, *Commentaire sur Rodogune.*

thrust reason in the same direction. The ethics of nobility, so frequently successful in its reconciliation of desire and virtue, occasionally reveals the defects and difficulties inherent in all idealism. It has trouble in establishing a satisfactory relationship between the two opposites of desire and virtue, to which it abandons man. This ethics attempts to reconcile extremes, and as a consequence its peculiar vices are those common to all peacemakers grappling with an awkward task—subtle ingenuity, forced or artificial syntheses, and *bel-esprit.*

This *bel-esprit* does not condemn extremes. It can serve to express the most violent feelings and the most atrocious actions, and confer upon them some extraordinary quality or value. It is seen in the unexpected solution Antiochus proposes when Rodogune asks that he or his brother, in order to win her hand, kill Cléopâtre, their mother:

> Of two princes who both yearn for you,
> Choose one as a victim and the other as a spouse.[69]

In *Pertharite,* Rodelinde, like Racine's Andromaque the prisoner of her husband's conqueror, and mother of another Astyanax, refuses to yield to her conqueror. But when he lets her choose for her son either death, if she is obstinate, or the monarchy, if she yields, she suddenly turns the threat into a challenge and answers that she will yield to him only if he has the courage to kill her child first:

> He who sets himself up as a tyrant must resolve to
> be one.
> To live up to the name must you acquire a teacher,
> And must a mother, at the price of her blood,
> Teach you to be worthy of this awful station?
> Do not suffer this shame and take all the glory
> Which this illustrious effort attaches to your memory. . . .
> At this price will I yield myself, at this price
> will I surrender. . . .[70]

[69] *Rodogune,* IV, 1.
[70] *Pertharite,* III, 3.

This illustration of barbaric *bel-esprit* is interesting in that it is followed, in the same scene, by a more rational attempt at self-justification. Rodelinde knows that her tormentor will kill her son even if she yields to him; given these conditions, she reasons,

> Since he must perish, better early than late.

Furthermore, once the child has been killed she will certainly marry the murderer, if only to kill him in turn. This rational reconstruction of her behavior (if one can call it that) is simply one more unexpected twist added to the surprise created by her earlier challenge.

Suicide for honor's sake, by one's own hand or with another's help, the obsession of so many of Corneille's heroes,[71] is one of the most frequent themes in this bloody subtlety. Rodrigue comes to ask Chimène to run him through with his own sword—

> In the name of a dead father, or of our love,
> Punish me for vengeance, or at least out of pity.[72]

Sabine, the wife of Horace and the sister of Curiace, asks the two heroes to kill her in order to break the cruel alliance between the two families—

> Let one of you kill me and the other avenge me:
> Then your enmity will no longer be something strange;
> And at least one of you will be a just aggressor,
> Either to avenge his wife, or to avenge his sister.[73]

After having killed Camille, Horace wants to kill himself to escape the dishonor of punishment; but then a struggle within him begins between the instincts of pride and the thought that his blood belongs not to him but to his father—

[71] It remains, however, only an obsession; one cannot point to a single case in which it is fulfilled.

[72] *Le Cid,* III, 4.

[73] *Horace,* II, 6.

But without your consent my blood does not dare to flow:
Since it belongs to you, your leave must be won;
To spill it otherwise would be to steal it from you.[74]

Examples of this type deserve at least the same attention as those in which intelligence induces acts of delicate generosity or tenderness. They all demonstrate that reason in Corneille is far from being ordinary.

Bel-esprit–subtle intelligence in search of beauty and grandeur–was for centuries the most admired trait in all intellectual life. One loved to see it accompany all the passions, refine and transform itself together with them, shine forth in their jousts, and surpass itself in their feats of valor. Since the Middle Ages the search for the good and the beautiful was cast in the form of a tournament for an audience of connoisseurs who enjoyed surprise and striking inventiveness. In Corneille, lofty poetry and morals remain faithful to this tradition; *bel-esprit* remains the most frequent form of intelligence in the thoughts that accompany and justify heroic behavior in his dramas. Not only the theory of virtue, but even the justification of specific acts reveal something rare and surprising. Glory commands, while intelligence contrives to attain the desired end and later justifies the action.[75]

When the impulse to glory is spontaneous enough and human enough, intelligence embellishes and sustains it. Judgment then plays the part of attendant and standard-bearer of glory, which would suffer to be at odds with intelligence and aspires to see all the highest powers of human nature bear

[74] Ibid., V, 2.

[75] The naturalistic writers of the second half of the century will say that this sublime *bel-esprit* manufactures fallacies in the service of vanity. But for its partisans it is just as wonderful as the glory it serves, which in human terms is the highest truth; and one cannot condemn it without condemning glory itself, a condemnation which, moreover, these adversaries did not shrink from. The same adversaries will also emphasize as strongly as possible the distinction between healthy reason and its overrefined counterpart. Very often in destroying a system we can best discover all its inner workings.

its seal and its coat of arms. But very often it happens that in search of deeds of valor and short of inspiration, glory obliges its servant to find some dignified retreat from an impasse, no matter what the cost. The servant then thrashes about outlandishly to comply properly, trying to rescue the cause of glory, and generally ending up in a contrived, cold subterfuge which makes them both look ridiculous. This difficulty usually occurs when the impulse to glory strains toward a particularly delicate or unreal level of sublimation, as in the platonic tenderness of the romances, or when *bel-esprit* focuses on subjects too crude and barbaric for its finesse, as is often the case with the horrors of tragedy. Since the role of *bel-esprit* is to accompany instinct from its most brutal to its most spiritual forms, when it can no longer carry out this connection and finds no way to retreat or advance, *bel-esprit* becomes confused and wavers.

Now the distance to be bridged between the crudeness of actual customs and the delicacy of virtue was almost always great. Between the violent instincts of noble pride and that quintessence of ideal magnanimity that constitutes chivalric virtue, there lies a long road; it has a hundred ruts and roadblocks; intelligence exhausts itself running from one end to the other without pause, and more than once it is halted en route. The fundamental flaw in all aristocratic literature is the sometimes labored stratagems of this *bel-esprit,* which does not always succeed in bringing together real life and the idea of virtue.

We have tried to distinguish in the ethics of Corneille diverse components born of different epochs or tendencies in the life of the nobility. With pride as the unifying thread, we have attempted to reweave the fabric of Corneille, heavily embroidered with the concepts of magnanimity, love, and duty. Into the forest of Corneille's work, where so many different growths are intertwined, where we discover century-old roots under fragile blooms, we have tried to introduce an order that is necessarily imperfect, and that should not make us forget the interdependence of the varying parts. Glory, pride, chivalry, love, stoicism, *bel-esprit,* magnanimity, and austere sacrifice—all these become tangled together and sustain one another in a constant and intimate connection that meshes the most delicate forms with the most primitive and archaic.

The moral problem posed by the work as a whole is whether or not a harmony is possible between virtue and the exaltation of the self. In essence Corneille's idea of the sublime gives this question an affirmative answer, formulated naturally in terms of idealist philosophy: the ego asserts itself and at the same time purifies itself under the sway of virtue. This is an idea whose influence reaches far beyond the limits of Corneille's theater, an idea which we will see questioned, in its most general form, in the ethical debates of the period. Consequently we will not be surprised to discover in those who disputed the concepts of the self, of glory, and of grandeur of soul, as in Corneille himself, the remarkable social significance with which these concepts were then imbued.

Political Drama in Corneille

Corneille's work is not merely influenced in a general way by the aristocratic spirit. Coming at a time of profound crisis in the relations between the aristocracy and royal political power, it bears the imprint of the events and discussions that witnessed its birth. Although at this time the nobles had long since lost real political power, they still fought for it in a confused and at times violent manner. The events contemporary with Corneille's tragedies–the vicissitudes of the ministries of Richelieu and Mazarin–constitute, in spite of the late date, a climactic moment in the ancient struggle between the monarchy and the aristocracy. To start with, there are the manifold conspiracies, rebellions, and military ventures of the nobility directed against the power and even the lives of Richelieu and his successor, detested ministers of absolutism. This period is followed by the long and violent upheaval of the Fronde, countered by the administrative and political reinforcement of the monarchy and Richelieu's harsh repressive measures. The final victory of the king marked the end of the Fronde and established the triumph of royalty for many years. During this entire epoch political rebellion was primarily the work of the high aristocracy.[1] This is as true in

[1] The bourgeoisie played only a timid part in the struggle against the king; in the Parisian Fronde it never rose up against the court without very soon repenting of its insubordination and demonstrating anew an active loyalty. The high magistrates, members of the Parliaments and the final courts of appeal, and in a general way the royal "officers" or functionaries, who were in absolute control of the rights conceded to them since the reign of Henry IV, were scarcely an exception. Lawyers, more important and more firmly established than the simple bourgeois, were already politically active; but still cut off from the aristocracy and fearful in proportion with their status as "bourgeois," they did not know if they should

literature as in life; in both spheres it is the aristocrats who have a bone to pick with the kings and who challenge the maxims of absolutism. The political literature of the aristocratic opposition of the seventeenth and eighteenth centuries is well known,[2] but there has been less research into the purely literary creations of the time–tragedies, poems, and romances–to see how they bear the imprints of the aristocratic upheavals. Yet it would be quite astonishing if the resistance and revolt of the aristocrats had not had some repercussions on their view of life or conception of virtues, and if literature had caught no echo of this. It would be especially strange in the age of Corneille and the Fronde, in which the political struggle was accompanied by a long spasm, undoubtedly the last, of feudal sensibility.

It is easy to see how an ethics like that of Corneille, based on pride and glorious nobility, gave support to the aristocracy in its fight against the monarchy's attempt to subjugate it. Horror of any humiliation to the ego is certainly the source of all valor in Corneille. Now for centuries it had been the lot of the nobles to be or to claim to be humiliated by the king. In asserting their pride in defiance of their cruel destiny, they asserted their freedom. Almost a hundred years after Corneille, Montesquieu, another interpreter of aristocratic traditions,[3]

---

imitate the nobles or denounce them, rebel or yield. The *petit peuple,* too, displayed no noticeable, independent political action; ignorant and inconstant, when they no longer obeyed the king they followed the nobles, and their agitation with few exceptions was as short lived as that of the nobles. Moreover, the conflict between the aristocracy and the king was the only one that seemed worthy of treatment in novels or in the theater.

[2] Joly, Retz, and others like them at the time of the Fronde have had many descendents. An extensive political literature paralleled aristocratic opposition to the very end (Fénelon, Boulainvilliers, Montesquieu, to mention only the principal authors).

[3] This characteristic stands out in all his work, one might almost say in every line he wrote. One must add that at the moment in which Montesquieu was writing, the alliance of the old aristocracy and the legal profession, to which he belonged and whose mentality he so well expressed, had almost been achieved.

analyzing the sentiment of honor in France, writes, "Glory is never the companion of servitude."[4] In political terms, the culmination of aristocratic pride in an age of absolutism is rebellion. The haughty Don Gormas, insulting the person upon whom the king's choice has fallen, is the incarnation of this rebellious pride. Urged in the name of the king to apologize to his victim, he refuses with these words:

> My lord, to preserve the high reputation I enjoy
> Slight disobedience is not such a heinous crime.[5]

A sense of one's own worth, the approval of the public, and glory—these are the values in open conflict with the ideal of obedience. Let us quote four lines, bolder yet, that Corneille deleted for reasons of prudence, and that were reinserted for the first time in the eighteenth century after a hundred years of oral tradition:

> Such amends[6] do not appease the soul at all:
> He who receives them has nothing, he who makes them dishonors himself.
> And the most common effect of such agreements
> Is that two men lose their honor instead of one.

These lines on the subject of dueling point to a more clearly defined problem than that of Corneille's general inspiration—the much discussed problem of Richelieu's hostility to *Le Cid*. Regardless of what may have been said, this hostility seems to be beyond dispute.[7] But its causes are not so clear. The one suggested as the most probable is that Richelieu's literary politics presumably sought to encourage a literature that would follow the rules and strengthen his Academy by censuring works conceived outside of the strict standards of the

[4] Montesquieu, *Lettres persanes,* letter 39.

[5] *Le Cid,* II, 1.

[6] The allusion is to a settlement commanded by the king.

[7] M. Batiffol's book on *Richelieu et Corneille* is not at all convincing. See G. Collas, editor of *Sentiments de l'Académie sur Le Cid,* 1911, and an article by the same author in *Revue d'histoire littéraire,* 1936.

theater, such as *Le Cid*. Perhaps there was no motive other than this; the subversive lines of *Le Cid* could have gone unnoticed by a government which was not overly sensitive when the established order was not under frontal attack and when the ruling authorities were not being called to account. One must not forget this personal side of politics, of capital importance at that time; a man was first of all numbered among one's friends or among one's enemies, and it is certainly clear that Corneille was not numbered among the Cardinal's avowed enemies. This fact, however, should not prevent us from recognizing in *Le Cid* the imprint of a state of mind that had little sympathy for the Cardinal's political methods.

In fact the play is full of aphorisms which, in spite of their abstract quality, could be taken as a condemnation of Richelieu's politics as the people of the time saw them. It is not likely that Corneille consciously intended this. He was expressing sentiments he found all about him, prevailing convictions that were naturally opposed to despotism even in the absence of any deliberate resistance. In any case, *Le Cid,* with its uncompromising code on duels, honor, and redress by arms, with its two single combats, one as glorious as the other for the hero, and with its atmosphere of pride and insubordination, had nothing that could serve Richelieu's purposes with the public. In the voice of Don Gormas, and even in that of Rodrigue and Don Diègue, the audience could recognize, as Sainte-Beuve says, "the echo of that proud and feudal arrogance that Richelieu barely managed to beat down and to crush."[8] In the monarchy's struggle against the nobles, the prohibition of dueling had the importance of a major administrative reform. It was a test of strength. It meant stripping the lords of the last symbol of that autonomy they had once possessed; it meant teaching them that from then on only the king could bear arms and only he could settle their quarrels. One must try and imagine the atmosphere of the times, and the clamor of protests which Corneille's lines echoed, before asserting peremptorily that Richelieu was unaware of the potentially dangerous aspects of the play.

[8] Sainte-Beuve, *Nouveaux lundis,* Vol. III, articles already mentioned.

Thus, after her father's death, when Chimène comes to plead her case before the king, beseeching him as the universal arbiter of justice (a notion dear to the monarchy), and declares,

> To the blood of his subjects a king owes justice,

Don Diègue replies in the very presence of the king,

> For just revenge there is no punishment.[9]

Here the law of feudal honor is placed above the authority of the king, very poorly defended, moreover, by the monarch himself, a good-natured and consistently conciliatory sovereign. In all of this Corneille knew exactly what he was doing, and was not unaware that he was depicting an archaic state of affairs in his portrayal of Don Fernand, the first king of Castile. "I believed myself justified," he wrote in his *Examen du Cid,* "in making him more compliant than would be the case in our times, when the king's authority is more absolute." Moreover, the atmosphere of the play suggests that a vague nostalgia for the past shaped Corneille's treatment of history at this point. Almost fifteen years after *Le Cid,* in *Don Sanche d'Aragon,* a queen of Castile (who is imaginary and thus of an undefined epoch), anxious to prevent a duel, allows her lady in waiting to tell her

> . . . It is a painful task
> To halt a combat that custom sanctions. . . .
> One cannot withdraw without shame,
> And to great hearts honor is dearer than life.

Confronted with this argument the queen can only yield—

> I understand your words and will not insist
> Upon a command that they would take as an affront.
> When dishonor sullies obedience
> Kings must question their omnipotence.[10]

[9] *Le Cid,* II, 8.
[10] *Don Sanche,* II, 1.

Castile had not changed since its first king, nor Corneille since *Le Cid.*

It is through magnanimity, as we have seen, that the relations between vassal and suzerain, aristocrat and king, must find their balance. A kind of covenant is established between superior and inferior, and around it revolve virtues and vices —the virtues to assure respect for the pact and the vices to destroy it. The virtues that constitute magnanimity vary according to situations and circumstances. On the one hand there is loyalty in obedience and a laying aside of envy, but also, in the stronger party, a casting off of tyranny and an honest offer of protection; on the other hand, there is assurance and authority in giving commands, but also, in the weaker party, refusal to yield to an injust command. In this double list of virtues Corneille has a predilection for the two terms most favorable to the vassal; of these magnanimous attitudes he chooses, as if by chance, heroic resistance to oppression, and a no less heroic resistance to the temptation to oppress. The hero in Corneille, as we have seen, is above all stoical or clement–stoical like Cinna, Nicomède, Suréna, or many others; clement like Auguste, César, Agésilas, or Nicomède himself after his victory. Of all varieties of greatness of soul, Corneille preferred above all whatever condemned the abuse of power. Thus one searches in vain in his dramas for the figure of the disloyal knight. This could certainly make for an edifying situation, should one consider the feudal system from the point of view of the strongest. But at the moment Corneille was writing the aristocracy was more inclined to invoke the duties of the sovereign than his rights. The crime which concerned the nobles was that of absolute monarchs who took the privileges of the aristocracy lightly. The crime of insubordination, which the aristocracy preferred to see only as the legitimate repudiation of an unjust sovereignty, was in their eyes likely to be tinged with glory. Honor, which Montesquieu will make the guiding principle of all monarchies uncorrupted by despotism, consists of both fidelity and dignity, and subjects agree to grant fidelity only when dignity is safeguarded. A failure to satisfy this fundamental exigency justifies rebellion.

Nevertheless, it would be false to believe that in this period the vassal's cause was always presented in as favorable a light as it appears in the theater of Corneille. There is no lack of contrary examples that contrast with Corneille, and, give further emphasis to his particular view of magnanimity.

In 1640, Desmarets de Saint-Sorlin's tragedy *Roxane* appeared, depicting the story of Alexander the Great and an ungrateful satrap, Phradate, upon whom he had heaped kindnesses and who rebels against him. Both are in love with Roxane. But all rights are ascribed to the king; even though he came after Phradate as a suitor, the author contrives to make him the most likable. He succeeds in this by imagining in a most improbable fashion that the satrap is jealous in advance of Alexander, even before the latter had met Roxane. This unjustified suspicion, accompanied by hatred, renders him culpable. Thus Phradate deserves to lose Roxane and to be punished, which in effect is what happens. He dies in the end in an attempt to assassinate Alexander. Alexander kills with his own hands another conspirator, a Greek of his retinue, who had once saved his life. As he strikes the blow he cries out,

> He saved his prince; is that such a great service?
> He did his duty; who among my men would not have done so?
> Did he have to conceive this treacherous madness?
> He who attacks his king is guilty of parricide.

When Alexander suffers from belated remorse, Roxane, by then won over to him, hastens to the rescue of the absolutist doctrine—

> . . . When one knows how to reign one never balances
> Services rendered against a great offense.

The play is strewn with maxims of this kind, which Corneille would have reserved for traitors. Desmarets was one of the Cardinal's staunch supporters, one of the authors allegedly willing to produce works made to order according to the Cardinal's specifications. Should the design and the general spirit of the tragedy of *Roxane* be attributed to Richelieu's influence? It is hard to say because here, as in most cases of this kind, all one has to go on are anecdotes and dubious traditions.[11] Nevertheless, one should take note of this absolutist tone, so contrary to what one hears in Corneille, in a writer undeniably very attached and devoted to the Cardinal.

It is not preposterous to imagine that Richelieu was preoccupied with the thoughts, the kind of reading, and the mood of the people. Since he was an unpopular ruler, he was naturally concerned with what people were thinking, and he naturally sought to modify or control public opinion. One must not forget that public opinion—which is to say, the opinion of cultivated people—was then fashioned in aristocratic circles. The role of the aristocratic salons was perhaps not so important as Saint-Simon, almost a century later, would have us believe when he asserts, on the strength of an undoubtedly embellished tradition, "L'Hôtel de Rambouillet was . . . a tribunal to be reckoned with in Paris and its decision had great influence in the world on the conduct and the reputation of members of the court, at least as much as on the works submitted there for discussion."[12]

Richelieu could indeed have worried about such circles. If one is to believe Segrais, the Cardinal dispatched his agent Boisrobert to the Marquise de Rambouillet to persuade her to keep him informed on what was said at her home. A similar attempt is recounted by another contemporary, Tallemant des Réaux, who concludes that the move was ineffectual. The desire to control opinion and literary output is evidenced in the same way in the foundation of the Academy, if it is true that its official character was authoritatively imposed on it at the private meetings of the first academicians. In his *Histoire de l'Académie,* Pellisson artlessly describes the public reaction

[11] It was presumably for having criticized *Roxane* that the Abbé d'Aubignac was not admitted to the Academy.

[12] Saint-Simon, note on the *Journal de Dangeau* of May 10, 1690.

to Richelieu's initiative: people "were afraid that this institution was but a new prop for his rule and that members were but hired help paid to uphold whatever the Cardinal did and to take notice of the actions and sentiments of others." If Pellisson, who is writing after the fact, is telling the truth, the public greatly exaggerated Richelieu's intent, but it is true that the Academy was obliged to serve the purposes of the government and those of the Cardinal. Shortly after it was founded this became apparent in the affair of *Le Cid.* All things considered, whatever the precise motives for Richelieu's animosity toward this tragedy, the success of *Le Cid* with the public and its censure by the Cardinal seem to be a single episode in a vaster and permanent conflict between public opinion and the man who was the embodiment of absolute authority.

Corneille's work does not merely touch on politics through the moral values it calls into play; it is itself organized like a vast political drama where one sees reflected, with all the symbolic intensity of drama, the conflicting ideas and forces that shook nations in this period. The sententious style and the sometimes conventional eloquence which characterize this aspect of his theater have erroneously led some to conclude that the politics of Corneille "are and could be only rhetoric."[13] Obviously Corneille is not Retz. He did not put into practice what he portrayed. Of political affairs, he knows only what his audience loves to imagine—great ambitions, great actions, and great maxims. But the very idea people have of politics is itself an important part of politics; and precisely because of his privileged role in the realm of opinion the writer, even if he is not personally involved in political action, participates in it. Corneille's "rhetoric" is inseparable from the living opinion of his times; following the tastes and the thoughts of the public, it interprets situations for which life furnished the model.

One should not, certainly, depict Corneille as a partisan or see in him the conscious defender of the nobles' cause. Such

[13] Brunetière, *Études critiques, loc. cit.*

a clear-cut position was inconceivable in his times. One did not belong to a party; or more precisely, what was called a party was not, as it is today, a group with clearly defined boundaries and with its own ideas and its own leaders. There were personal intrigues and private groups, as shifting as politics itself. If the nobles themselves alternated between loyalty and rebellion, and in rebellion shifted from one clan to another, more often spurred by temporary advantage than by sustained political views, why should one expect Corneille, a man of no importance and at some remove from these affairs, to be more consistent? At the time of the imprisonment of the Duke of Longueville (one of the leaders of the Fronde), he readily accepted an appointment in Normandy that was being taken away from one of the Duke's followers. He seized this opportunity as the most illustrious of the rebel princes and dukes seized greater ones. By definition, in politics and aristocratic custom, everything revolved around self-interest. Inconstancy was among the most common characteristics of the period. Poets shared in it in their sphere, furthering their own reputations by every means, telling people what they wanted to hear without being held truly responsible for what they said. It is quite remarkable that Corneille's work was so consistently hostile to the spirit of despotism. This uniformity of sentiment was rare, and no doubt it was based on a profound inclination in his character, which we know to have been proud and sensitive. Yet the general inconstancy did not prevent a certain tendency of feeling and thought to dominate in the public as a whole, especially among the nobles and their admirers. Corneille's work expresses both this general tendency and his own particular bent.

Moreover, calculating ambitions and the spirit of intrigue have a far from negligible place in the theater of Corneille. "These are court intrigues which negate themselves," says Corneille himself of his tragedy *Othon*,[14] without any negative implications. To understand how much the public admired skillful machinations, one must read Retz; his cynicism would be inexplicable if his readers had not considered

[14] *Othon*, To the Reader.

it a normal political attitude. The aristocracy had always felt a certain inclination to seek greatness in a contempt for scruples, in the undisciplined exercise of the "right of war," which, if one thinks about it, justifies usurpation as well as conquest, and guile as well as force. The Fronde knew this breed of cynical gentlemen, who placed politics as they placed themselves above every rule. They were *libertins,* as that word was then understood, and as contemptuous of virtue as they were of the rabble. Retz is not too far from this type.

Let us add that as a result of its amoral aspects the aristocratic spirit has in it the seed of absolutism, and justifies absolutism. Why should the nobles be shocked if the arm of the king be above the law when each among them claims the same privilege? The idea of a supreme will, acting freely and wantonly, or of a majesty without restrictions, is an obsession with the nobles. Their own dream of power and glory is realized for all time in royalty, in which they have always wanted to see something unparalleled. The institution of absolutism was greatly facilitated by this state of mind; fundamentally the sacred character of the royal person had never ceased to be acknowledged. Consequently one should not be surprised to find it affirmed so frequently in Corneille, who also thinks, as does Camille in *Horace,* that one must seek the direct inspiration of the gods in kings,

> Whose free and holy authority
> Is a hidden ray of their divinity.[15]

But at the time of Corneille the aristocrats' tendency to Machiavellianism or to the deification of authority is counterbalanced by a contrary tendency. The nobles, victims of the kings' power, sought in tradition itself a counterweight to certain political maxims that worked to their disadvantage. And as a matter of fact the right of the strongest or the most astute, when abusively interpreted, went against their own interests. Thus, the critique of the *maximes d'Etat*[16] and of despotism in the name of a magnanimous ethics takes prece-

[15] *Horace,* III, 3.

[16] Machiavellian political maxims (*Tr. note*).

dence in the period that concerns us; the image of the evil king who misuses and abuses his power, of the "tyrant" as he was already called, is present throughout Corneille's theater in *Cinna, Pompée, Héraclius, Nicomède, Attila,* and *Suréna.*

Consequently the aristocracy, at one and the same time the admirer and the victim of absolute power, found itself in an uncertain position with respect to royalty. It would have wanted the power of the kings to be at once sacred and limited. Not knowing how to resolve the contradiction, the nobles had recourse to an artifice that reconciled conformism and revolt; they put the blame on a scapegoat, who was held responsible for all the sins of royalty, while royalty itself was held innocent; rather, the evil counselor of the king, the cunning scoundrel who has caught the monarch off guard or humored his evil inclinations, is to blame. The abuses of kingly power are the consequence of his pernicious counsels. The independence and the sacred sovereignty of the royal person must be defended against this evil person. Those who want to say to the king, "Rule less strongly," say instead, "Rule completely, rid yourself of your wicked demon."[17] Furthermore, the introduction of this third person was not only convenient for the requirements of the polemic; it corresponded to reality. The kings of France had at all times surrounded themselves with private counselors, loyal supporters of their absolutist designs. The latter had always incurred the hatred of the aristocracy who, detesting in them the instrument of their abasement, pretended to make them solely responsible for the crimes with which they did not dare charge the king.

An anti-absolutist theoretician of the Fronde, Claude Joly, while manifesting a religious respect for kings, attacked "the malice of their favorites and ministers."[18] "The royal author-

[17] Cf. the sonnet, attributed to Corneille, on the death of Louis XIII, which occurred some months after that of Richelieu:

> After thirty-three years lost on the throne,
> Beginning to rule he ceased to live.

[18] Claude Joly, *Receuil de Maximes véritables et importantes pour l'institution du Roi contre la fausse et pernicieuse politique du cardinal Mazarin,* 1652, *Avertissement au lecteur.*

ity," he claimed, has been usurped by these ministers, who have left their masters only the name of King."[19] Now one can grasp the importance of Corneille's "villains"–these cynical tools of despotism are not conventional creations in Corneille; their role is central in the drama as in the reality it depicts.

In Corneille's tragedy the fainthearted monarch, the ministers who give him bad counsel–in short, the court–constitute the milieu in which deceits and betrayals are hatched. Only the most ignoble ethics govern there, forming as it were the somber antithesis of the virtues that shine elsewhere. This realm is the reverse of Corneille's magnanimity–cowardice in place of courage; cruelty in place of generosity, for

> . . . Such is the infamous nature of a tyrant . . .
> If he is not afraid he oppresses; if he does not oppress, he is afraid.[20]

A wicked queen invokes "disguised hate" as the tutelary goddess of her throne,

> Worthy virtue of kings, noble secret of the court.[21]

Another villainous queen, as she is plotting for her son, fears that he

> . . . might misunderstand that there is no deceit, no crime,
> That a throne acquired thereby does not justify.[22]

And when she sees that her fears are well-founded she predicts to this same son that

> Time and new experiences will teach you
> The virtues of which kings stand in need.[23]

[19] Ibid., Chapter VI.
[20] *Héraclius,* V, 5.
[21] *Rodogune,* II, 1.
[22] *Nicomède,* I, 5.
[23] Ibid., III, 6.

Nowhere in Corneille is the spirit of the court painted in pleasant hues. In *Polyeucte,* Félix, an old courtier blinded by his own baseness, interprets Sévère's generous plea to spare Polyeucte as a trap meant to test his loyalty to the Emperor—

> I know what politics is among people of the court;
> I know better than he its skillful practice.[24]

Turning away from magnanimity, courtly politics seeks immediate gain at the expense of glory; it looks on faith as an empty phantasm—

> My Lord, when questions are settled by the sword,
> Justice and right are hollow ideas,
> And he who would be just in such times
> Weighs power, and not reasons. . . .
> Justice is not a virtue of State. . . .
> When one wants to be just, one lives in fear;
> And he who would want all power, must dare
> to transgress all laws.[25]

Hostility to the court and to the ministers reached its high point, or rather appeared most overtly after the death of Richelieu. The nobles, who had considered this death a liberation, had expected a great deal from the regency of Anne of Austria, a faithful ally of the aristocratic conspirators during Richelieu's lifetime. Anne of Austria's conversion to absolutist politics and the elevation of Mazarin bitterly disappointed them without overly intimidating them. Mazarin had neither the birth nor the prestige of Richelieu. In him the abhorred image of the wicked royal counselor was shaded with a tinge of baseness and common birth from which his predecessor had been free. The nobles preferred to imagine scoundrels in the royal entourage as commoners, *parvenus.*

[24] *Polyeucte,* V, 1.

[25] *Pompée,* I, 1, the counselor of the King of Egypt speaking to his master. Here we have the *maximes d'état* introduced by absolutism that are usually elaborated by Corneille's traitors and stigmatized by his heroes. See also *Nicomède,* line 850 and *passim.*

Mazarin was a perfect illustration and embodiment of this traditional notion. In November 1643, in his *Discours à la Reine Régente,*[26] Balzac asks Anne of Austria to establish true peace in the realm, one that "will not elevate to high office servants who would drive the children out of the house." This discourse appeared at the moment when Mazarin had just imprisoned the Duke of Beaufort, the grandson of Henry IV and the chief leader of the conspiracy of the Importants. A year later Corneille, whose tragedy *Pompée* was being printed, felt the need to dedicate it to Mazarin, who was also thanked in a dithyrambic tone for some favor in a few lines of verse at the beginning of the work. Now in *Pompée,* written and performed before Mazarin's accession to power, there are certain lines that were hardly likely to please the minister. Cléopâtre, for example, reproaches her brother, the King of Egypt

> . . . for listening to these cowardly advisors,
> Who inspire in kings only habits of tyranny:
> Not only their birth, but their minds are base,
> In vain does one raise them up to govern nations:
> A heart born to serve knows not how to command.

She pleads with him to drive out his wicked counselors–

> Free yourself from them and their tyranny,
> Summon once more the virtue their counsels
> have banished,
> That high virtue with which heaven and blood
> Always swell the hearts of those of our lineage.[27]

Lines like this could have troublesome reverberations: it is precisely the language that the aristocratic enemies of Mazarin had begun to employ and this, in all probability, explains the precaution of the dedication. In any case these

[26] One finds there all the aristocrats' demands–an end to the war with Spain, the toning down of absolutism, the re-establishment of the rights of Parliament and the princes, etc.

[27] *Pompée,* IV, 2.

lines expressed a deep-seated conviction of Corneille, since he reiterates the idea twenty years later in *Othon,* where he shows us a noble Roman woman heaping scorn on a freedman, the all-powerful counselor of the Emperor Galba, who dares to think himself worthy of becoming her husband—

> I had been told, though, that Nature
> Retained in your kind her first colors,
> That those of our Caesars who have listened to such men as you
> Have all sullied their names by cowardly deeds.[28]

The kings of France, too, had aspired to change men's natural state. They had raised simple commoners up to the highest posts in the State. They had made them their trusted counselors, ministers, Secretaries of State, and commissioners, giving them the real power and leaving to the great lords only the honorary semblance of power. When Corneille stigmatized the low birth of these tools of despotism he was echoing not only a generally accepted platitude but at the same time an old aristocratic charge, the one the historian Mézeray, who also wrote at the time of the Fronde, voices in retrospect when he reproaches Louis XI for "the abasement of the nobles and the elevation of worthless people."[29]

In Corneille the situation thus brought about by absolutism is the point of departure for the political drama. In this drama nobility, confronted with tyranny, will arrogate to itself the fine role of legitimate and lifesaving rebellion. What justifies the nobility in its rebellion is the unjust treatment to which it has been subjected;[30] the nobles, if they are to be

[28] *Othon,* II, 2.

[29] Mézeray, *Abrégé chronologique de l'Histoire de France,* Vol. II, p. 155.

[30] Claude Joly censures the revolt of the nobles but is of the opinion that "the ministers are the reason these illustrious people . . . are brought to these unfortunate extremes, sometimes wantonly provoking quarrels with them and harassing them so that they are forced to hurl themselves into the abyss." *Recueil de maximes,* Chapter VII.

believed, would serve faithfully if their devotion were recognized and rewarded. But the failing of kings lies precisely in not knowing what gratitude is, in even mistrusting anyone who wins too much luster in their service. In their eyes a too glorious servant is not dependent enough. Prusias mistrusts his son Nicomède, who wins victory after victory for him. And Araspe, the king's counselor, busies himself with confirming him in his fear, and discrediting "great hearts" in his eyes–

> It is usually in this way that his kind act:
> The pursuance of duty would dim the brilliance of noble deeds;
> And these great hearts, swollen with the din of their combats,
> Supreme in the army and among their troops,
> Acquire an easy habit of command
> And obedience becomes an arduous calling.[31]

The drama of the unjust persecution of Nicomède was presented for the first time in 1651, perhaps early in the year, when "the princes," namely Condé, his brother Conti, and his brother-in-law the Duke of Longueville, were still in prison by order of Mazarin. The imprisonment of the princes, especially of Condé, to whom the royal house owed so many victories, as Prusias did to Nicomède, had just occurred in February 1651. One can imagine what echoes the play must have awakened in the audience. Corneille reproduced the arguments with which the court justified the arrest of the princes–namely, their insubordination, their pretensions, and their arrogance–and as we have just seen he changed them into servile sophisms in the mouth of a base courtesan. Nicomède, moreover, accurately symbolized the type of hero that one usually lauded in Condé. In the course of the play he is called "conqueror," and "taker of towns," the very titles contemporaries bestowed on Condé. At the beginning of the *Grand Cyrus,* Scudéry's dedication to Mme. de Longueville alluded to her brother, "the taker of towns and the winner

[31] *Nicomède,* II, 1.

of battles." This dedication is dated 1649. In the first volumes of their romance the Scudérys were to dwell at considerable length on the theme of the great captain persecuted by a mistrustful king who forgets that he owes him his throne. Artamène, like Nicomède and like Condé (with whom the *clefs* of the time identify him) is unjustly imprisoned by his king. Remember, however, that the first books of the *Cyrus,* which contain the story of the imprisonment of Artamène, appeared before 1650, that is to say before the imprisonment of the princes. It is well to keep this in mind in order to understand that in all of this, actual events of the time did not influence literary works in terms of precise details but in terms of general conditions and atmosphere. The Scudérys foretold the misfortunes of Condé because the nobility was obsessed with the idea of similar misfortunes. Moreover, when dealing with the subject of royal ingratitude, as with many other subjects, the spirit of aristocratic rebellion lived on in Corneille far beyond actual circumstances. In *Suréna,* his last tragedy produced almost thirty years after the defeat of the Fronde, Corneille again has his hero, persecuted by the royal family, utter these words in which all the old bitterness of the nobles reappears–

> The more I serve them the guiltier I will be;
> And if they wish my death, then I must die. . . .[32]

The reaction of the nobles to so much injustice can range from outright conspiracy to a sort of muted and haughty insubordination mixed with protestations of intense devotion. Artamène defends himself before his king, who suspects him of treason, in these proud terms: "It is not easy to imagine who could corrupt at his pleasure the allegiance of one who disposes of crowns at will."[33] This allusion to his services and his power is, it is true, the only sign of disrespect he permits himself; elsewhere there are only declarations of blind obedience. All the same, he resists the wishes of the king and a rebellion of the nobles, presented in a favorable light, breaks

[32] *Suréna,* V, 3.
[33] *Le Grand Cyrus,* Part I, Book I, p. 141.

out in his favor. Suréna, too, knows how to recall all that is owed to him:

> I have lived for my glory, as much as one should;
> I leave a noble example to him who can follow me;
> But if you deliver me up to your jealous anger
> I will perhaps not have lived enough for you.[34]

The tone is always the same; although one proclaims his devotion in vain, there is a point at which he ceases deep down to believe himself held to complete submission—

> Although we owe everything to the supreme powers,
> Madam, we owe something to ourselves.[35]

With absolutism challenged and the nobles arrayed against the royal power, how will the drama unfold?

Ultimately the goal toward which Corneille is striving is the reconciliation of royalty with the *gens de coeur,* the valiant nobles. But in the meantime there is no dearth of violence. The valiant nobles themselves can take up arms; or the people could take them up for the nobles and defend their rights against tyranny. And indeed in this age of conspiracies and riots the nobles will often find themselves allied with the common people, or more precisely they will often make use of them. In this way Condé, with all the disdain that one can imagine, supported the extremists of the *Ormée* of Bordeaux. Even in Paris the people played a part in the plans and the intrigues of the nobility. Certainly the nobles did not use this dangerous tool out of sheer wantonness. Like the rebellious princes in *Cyrus,* their adoption of so perilous a remedy betrayed their desperation, for "there is nothing in the world more to be avoided than the revolt of the people."[36] Corneille's dramas are full of popular uprisings—the people riot for Polyeucte, for Héraclius, for Nicomède—but obviously

[34] *Suréna,* IV, 4.
[35] *Othon,* III, 1.
[36] *Le Grand Cyrus,* Part III, Book I, p. 32.

there are no representatives on the stage; the people play the role of a distant ally. Those whose cause they serve barely mention them, and then it is with contempt. Laodice, who has stirred up the people against Queen Arsinoé, tells her,

> Your people are guilty, and in all your subjects
> These seditious cries are so many heinous crimes;
> But I am a queen and to triumph over you
> In our disputes I have made them rise against you;
> The rules of war have always allowed one
> To kindle rebellion among his enemies.[37]

It was in this way that the nobles at the time of the Fronde used the people to make themselves feared by the court. The people had only to disappear as soon as the nobles received satisfaction. The riots of which the nobles dreamed were not meant to sow discord between themselves and royalty but to command the king's respect and to lessen his severity. In these Frondes of fantasy, to which their imagination gave a happier ending than that of the real Fronde, the nobles emerged as the saviors of a repentant and grateful monarchy. They came generously to offer peace and general tranquillity to the distressed king. Nicomède and Laodice protect the royal couple against the mob they themselves have unleashed; Nicomède says to the king,

> All is calm, my Lord: one moment's glimpse of me
> Has suddenly appeased the angry rabble.[38]

The riot in *Cyrus* ends the same way–Artamène throws himself at the feet of the king the moment the king is at the mercy of the victorious conspirators. In this instance, too, the monarch receives a lesson in mercy from his rescued victim. Here, too, the defeat of tyranny opens the way to good monarchy.

Nicomède, then, traces the picture of an imaginary Fronde,

[37] *Nicomède,* V, 6.
[38] Ibid., V, 9.

a Fronde crowned by victory and the triumph of the princes;[39] at one time the real Fronde had allowed of such hopes. But in general it was necessary to be more modest. Spontaneous leniency on the part of the kings was still the most likely among happy endings. This is the ending of *Cinna.* If any tragedy of Corneille is difficult to separate from the times in which it was written, it is certainly this one. Without claiming to perceive there the echo of any precise event, the Normandy revolt or the Conspiracy of the Noblewomen, it will suffice to recall that under Richelieu a dozen artistocratic conspiracies followed one another, that the members of high society were very much interested in them, and that they could not but see in the political intrigues of Corneille's tragedies the reflection of contemporary events presented in a way pleasing to them. "The first spectators," writes Voltaire in his *Commentaire sur Cinna,* "were those who fought at la Marfée[40] and who participated in the war of the Fronde." We need say no more, as long as one applies the remark not only to *Cinna* but also to other plays.

The emotional impact of the ending is perhaps even greater in *Cinna* than in *Nicomède.* In *Cinna* we have a crime committed, an open revolt; and then sudden failure, the suspended bolt of lightning, the atmosphere of imminent martyrdom, when abruptly reconciliation comes from on high, the crime is forgiven, and oppression turns into magnanimous lordship. They say that when Condé, whose traits one may recognize in the character of Nicomède, attended the first performance of *Cinna* at twenty years of age, he wept at the moment of Auguste's pardon. Ten years later he himself was to play a new *Cinna,* this time a real one, and before being pardoned he would know imprisonment, defeat, and exile. The real-life *Cinna* explains the tears shed, if the story is true, for the fictitious *Cinna.*

[39] The fact that Nicomède, a rebel prince, is at the same time heir to the throne changes nothing; on the contrary, in this case the identification of the rebellious prince and the future good king is highly significant.

[40] A battle delivered against the king's armies by the Count of Soissons, who was killed there (1641).

It does not matter who plays the most glorious part in the final reconciliation, king or nobles. Reconciliation is brought about, and brought about by casting off tyranny for the greater glory of true and good monarchy. One question remains–where does kingship end and tyranny begin? Corneille certainly did not have to work out this theoretical problem. He limited himself to staging the situations, the personalities, and the attitudes springing from the conflict between the nobles and absolutism. He sought not to specify the terms of the debate but to draw from it the most intense dramatic effect.

There were others, and in the same period, who dealt with the intellectual bases of that problem which Corneille posed and resolved in terms of drama. All the political writers of the aristocracy up to the revolution of 1789 sought to establish criteria for distinguishing kingship from tyranny and monarchy from despotism. Montesquieu's whole work rests on this distinction. The criterion they ultimately stressed was the existence of a contract which should order the relations of a true monarch with his subjects, a sort of constitutional law which was a modernized form of the old feudal pact. It would be a mistake to believe that constitutional doctrines, at least in France, originated with the middle class. Those ideas bear the deep imprint of aristocratic thought, which mingles its hopes for a constitution with its memory of the "old laws" or the "old government," that is to say feudal institutions. As a matter of fact feudal government never knew laws in the proper sense of the word; it was never a legal arrangement that limited authority, it was the state of things and the physical inability of all authority, of whatever kind, to exceed certain limits. But the apologists of feudalism were apt to represent as a legal harmony what in fact had never been more than an anarchy systematized into custom. For purposes related to their own epoch, they set up against absolutism the idea of law and of the contract. Thus Claude Joly, whose feudalist tendencies are beyond dispute and who anathematizes the "new views" introduced in France by recent ministers, gives this ideal definition of law: "A bilateral contract composed of two equally essential parts, that is, on one hand a proposal by the king or the people, and its free acceptance by the other party."[41] For Retz, as well, "the most established monarchies and the monarchs invested with the strongest authority keep themselves in power only by joining force and laws." Obviously Retz is speaking of laws that could be imposed on the royal power itself; and since Richelieu had destroyed the last remains of such law, the Cardinal, according to Retz, "established in the most legitimate of monarchies what was perhaps the most scandalous and dangerous tyranny that had ever enslaved a nation.[42] It was necessary, in order to reconcile the king and the nobles, to double back along the path traveled by Richelieu. But should one then set explicit limits to the power of the kings? The monarchs of earlier times were weak by necessity; should modern kings be kept weak by the strength of laws and of men? Occasionally but rarely, especially in the seventeenth century, theoreticians dared to argue this case openly; but in general the people, less audacious and finding no proper legal restriction of royal power in tradition, gave no expression to such a demand. They dreamed of a sort of generous consent by which the monarchy voluntarily imposed certain limits on itself without surrendering its prerogatives. The literature of the romances of the seventeenth century often took great pleasure in the image of a paternal monarchy whose glory lies in imposing limitations on itself. In *L'Astrée,* King Mérovée, upbraiding his son Childéric for his tendency toward dissoluteness and despotism, expresses himself in these terms: "Every prince who wants to command a people must make himself wiser and more virtuous than those by whom he wishes to be obeyed, or he will never succeed except through tyranny, which can be neither safe nor pleasant for the one who practices it."[43] In *Cyrus,* King Cambyse "lets himself be governed by the laws, and governs only through them, so that from the way he acts toward his subjects he seems not

[41] Claude Joly, *Recueil de maximes,* Chapter V.

[42] Retz, *Mémoires,* éd. des Grands Ecrivains, Vol. I, pp. 275, 278–79.

[43] *L'Astrée,* Part III, Book 12, p. 679.

so much their king as their father."[44] Corneille conceived the ideal monarchy no differently:

> I shall never abuse absolute power,[45]

says Queen Isabelle in *Don Sanche*. And in *Pertharite,* a king answers the counselor who urges him to do violence to his captive–

> Offer, offer to tyrants your detestable maxims,
> I hate the art of governing that permits itself crimes.
> How impudent I would be to give an example today
> That tomorrow my laws would punish in another.[46]

Corneille is not a speculative thinker. But his characters often debate, thereby introducing into the drama the echo of contemporary political discussions. In Corneille's time the enemies of absolutism were already beginning to form the habit (one they were to have for a long time) of making shrewd comparisons of different political regimes. In his tragedies Corneille simply did in an unsystematic way what Montesquieu was to do, stressing the diversity of the systems of government and analyzing the strengths and possibilities of each so as to abstract from them the idea of that perfect milieu, somewhere between the people's state and the despotic state, that constitutes the old-style moderate monarchy. Thus in *Cinna* Maxime recommends to Auguste that he lay aside his power–

> I dare to say, my Lord, that in different climes
> Not all sorts of states are well received;
> Each people has its own according to its nature,
> Which could not be changed without doing it injury:
> Such is the law of heaven, whose judicious fairness
> Scatters the seeds of diversity throughout the universe.
> The Macedonians love monarchy
> And the rest of the Greeks love liberty,

[44] *Le Grand Cyrus,* Part I, Book 2, p. 228.
[45] *Don Sanche,* II, 2.
[46] *Pertharite,* II, 3.

The Parthes, the Persians want sovereigns,
And only the consulate is right for the Romans.

Cinna, who in the same scene pretends to defend the absolutist regime, opposes this geographical relativism to the idea of inevitable changes in history. These were the two common arguments in the political controversy–one invoked the temperament of the French people to justify the preservation of the old institutions; the other invoked the sweep of history to justify the advance of absolutism–

It is true that the infinite prudence of heaven
Dispenses a different genius to each people;
But it is no less true that this order of the heavens
Changes with time as well as with place.[47]

Freedom in the past, despotism today. In the debates of Corneille's characters, as in Montesquieu, the point of the theory of different climes is to refute the idea of historical necessity and to oppose absolutism. Here now, in *Agésilas,* is the panegyric of moderate government contrasted with the specter of Asiatic despotism, of which Montesquieu will also make ample use in his *Esprit des lois*. Here the historical example is offered by the Persians of antiquity, who for Corneille were more like Montesquieu's Persians than like those companions of the great Cyrus in Mlle. de Scudéry's novel–

In Persia there are no subjects;
There are only abject slaves,
Whom sovereigns crush with a glance:
The monarch, or rather the tyrant,
Whose only law is his caprice,
Wants no other rule and no other justice
And often even considers as a capital offense
The most singular merit and the greatest service;
He humbles at his feet the most sublime virtues,
He insolently sacrifices the most illustrious lives,[48]

[47] *Cinna,* II, 1.

[48] This is obviously a reference to despotism as the enemy of the nobles.

And today only the disheartened
Are safe from his tyranny. . . .
Greece has holier laws,
She has people and kings
Who govern with justice:
Reason presides there, and judicious fairness,
Sovereign power, limited by them,
There grants no rights to caprice.[49]

These lines, written in 1666, did not keep Corneille from flattering the omnipotence of Louis XIV about the same time.[50] Corneille the flatterer by training and by profession is always found alongside of Corneille the enemy of tyranny by inclination and by eloquence; this was the temper of his whole generation.

Another echo of the current political debates in Corneille, which the following century will re-echo and amplify, is the idea of the greater stability of the moderate government that rules by consent rather than by force. We have seen the role that rivalry in magnanimity plays in Corneille; theoreticians who favored aristocratic government based good government on a similar technique operating between the ruler and the ruled. The generous acts at the end of *Cinna* present in shortened form the working of a perfect monarchy–Auguste has never been more assured of the obedience of his subjects than after the pardon. According to Joly, tyranny, "being accepted only by force, can produce nothing but wars, public disorders, and divisions, which destroy true authority."[51] Similarly in *L'Astrée,* Childéric, having spurned his father's counsels on justice, is overthrown by an uprising and places all his hopes of being restored to power in the intrigues of one of his friends, who deliberately encourages the new king along the path to tyranny to lead him, too, to his downfall.[52] The same situation, which is also an argu-

[49] *Agésilas,* II, 1.
[50] See *Attila,* line 221 ff.
[51] Claude Joly, *Recueil des Maximes,* Chapter VII.
[52] *L'Astrée,* Part V, Book 3, p. 148.

ment, is to be found in Corneille, when a royal counselor, who secretly wants to supplant the king, plans accordingly

> To set him up as a tyrant by my own counsels,
> To have him prepare the instruments of his own
> downfall. . . .[53]

Tyranny is the ruination of the monarchy; it opens the door to total subversion. This argument will be picked up again by all the theoreticians of aristocratic government. From Fénelon to Montesquieu they will try to show the kings that their ruin lies where they think they see their greatness. On a very different plane, and right up to our own times, this will also be the argument of liberalism against dictatorship, accused of breeding violence and disorder. There is a curious kinship, but one that can be observed at many points, between the political themes of the restive nobility and those of the liberal parties of the last century and of our own, though their social basis is completely different. For this reason alone it is rash to see Montesquieu as the first liberal, in the modern sense of the word.

In effect, all this anti-despotic literature, born of the difficulties of the aristocracy, was bound to turn to their disadvantage. The people were inflamed with the idea of freedom and laws but behind these words they saw something other than nostalgia for an aristocratic regime. This misunderstanding, which was not to be cleared up until 1789, became more and more pronounced up to that time and is much more conspicuous in the eighteenth century than in the seventeenth. But it was already perceptible at the time of Corneille and particularly in that paradoxical enthusiasm for Roman patriotism so prevalent in the aristocracy and its favorite authors.[54] Yet it is hard to imagine anyone further from the Prince of Condé or the Duke of Beaufort than were the citizens of the Roman Republic. And what purpose could Cinna and Sertorius serve at the time of Louis XIII and

[53] *Pertharite,* II, 2.

[54] See especially Balzac's discourses to Mme. de Rambouillet on *Le Romain, La Conversation des Romains,* and *Mécénas.*

Louis XIV? The fact was that the high nobility instinctively compared its lot with the lot of that Roman aristocracy and that Senate which despotism succeeded in debasing at the same time it destroyed the old freedoms. Remember Cinna, like an aristocrat adherent of the Ligne or of the Fronde, speaking to the conspirators of their "illustrious forebears." A knowledge of history and of Roman institutions was useful not only to the French theoreticians of absolutism and *raison d'état,* who sought in it above all the idea of imperial majesty and the omnipotence of the prince and of the State. Seen from a different angle, Roman history appeared to be the startling representation of the decadence that was part of the course of despotism.[55] In this sense, the debate in *Cinna* between Auguste and his counselors on political liberty and absolute government, initiated at the moment Rome had passed from the one to the other, was not a simple rhetorical exercise for Corneille's contemporaries.

Yet there is a great difference between the two worlds. Corneille tries in vain to make Cinna a faithful knight, to attribute to his Romans the vainglory and courtly manners of the heroes of his own time. The fact remains that the Roman republican character that disdains royal grandeur, and the Roman civic and patriotic ardor that edified Corneille's aristocratic spectators have little to do with the moral realities of that aristocracy. In the fifth of his *Essais sur l'histoire de France,* Guizot makes a profound distinction between feudal government and aristocratic government of the patrician type practiced by a body of men or a senate, of which the Roman Republic is the most celebrated example. In the first, sovereignty is completely individual; it is a "collection of absolutisms," in which assemblies are but temporary groups. In the second, there are laws superior to the individual, that express a collective sovereignty. All sorts of distinctions re-

[55] The aristocratic polemic was so conscious of the profit it could draw from Roman history that Montesquieu (one always comes back to him as the perfect representative of this school) found it worthwhile to dedicate a special work to it. The *Considérations* are nothing more than the history of Rome interpreted according to the spirit of aristocratic liberalism.

sult from this difference. In the moral order the one that is most obvious to us is that established between the ethics of the ego, the only truly feudal ethics, with its perennial tendency to megalomania and to boundless ambitions, and the Roman ethics of law and the commonweal. The French nobles, in spite of their verbosity, were never capable of passing from one formula to the other. There was also a good deal of imprudence in the Roman declamations of the aristocrats: this legalistic notion of patriotism was itself eventually to condemn the type of prerogatives that the aristocracy was trying to defend. In its beginnings the Revolution was merely the sudden clarification of this misunderstanding. Yet this distant repercussion, as many lessons as it may hold for the historian of ideas, does not change the meaning of the political maxims of the aristocracy. In the form they assume in Corneille's theater, they were entirely inspired by the political traditions and problems of old France.

The Metaphysics of Jansenism

It is not easy at first glance to attribute a precise meaning to the seventeenth-century current of thought that we call Jansenism, which by common consent profoundly marks the spirit of this period. The fundamental ideas of Jansenism and the most important events in its history are, however, so well known that it will suffice to recall them briefly.

The movement originated in the exchanges of ideas and projects that took place, from about 1617 to 1635, between Du Vergier de Hauranne, Abbot of Saint-Cyran, and his friend Jansen (or Jansenius), Bishop of Ypres. They were secretly planning a reform of the Catholic Church, actually an ill-defined one. All that still survived of their projects a generation later was a Latin book of Jansenius, the *Augustinus,* a sort of compilation of St. Augustine, and the imprint Saint-Cyran left on the convent of Port-Royal. Richelieu imprisoned Saint-Cyran in 1638 and as early as 1653 the papacy unequivocally condemned Jansenius' book, which was published posthumously; in 1656 the Sorbonne debarred Arnauld, who was carrying on Saint-Cyran's work and defending Jansenius. Jansenism endured, however, adhered to by two groups. On one hand there was the convent of Port-Royal, whose nuns refused to sign the formulary imposed on the French clergy in 1656 condemning Jansenius. On the other hand there were the scholars and *solitaires* of Port-Royal, especially the great Arnauld and Nicole, and the friends of the convent, the most illustrious of whom was Pascal. The Jansenists believed that the salvation of man after the sin of Adam and the fall could come only as a free gift of God and not from human effort, which could no more win grace by itself than it could resist it. To believe otherwise, they maintained, was to place man on a level with God and to render Christ's coming and sufferings useless; it was to attribute to the creature the power to save himself. The Jansenists were champions of the most rigorous ethics; they condemned laxity of morals and the corruption of Christian principles whether dealing with the ethics of the individual or the organization of the Church. In this twofold domain of theology and ethics they clashed with the Society of Jesus, which argued the case for a more easygoing religion and morality, inspired by the views of the Jesuit theologian Molina and the casuists. The monarchy and the clerical hierarchy as a whole persecuted the Jansenists almost incessantly, and Louis XIV finally went as far as to have the convent of Port-Royal razed to the ground in 1710. In any case this long crisis, which was to continue all through the eighteenth century with many political repercussions, left a profound impression on the ideas and the literature of the age of Louis XIV. Not only the writings of Pascal but also those of La Rochefoucauld, Racine, and Boileau reveal the effects of the Jansenist influence.

Seen in bold outline, this is the complex of events and ideas that we know as Jansenism. But if we ask ourselves what it all means, or what its precise place is in the history of French society, difficulties immediately stop us short. Here we are no longer dealing with neat formulas or with the clearly defined characters of heroic literature. In heroic literature a certain idea of man and of life was forcefully affirmed. With Jansenism everything is complex, all things dissolve into controversies, reservations, and subtle distinctions. In heroic literature the actual ways of a class and the spirit of an environment openly and triumphantly asserted themselves. In the case of Jansenism the conflict was one of theological notions whose practical implications were obscure and remote. Thus we generally conceive of Jansenism as pure theory, with no other attributes but those imposed by its own logic, which we seek to follow and understand. We concede that the social role of Jansenism, its history as a party, was subject to outside influences, but we do not consider this part of its history important. In any case we consider it something apart from what constitutes the greatness of Jansenism; we abstract from the vicissitudes of the real

Port-Royal a sort of eternal Port-Royal that owes almost nothing to history, a pure response of the mind to the problems of liberty and the good.

Yet as convenient as this attitude toward Jansenism might be, one should not adopt it too hastily. Such an attitude is above all possible when we dwell exclusively on the core of the fundamental doctrine of Jansenism, according to which human merit plays no decisive role in salvation, and when we refuse to approach that doctrine in any other way than from within. Obviously from this point of view another hundred years of meditation will still not uncover any other meaning in the doctrine than a specifically theological one. But if, on the contrary, we believe that the true import of a doctrine or theory lies in the human intent that inspires it, in the conduct to which it leads, and in the nature of the values it defends or condemns, then all this will appear to be much more important than the speculative aspect of a statement or creed. There is hardly one idea that does not have this ethical aspect or dimension, these practical consequences whose study does more to clarify a doctrine than does a pure meditation on the doctrine's formulas. Jansenius, following St. Augustine, believes that since original sin radically corrupted man's nature he no longer has in himself, in his powers alone, the means of advancing, however feebly, toward his salvation. Therefore grace must be absolutely independent of our natural merits or demerits, it must be absolutely gratuitous and irresistible. It is not hard to imagine the disputes that could arise from such a statement. Of what use is man's free will if everything depends on God's election? What becomes of God's justice if he does not choose according to merit? Other questions can be opposed to these upholding the contrary thesis. Where is God's sovereignty if, our choice being free, His ceases to be? Where is our corruption if salvation is all one with the merits of our nature? And so on and so forth, a middle position being impossible, since the whole debate can hang on the least spark of initiative left to man. But beneath these dilemmas, apparently unresolvable on the plane of pure reason (Bossuet himself says so, and concludes that it is a mystery), there is a clash of two strong divergent views of life. The theological arguments draw their haunting strength from a stronger human source than mere logical exigency. The debate centers principally on two ways of judging man and human values. To reduce the discussion to its theoretical terms is to stress, whether consciously or not, the excessive and vain character of a purely metaphysical attitude. To give meaning to the debate and human relevance to the conflicting arguments one must look for the profound motives, that is, *passion,* that actually produced them.

The doctrine of efficacious grace rests on a particularly somber notion of original sin and man's subsequent fall. But such an unrelieved notion of the fall is in actual fact simply the theological version of a harsh and suspicious position taken toward man as we know him, his nature and impulses. The doctrine of efficacious grace is linked with an indictment of humanity. It is the speculative and metaphysical culmination of this indictment rather than its source.

It has often been argued that like the Reformation, Jansenism is a violent Christian reaction against that rehabilitation of human nature initiated in the Renaissance which was to shake the whole Christian structure down to its foundations. According to this view, Port-Royal opposed principally the *libertins* of the seventeenth century, and constituted a sort of advance condemnation of the next century's tremendous surge of naturalistic thought and ethics. One may accept this view of Jansenism if he wishes; but then it will lose its originality in the whole Christian mainstream and its writers will resemble all those in the Church who have fought "innovations" and the godlessness of the world since the beginning of modern times and even earlier. From this perspective, those characteristics that distinguished Jansenism from other groups in the Church remain unexplained. Now Port-Royal's struggle was principally with other groups within the Church. That is why historically it stands out in relief. Jansenism is more clearly defined by its condemnation of a certain form of religion than by its denunciations of godlessness. Its peculiar impulse, like that of all intransigent doctrines, was to attack its closest neighbors, those who lack the supreme rigor that is the necessary mark of truth. This impulse is quite evident in Pascal's *Pensées* which, though written to serve as a defense of the Christian religion against freethinkers, are most striking in that which sets them against the common religion. Their originality continues to rest on that opposition down to our day.[1] Jansenist theology is designed to crush not materialism but rather all forms of spiritualism, even Christian ones, that are not accompanied by an absolute negation of human values, of all forms of virtue or greatness suspected of compromising with nature and instinct. The seventeenth century was acquainted with an optimistic idealism that trusted up to a point the impulses of man's nature. This optimistic idealism was Jansenism's true adversary and we must recognize it and put it in context if we want to explain Port-Royal. Throughout Corneille's work we have seen a similar notion of idealism expressed, undoubtedly opposed to nature to the degree that it constantly opposes the sublime to the base, but strongly opposed to the zealous exigencies of Jansenism, since in Corneille the sublime itself springs from a glorious impulse born of nature and sufficing to ennoble it. It is this confidence in man that Jansenism denounces as a criminal illusion. But in the seventeenth-century moral optimism is still feeling the effects of its aristocratic origins; this projection of the ego into the realm of greatness is above all a trait of the aristocracy. Port-Royal would call it the chimera of a fallen creature still blinded by the very pride that led to his downfall; and this

[1] In the course of the following pages we assume Pascal's close association with Port-Royal and Jansenism. Yet this association is still disputed in varying degrees by several Catholic writers, who are as anxious to rid themselves of Port-Royal as they are to hold on to Pascal. This is not the place for a detailed discussion of this subject; we know that the dispute has been complicated by the alleged discovery of Pascal's hostility to Jansenism at the end of his life and his so-called final retraction. All the erudition that has been expended in this direction, and in such an unconvincing fashion, carries very little weight in view of the text of the *Pensées*. Pascal still belongs to Port-Royal and no one seems to be able to steal him away.

condemnation, however broad and metaphysical, will strike the noble man to the heart. At Port-Royal the meditation on the Christian myth of the fall was more than a theological position; it led to the condemnation of an entire morality, of a whole set of ideas on man, and beyond these ideas, of a whole system of social relations. Port-Royal helped to break down the ideals inherited from the Middle Ages by openly setting aristocratic idealism in conflict with religion. Jansenism, in the guise of a strengthened Christianity, was in its own way a modernizing force.

The conflict between Christian law and the values that sprang from aristocratic individualism was undoubtedly a perennial one. Christianity had within it a principle of universality and of constraint, a law from on high that could oppose the pride of the nobles and that could permit the Church to maintain universal discipline. But in actual fact under the pressure of circumstances and concern for its own interests, the Church had always exercised this function very prudently. Its history was in part that of the lay world, its institutions and customs were modeled on those of that world. In the realm of ideas and ethics the distinction of sacred and profane had not prevented their interpenetration and their reciprocal accommodation. All chivalric idealism was built on this compromise, and one might say that it represented both Christianity's conquest of secular society, and at the same time, its retreat before the values which sprang spontaneously from the conditions of aristocratic life. In chivalry, human glory and Christian charity harmonized up to a certain point; at least they ceased to battle each other openly and arranged themselves in hierarchic order. They were two links in the same chain. Undoubtedly this tradition of compromise was not the whole of Christianity; the Church remained apart and always preserved its right to censure and to fulminate. The tendency to synthesize and reconcile opposing values, however, was so old and so strong that its contrary, the awareness of the distinct and opposed poles of nature and grace, or earthly glory and Christian merit, appeared in the course of centuries more like a subversive innovation for society and for the Church than a return to an elusive original doctrinal purity. In fact all the so-called restorers of the strict principles of Christianity–and the Jansenists, alongside of the Protestants, were among their number–had a quarrel with the real Church.

The secular compromise between religion and the world, grace and nature, was still in force after the failure of the Reformation; a certain appreciation of natural man and his ambitions continued to have a place within Catholicism to the degree that they could be reconciled with basic dogma. Henri Brémond has well described the phenomenon as *devout humanism,*[2] and has given a good account of the value this school assigned to human nature, its gifts, its spontaneous powers, and its central place in the universe–all of which were pitilessly criticized by the Jansenists. For this group virtues and natural talents form so many bridges that lead from purely human excellence to excellence in the sight of God. We are poles apart from Pascal's phrase, "If we take all bodies and all souls together they would still not yield one impulse of true charity. That is impossible; the quality of charity is of another order, it is supernatural."[3] In place of this unbridgeable gap, devout humanism works out successively accessible levels of perfection between nature and charity. Obviously, without claiming that it is entirely within man's power to pass through all these stages, especially the last, and without denying the necessity of grace, it was loath to condemn what had already been accomplished without grace, all that prefigures it and all that grace cannot help but reward. This essentially optimistic doctrine leads to the creation of a whole intermediate zone between concupiscence and sanctity, an area rich in moral works that are both delicate and spiritual, where human nature, freed from its own baseness and barely feeling the effects of the original stain, reaches almost up to God without ever ceasing to be itself. It is like an ideal nature above ordinary nature; man divides himself in two and in so doing he manages to escape half of

[2] Brémond, *Histoire littéraire du sentiment religieux en France,* Vol. I.

[3] Pascal, *Pensées,* Brunschvicg edition, 793.

the effects of his fall, from that point on considered partial rather than absolute. Within him there is still a bit of Eden.[4]

Undoubtedly this re-establishment of man's pre-eminence within the limits of Christianity, as it appeared in the seventeenth century, borrowed a good deal from the humanism of the Renaissance. But the renewed influence of classical thought affected only the forms of an already existent tradition of reconciliation between natural man and Christian law. This exalted zone, constantly described by the disciples of Francis de Sales in the seventeenth century–no longer a zone of brutish nature and yet not quite the realm of grace, this region of human and spiritual wonders that is the antechamber of heavenly glory–is it not the glorious field in which aristocratic tradition finds the ideal source of all virtue? Christianity had long flourished in this region because it had long been bound to the ethics of the aristocracy; and in the seventeenth century to defend human excellence while embracing Christian doctrine was still to defend the harmony of charity with glory, perfect love and *bel-esprit*.

This was the path chosen by Desmarets de Saint-Sorlin, one of the best-known enemies of Jansenism, a curious and remarkable mind in spite of the mediocrity of his talents, who took part in all the polemics of the great century. In the *Délices de l'esprit,* his now quite forgotten work, published in 1658, he described all the intermediate stages that lead man from the pleasures of the flesh to union with God. The book presents an unbeliever whom a Christian converts by making him appreciate in succession the ever more delicate pleasures that can be enjoyed by the human spirit which, though not yet united to God, has by its natural powers already gone beyond the satisfactions of crass concupiscence. All the characteristic beliefs of this school are found in this work–the glorification of man's capacity for nobility, moral and theological optimism, and finally the profound aristocratic nature of those "delights" on which Desmarets bases his

[4] All the writers of this school insist on this duality in man, the result of a partial fall, especially Francis de Sales, who dominates this whole school of thought. Jansenism rejects both this idea of man and this theology.

optimism and whose temples he places in the outlying areas of the divine city of True Voluptuousness.

First there is the delight of the Arts. The author sees them in the light of traditional *bel-esprit,* broadened and embellished by the theorists of the Renaissance, and in this guise still very powerful in the seventeenth century. For him the delights of the Arts are the fruit of a constant refinement of taste "that is sharpened by knowledge,"[5] and to which glory adds its charms, because if one loves works of art it is because "man, by the self-love that brings him to love the glory of his species, loves the Imitation of nature much more than Nature itself."[6] Then come the delights of the Sciences, still more spiritual than the arts, which the author, in spite of a completely mystical mistrust of purely intellectual research, repeatedly praises in a style reminiscent of the *Femmes savantes.* Then there are the delights of Reputation, which Desmarets situates without too much difficulty in the outlying areas of the city of God; indeed the love of glory derives from the fact that "the soul, which is immortal, wants a good action or a good work to be immortal, too."[7] "Thus honor or fame is in harmony with God and with the soul, as the fifth in music is in harmony with the two octaves."[8] Then follow the delights of Fortune, that is to say of power or greatness, pleasures that are even stronger when they are bound more to the thought of power than to its reality, when they are more highly spiritualized. The delights of magnanimity or clemency are the crowning touch because one of the greatest and most noble pleasures "is not to avenge oneself when one has the power to do so. For you triumph over another potentially, which is worth more than to triumph over him in effect. You triumph over yourself, and all tongues enviously proclaim this great victory."[9] Finally come the delights of Virtue, the

[5] Desmarets de Saint-Sorlin, *Délices de l'esprit,* fourth day.

[6] Ibid., fourth day.

[7] Ibid., sixth day.

[8] Ibid., fourth day.

[9] This beautiful description of magnanimity as the nobles saw it, written by a man who unquestionably understood Corneille's notion of the sublime better than most modern critics do, is a perfect description of Auguste in *Cinna.* (Ibid., seventh day.)

last before those of the mystical union: "The lover of virtue enjoys the glory of his own triumph and at the same time enjoys even more the glory of the virtue he loves when it triumphs in him."[10] Man is drawn to the path of salvation by the irresistible attraction emanating from this realm between nature and God; Christian doctrine adopts the charming ways of aristocratic idealism–sublimation of the desires or glory and refinement of reason or *bel-esprit.* In this aristocratic vestibule of the faith or, if you prefer, in this Christian extension of glory, the impulses of the ego are utilized, not suppressed.[11]

The link between conciliatory Christianity and aristocratic idealism is evident all through the literature of the seventeenth century. Objecting to those who claim that an irreducible opposition exists between the glory of the world and that of heaven, Balzac writes in his discourse on *Glory,* "The noble passion with which we are concerned here is in accord with the highest sanctity, with that closest to the divine." And his whole discourse is but a long panegyric of the old sentiment of honor. Nothing could be further from the truth than the rapprochement that is sometimes effected between Corneille and Port-Royal. They are poles apart from one another. How could Corneille's concept of glory be acceptable to the Jansenists? Sainte-Beuve himself, who tries to link Corneille with Port-Royal through *Polyeucte,*[12] is forced to recall that the writers of Port-Royal always judged this tragedy harshly. The sudden conversions, the unexpected illuminations of grace in this play have nothing properly Jansenist about them, but belong rather to the most common Chris-

[10] Ibid., eighth day.

[11] Desmarets is not the only one in whose writings the aristocratic inspiration is perceptible; cf. especially in *Humanisme dévot,* the work of Brémond already cited, the chapter on Yves de Paris—a Capuchin of noble birth, he pleads for the sentiment of honor and for its moral usefulness, and he defends the beauty of purified and spiritual love even when it is addressed to earthly creatures, etc.

[12] Sainte-Beuve, *Port-Royal,* Book I, Chapters VI and VII.

tian tradition. Moreover, the thoughts expressed there on God and grace are quite consonant with the Jesuits' ideas:

> He is always all just and all good, but His grace
> *Is not always equally efficacious,*[13]
> After certain moments *that our delays allow to slip by,*[14]
> It lays aside those shafts that pierce the heart.
> Our heart hardens, spurns it, loses it:
> The hand that poured it out becomes more sparing with it;
> And that holy ardour that should lead us to good
> Falls more rarely,[15] or no longer works within us.[16]

A fundamental opposition separates Corneille, whose whole work glorifies man's "fine actions" and their accompanying thoughts, from those who deny all greatness to fallen man and all lucidity to his judgment.[17] And let us not delude ourselves that the lofty stoicism of Corneille's characters was in any way pleasing to the Jansenists. Jansenism and stoicism

[13] The Jansenists themselves call their doctrine the doctrine of efficacious grace, that is to say, grace that is always irresistible when it manifests itself, and they believe that it manifests itself rarely. The opposite holds true in this passage, in which grace is thought to be present at all times but of varying efficacy according to the merit of the subject.

[14] It is clearly man who is at fault, who discourages divine favor.

[15] There always remains a little from time to time; no one is completely deprived of it.

[16] It becomes completely inefficacious, and by the fault of man who has the power to resist it. The tragedy *Oedipe* (III, 5) contains a long defense of free will, one of unequivocal import. Sainte-Beuve cites it and carefully notes its anti-Jansenist sense, but only in a footnote (Book I, Chapter VIII, *in fine*). He needed a Jansenist Corneille to embellish his theory, but he could not have more than half believed it.

[17] M. F. Strowski underlines this contrast when, in his account of the Pascal-Arnauld polemic against the Sorbonne theologian Lemoine on man's merit and his lucidity, he writes, "Auguste and Rodrigue are figures drawn in the spirit of M. Lemoine." (*Pascal et son temps*, Vol. III, p. 83.)

were at swords' point. Jansenius is understandably violent with respect to the stoics. Stoicism, very much in fashion in France in the cultured society of the classical period, seemed in spite of its severity to be the glorification of human liberty and the philosophical apotheosis of pride. The stoic acceptance of misfortune, *la constance* as it was called, was too brilliantly ostentatious for Jansenist taste. Port-Royal demanded a more rigorous self-denial. It is not by chance that Pascal takes it upon himself to refute Epictetus, who is ever-present in his thoughts. Because of its exaltation of man and because of its popularity among the *grandes âmes* of the aristocracy, whose natural tendency it seconded, stoicism was obviously an enemy creed from Port-Royal's point of view.

Among all the manifestations of the aristocratic spirit, those that deal with the idea of love are perhaps the most frequently mingled with optimistic Christianity. In Savoy, Francis de Sales frequently visited Honoré d'Urfé, author of *L'Astrée* and theorist of love as it was conceived in the romances of the time. One of his friends and neighbors, Camus, like him a bishop, wrote romances in which the usual spirit and style of the genre concealed edifying narratives meant to glorify divine love. The sweetness of the inspiration and of the language, the use of flowery metaphors, and the very shading of the sentiment reveal some curious resemblances between *L'Astrée* and the *Introduction à la vie dévote*. Optimistic Christianity plays on the courtly idea of love, and it sees in purified earthly love an imperfect but precious approximation of the love of God and of heavenly things. Since the time of the troubadours it had been customary to place side by side, in a more or less orthodox fashion, purified profane love and a kind of worshipful devotion addressed to the mediators between man and God—the saints, the Virgin, and the angels. This worship, when added to courtly profane worship, crowned it, raising its *élan* to the very heavens. It too was based on the idea of the potential excellence of human love once it is freed from its vulgar attachments.

This Christianity, which we could call a Christianity of sublimation since it transfigures and lifts the heart up to the divine, culminates in mystical prayer. Consequently it is not surprising that the states of prayer, in spite of all the precautions with which religious discipline surrounds them, should be suspect to the Jansenists. From the time it formulated its doctrine Port-Royal could not but be very hostile to that mysticism which held that it was possible for man, while still in this world, to enjoy God.[18] Pascal consistently distinguishes between *grace,* which touches the elect on earth, and *glory,* which they will only enjoy in heaven. On the contrary Desmarets' convert is no sooner touched by grace than he declares himself in a state of an "incomparable glory."[19] In return for its sacrifices human instinct receives here a foretaste of the highest good. In aristocratic ethics all virtue has lures of this type–charity follows this rule.

Beneath the debate on mysticism lay a concrete problem already perceived by an uncomplicated moral sense–is it really possible for man's instinct to purify itself, is it possible for him to find satisfaction in an ideal object, to dedicate his natural zeal to the service of the good? Aristocratic virtue cannot forego this possibility; Jansenist ethics, on the contrary, mistrusts the sublimations of instinct and justifies that mistrust with the doctrine of man's fundamental corruption. The discussions relative to the states of prayer raise the whole problem of the so-called ideal impulses, their value and their existence. Now the modern era at its beginnings incessantly posed this problem to the fading Middle Ages, and very often resolved it, as did Port-Royal, in the most realistic fashion.

Nothing is more significant in this respect than the dispute that set Nicole against Desmarets around 1665. Desmarets accused the Jansenists of wanting to abolish prayer completely,

[18] Of course antimysticism became completely clear at Port-Royal only in the generation of Louis XIV, but doctrinal Jansenism, too, hardly existed before that.

[19] *Délices de l'esprit,* twelfth day. Desmarets is not a great mystic nor a very reliable authority, but he gives one a good idea of the genre, and does so artlessly. That is what interests us most of all here. What we call the weak or lesser side of things is often of the essence.

of "never having felt an attraction to things divine or to the spiritual joys,"[20] in short of not understanding "interior spirituality" at all. In *Visionnaires,* Nicole answers him with a psychological critique of the states of prayer that questions the very existence of an ideal sensibility in man. In substance he says that it is extremely difficult to distinguish natural from supernatural prayer. In natural prayer the movement of the soul toward God is a purely human impulse inspired by self-interest; grace has no part in it and consequently it is of no value. The impulses of supernatural prayer are inspired by God himself. Indeed we cannot clearly distinguish these two kinds of prayer in ourselves, nor have we the right to attribute these impulses to grace simply because we feel that grace is their source. Since we have a stake in the matter and since we have no other light to illumine the argument than a thoroughly unreliable feeling within us, we can again and again take the disguised effects of concupiscence for impulses of true piety. The danger is all the greater since there are deceitful forces within us and without that work to put us on the wrong scent—our "self love" which colors all things, and the Devil who uses it to his advantage.

This completely pessimistic psychology, then, is inseparable from Jansenist theology. A refined mystical spirituality that one attributes to grace is nothing but a "refinement of pride"; we flatter ourselves that we are enjoying God and in reality we are simply enjoying the pleasure of a rare privilege with which we believe ourselves to have been favored. Nicole is convinced that in the fervor and outbursts of devotion he can discern the wicked stirrings of the human heart, spiritualized by a false mystical language. The perfect rapture that we experience in prayer is only "the undisturbed reign of self-love";[21] if the soul that believes itself united to God in its ecstasies feels reassured, it is because "the devil procures for him that peace he gives to those he possesses."[22]

[20] Desmarets, *Réponse à l'insolente apologie des religieuses de Port-Royal,* Part II, Chapter XVI.

[21] Nicole, *Visionnaires,* 7.

[22] Ibid., 3.

The end result of all these criticisms is to cast doubt on the value of the feeling each individual can experience, even sincerely, about his own state of soul. This doubt is readily generalized and can eventually affect all introspective knowledge of man by declaring it subject to the deceitful powers of self-love. As a result man becomes to himself an obscure being who ignores his own motives and who acts without self-knowledge. Our knowledge of ourselves extends only to the exterior of our being, or rather it fashions that exterior; it imagines beautiful thoughts that it takes for fundamental inclinations by virtue of "a natural tendency of self-love that leads us to take our thoughts for virtues and to believe that we have in our hearts everything that floats on the surface of our minds."[23]

A similar distinction drawn between the surface and the depths of man leads one to deny all validity to conscious thoughts—"Out of self-love one can wish to be freed from self-love; one can desire humility out of pride. In the movements of the soul, an endless and invisible circle is traced by coming back again and again to the same point, from reflections to reflections, and *there is always within us a certain depth and a certain root that remains unknown and impenetrable for all of our life.*"[24] This determination to seek out the truth about man in a sphere other than his inner consciousness is common to all those in the seventeenth century who set out to destroy the aristocratic idea of the sublime. Recourse to the unconscious elements in man is, as will be seen, their most powerful weapon when they want to challenge the assertions of idealism. Jansenism knew how to make use of the old Christian obsession of the devil, and how to turn to the same end the myth of the devil and a lucid analysis of human nature by confusing the snares of the Evil One with those of instinct.

[23] Ibid., 7.

[24] Ibid., 7. Saint-Cyran speaks in the same way of the "deep abysses" of the soul and the "invisible world" of concupiscence, more difficult to destroy than the visible world. This notion, of course, is common to all Christianity but it is of primary importance in Jansenism.

One can see how integral Jansenism is and how the theology, religion, and psychology of Port-Royal are animated by the same basic impulse of the denial of every heroic or godlike extension of our nature. This denial extends to the whole range of human ambition, from simple virtue to the heights of mystical prayer, and manifests itself both in the analysis of the human heart and in the debates on grace. Obviously the most effective subversion is accomplished in the areas closest to life, in the discussion on ethics and on man. But the other areas should be of no less interest if one wants to show how the primary impulse of Jansenism constructs its own speculative philosophy, how a need creates and develops a doctrine.

Is there anything that has not been said of Pascal's dizzying metaphysics, of those sudden contrasts of thought, and those constant surprises by means of which he passes from one order of things to its opposite, transforming reason into doubt, contradiction into certitude, and an ignorance similar to that of brute nature into insight? But this metaphysics of sudden leaps, turnabouts, and unexpected relationships was the only possible expedient for one who wanted, as Pascal and all of Jansenism did, to cut the bridges between man and God without ceasing to make one exist for the other. Optimistic Christianity, on the contrary, tied the natural order to the divine by an unbroken rising scale of perfections. Certainly dogma imposed distinct planes—that of grace, that of nature at its highest point, virtue and knowledge, and that of brute nature; in other words, God, Eden, and fallen man. Two moats had to be dug, one between concupiscence and the good, the other between the good and charity. But the problem was not so simple; there was discussion as to the middle term, the heritage of Eden. If one allowed, as optimistic Christianity did, that there remained something in man of the lost paradise, something real and active, greatness, an instinct for the good, a sovereign intellect, then the lines of demarcation became blurred. The moat that surrounded grace was then half-filled, and that which separated man's greatness from his baseness was crossed from the start by certain natures whose impulses spontaneously assumed their most exalted form. On the philosophical plane the rehabilitation of man was consequently expressed by a tendency to obliterate and to soften the differences between the orders. Pascal's tendency is in the opposite direction. He also distinguishes among the three orders, but emphasizes the differences between them and the absence of continuity from one order to another. "The greatness of wisdom, which is nothing if it does not come from God, is invisible to carnal men and also to men of mere intelligence. These are three orders differing in kind. . . . All bodies taken together are not worth the least of minds. . . . All bodies and all minds together, and all their achievements, are not worth the smallest impulse of charity."[25] But this absolute heterogeneity of orders is possible only through a particular interpretation of the middle term; the separation of the orders is tied to the destruction of the intermediate order, that which Pascal calls the order of the mind or of the greatness of man. It is no longer a state of transition, as real as those states of concupiscence and grace, and leading from one to the other. Human greatness, effectively demolished after the fall, no longer exists except as a faint trace or rather as a painful lack. The pre-eminence of man, tainted at the root, manifests itself only in his awareness of his degradation—"Man's greatness lies in the consciousness of his wretched state."[26] Thus the only greatness of man is that he is aware of his wretchedness; his nature is exalted only because it cannot reconcile itself to baseness, and when Pascal defends the greatness of man it is always a restless and anguished greatness. All that remains is between the two end terms; and in man's present condition the surviving traces of his first state, far from softening this contrast, only serve to heighten it. Pascal does more than deny human greatness; he forces it to deny itself and to dig its own grave.

For example, it was a commonplace of idealist philosophy from ancient times to trace the desire for glory to a confused consciousness of the soul's immortal destiny. Pascal will

[25] Pascal, *Pensées,* Brunschvicg edition, 793.

[26] *Pensées,* Brunschvicg edition, 397.

take up the same idea, under the title *Grandeur de l'homme*—"We value man's soul so highly that we cannot endure being held in contempt."[27] Another thinker would conclude with an ideal rehabilitation of glory; but Pascal's intent is quite different. Let us not deceive ourselves on this point; it is a question of emphasizing the intolerable nature of our actual condition when compared with an ideal aspiration—"If he boasts, I humble him; if he humbles himself, I praise him, and I always contradict him until he understands that he is an incomprehensible monster."[28] Since man's greatness stems from his wretchedness, and his wretchedness is the result of his greatness, his praise is but one element or one moment in a dialectic that aims to destroy, along with his serenity, the idea of any sound value inherent in man, and that ultimately leaves him no hope but in the supreme leap of grace.

What Pascal thinks of glory can be applied as well to the intellectual sphere, since knowledge, too, is one of the bases of man's pre-eminence. Human dignity presumably would find its ideal in rational knowledge, made up exclusively of clear definitions and incontestable proofs; only knowledge of this sort would truly satisfy the aspirations of thought. Those are the sentiments of mankind, which sees a lessening of its worth in imperfect knowledge; that is the judgment of Pascal himself, who attributes the "highest excellence"[29] to this impossible perfection. It is impossible because obviously we cannot define everything and prove everything; when we have gone as far as we can go, reason itself compels us to acknowledge undefined concepts and unproven axioms. Consequently in the last resort all certitude is going to rest on fundamental evidence that owes nothing to reason but originates in a totally different sphere—the heart, instinct,[30] and natural insight,[31] these are the names Pascal gives to this intuitive

[27] *Pensées,* Brunschvicg edition, 400.

[28] *Pensées,* Brunschvicg edition, 420.

[29] *De l'esprit géométrique,* petite édition Brunschvicg, p. 465.

[30] "It is on this knowledge of the heart and instinct that reason must base itself and elaborate its concepts." *Pensées,* Brunschvicg edition, 282.

[31] *De l'esprit géométrique,* p. 168.

faculty, in his opinion the only one capable of affirming or propounding anything, since reason is limited to working on the data it furnishes. But Pascal generally sees this intuitive evidence as something makeshift in comparison with the ideally conclusive knowledge that we have been denied. Consequently the only form of certitude we have at our disposal, which forces itself on us from outside of reason, contributes nothing to our glory, for how can we be proud of knowing what we have not proven? The certitude that comes from the heart does not presuppose any effort on our part and proceeds from no inherent excellence of our being but rather from nature, which compels us to believe without asking our opinion. When reason, prompted by its ambitious hunger for proofs and after passing from one doubt to another, finally arrives at a complete void, it is nature that sustains it and "keeps it from falling into extravagance."[32] Our certitude depends on the order of things, not on reason. But such certitude, as it elaborates itself in irrational terms, falls into the arbitrary and keeps us there.[33] If it is true that Pascal seems to make an exception for geometrical proofs without, how-

[32] *Pensées,* Brunschvicg edition, 434.

[33] The order of the heart and instinct is inferior in dignity and clarity to that of reason. It is true that at times Pascal's thought seems vague on this point. Thus in his *Esprit géométrique,* after having asserted that the order based on intuition is "inferior in the sense that it is less convincing but not in the sense that it is less certain" (p. 168), he writes that "the lack of proof is no shortcoming, but rather a perfection," and that "natural clarity . . . persuades reason more tellingly than argument" (p. 175). The apparent contradiction disappears if one remembers that, in accordance with his usual dialectic, Pascal wants to use each of the two sources of belief to humble the other. In the last analysis he would judge the purely rational method more satisfying for our intelligence and for the dignity of the human mind, but inapplicable, and the intuitions of the heart more substantial but less illuminating. The whole originality of Pascal consists precisely in destroying neither reason nor instinct, in making use of one against the other without building on either, and ultimately, for want of a better solution, assigning all value to instinct, while waiting for grace to touch it.

ever, justifying this exception, he still destroys the whole theoretical foundation of intuitive certitudes when he writes, "All our reasoning ends in a surrender to feelings, so that we cannot distinguish between these two opposites. One says that my feelings are mere fantasy, the other that his fantasy is feeling.[34] We need a rule. Reason is willing, but it can be twisted in all directions; and so there is no rule."[35] In this way man has carefully preserved the idea of and the desire for a perfect knowledge; but this desire, like the intellectual ambition that is its expression, operates in a vacuum. The little effectual knowledge left to man is attached to the part of his being that is least responsible and least susceptible of proof. Pascal does not wish to deny either the dignity of thought or the certitude of knowledge but he separates them irreparably; he creates a void between the conditions necessary for ideal thought and those of true certitude, between reason and obviousness.

As a consequence of this separation, reason, seeking certitude and finding it out of reach, is induced by virtue of its own laws to abdicate, to place functions that it cannot exercise in the hands of an extraneous power. All of its steps thus testify to a lacuna in man's faculties. Not that Pascal annihilates reason; it must subsist so that its steps may lead right up to the abyss that opens beneath it, and give us an idea of the depth of that abyss which we could not know otherwise. "Reason," says one of Pascal's commentators, "is the aspiration to greatness but the consciousness of wretchedness."[36] It is always operative and always great provided it succeeds in disqualifying itself. Consequently the same conflict that exists between greatness and wretchedness is established between reason and the heart, one alternately destroying the other and reinforcing it, and each hurting itself as

[34] *Fantasy* means illusory evidence, *feeling* means true evidence.
[35] *Pensées,* Brunschvicg edition, 274.
[36] Brunschvicg, introduction to edition of the *Pensées* (coll. des Grands Écrivains). Concerning Pascal's theory of knowledge see also other works by the same author, particularly *Spinoza et ses contemporains,* Chapter X.

much as the other. But it is a struggle in which the heart ultimately wins out, as wretchedness won out before. Certainly what natural feeling perceives as true can be an illusion traceable to our frailty, which reason can at any moment correct. The *sentiment naturel* that Méré invokes against the idea of the infinite divisibility of space cannot stand close scrutiny, which soon reveals the absurdity of the opposite proposition. But such evidence is nevertheless distressing for reason, which wants to understand the truth. As Pascal says, it would like to possess it directly, and it is precisely this ability that is denied it.[37] For Pascal the great lesson of mathematics lies in the final defeat of reason before the facts —"All that is incomprehensible does not cease to be."[38] With respect to ethical knowledge there is the same endless struggle, the same helplessness of reason banished from truth.[39] It is undoubtedly reason that will dispel the false evidence with which the "deceitful powers"—custom, imagination, and sickness—fill a corrupted sensibility; it is reason that will force man to consider those truths that *divertissement* expressedly hides from his view. But apart from the fact that these corrupting influences can spread to its own functioning, reason cannot criticize with one piece of evidence without having recourse to another, which is also independent of it. Thus, having made us feel how imperfect everything is without it, reason is forced to acknowledge its own imperfection. Because "the last step of our reason is to recognize that an infinite number of things surpass it; it has no strength at all if it does not go far enough to know this."[40] Its function is not to crown our sensory faculties in order to bring us closer to a knowledge of God, but to widen still further the chasm that separates fallen man from the truth. Between human knowledge and an object beyond its understanding, reason allows of no passage but the abrupt passage that only grace

[37] *De l'esprit géométrique,* p. 175 ff.

[38] *Pensées,* Brunschvicg edition, 430.

[39] See especially the fragments *Pensées,* Brunschvicg edition, 381, 382, 383.

[40] *Pensées,* Brunschvicg edition, 430.

can effect, leading from the realm of natural evidence to that of supernatural evidence, and from instinct to the awareness of God.

In Pascal everything leads to this final leap. With the intermediary order eliminated and what is left of the first state of Adam serving only to underscore the wretchedness of his present state, man can reach God only by a sudden change of order that depends on Him alone. Pascal's apologetics tend simply to prepare the ground for this change by making man conscious of wretchedness as such, with all the loathing attendant on this awareness, to make him wager for God and act outwardly in a Christian way while waiting for grace. Pascal creates a void, sets up a counterfeit, and waits for everything to come suddenly out of nothingness by a gratuitous act in which man plays no part at all. All concupiscence then miraculously turns into charity, and shadowy understanding becomes a proof of the "hidden God."

This is Pascal's dialectic, a "constant inversion of pros and cons"[41] that extends to all realms of his thought, even the most subordinate, and enlivens every page of the fragments of his *Apologie*. This dialectic replaces the rising scale of perfections with an irregular and dramatic scale. The first step of this dialectic is the denial of an enduring middle term between nature and God, and the refusal to allow of the existence, to any degree at all, of a purely human value. This is so much so that Port-Royal does not find that value even in the state of grace. The human heart does not change its nature when it loves God. The object of its enjoyment has changed by the grace of God, but it remains brute enjoyment and is obviously still comparable in the psychological order to natural enjoyment. That is why the Jansenists' enemies within the Church reproached them for their crude notion of prayer and their description of prayer as crude emotionalism.[42] But

[41] *Pensées,* Brunschvicg edition, 328.

[42] Among contemporaries cf. Brémond, op. cit., the chapters on Pascal and Nicole in the volume on Port-Royal. It would be idle to go into this polemic in detail but one can see clearly enough the difference between Pascal's God, who can be perceived by the heart, and the God of the optimistic Christians and mystics, no less

the point is that Jansenism would no longer be itself—and again we are dealing with the all-important human aspect of the dispute—if it believed in sublimated, enlightened forms of instinct and if it did not, without transition, superimpose grace on the natural appetites, a grace that redirects them without transfiguring them in essence.

Far from reconciling the real and the ideal as aristocratic idealism did in such an ingenious manner, far from exhausting itself in the brilliant reconciliation or the harmonious systematization of the conflicting forces of human mind into a hierarchy, Pascal's whole dialectic does its utmost to deepen the opposition between them. That dialectic ultimately isolates the natural appetites and irrevocably prevents them from being transformed in any ideal way. The last leap of grace does not alter or attenuate Jansenism's image of man as something low and common. It is that image we must come to now, since this is the real heart of the polemic.

---

perceivable by the heart. For Pascal the heart is a brutal power but the only one that truly defines us, and God reveals himself to it in joy or fear, in anguish or certitude. For the mystics the heart is the ineffable locus of our spiritual experiences, the road that leads from our lowliness to divine union.

The Destruction of the Hero

The hero as Corneille conceived him a nature greater than nature, a man who is more than man, and the ideal model of the aristocracy as long as it remained faithful to its traditions has no worse enemy than the moral pessimism that goes hand in hand with the doctrine of efficacious grace. This aggressive pessimism, more or less explicitly based on Jansenist theology, was very widespread in the seventeenth century. A vast current of ethical theory accompanies and carries along what can properly be called Jansenism, gathering strength in the second half of the century at the very moment when the old heroic ideal of the aristocracy appears utterly obsolete with the triumph of absolutism under Louis XIV. The reflections on human nature contained in Pascal's *Pensées,* the *Maximes* of La Rochefoucauld, and contemporary works of this type are a part of this current of thought. It even seems that the genre of disconnected reflections was occasioned in large part by the debate on human worth, and especially by a negative attitude taken toward human worth. The salon of Mme. de Sablé, half *précieux,* half Jansenist, seems to have been one of the principal centers for such discussion. La Rochefoucauld frequented it; Abbé Esprit's treatise, *La Fausseté des vertus humaines,* was published in 1678 through the good offices of Mme. de Sablé and Mme. de Longueville after the author's death. In the same year, the year of Mme. de Sablé's death, the Abbé d'Ailly's *Pensées diverses* appeared along with her *Maximes.* Nicole's *Essais de morale* appeared about the same time. But whether one is dealing with ponderous treatises or brief reflections, doctrinal works or secular writings, the literature of morals of the age of Louis XIV seems to be centered around the problem of the greatness of man or his lowly state, the nobility of his instincts or their brutality. In this polemic, in which every resource of subtlety and of psychological insight known to that period was put to use, a polemic that constitutes one of the most profound debates on man, of any period, the verdict was the condemnation of a past age. If pessimism is the dominant note, that is because under Louis XIV the aristocratic superman was in very bad straits.

Jacques Esprit, from his preface on, prides himself on dissuading men "from thinking themselves heroes and demi-gods." And as a matter of fact all of Esprit's arguments will seek to establish that man is at the furthest remove from that invincibility and that knowing faithfulness to oneself which mark heroes and demi-gods as the aristocracy imagined them and as they appeared in Corneille. Seen with new eyes, man becomes the weakest, most inconstant, and most faithless of creatures. He was an *ego* above things and he becomes as it were one *thing* among others–a brute nature, no longer a will or a reason. Will and reason made him master of himself, the recipient of a unique power in the midst of the universe, and they rescued him from the stream of things; suddenly he is nothing but the plaything of natural powers that control him, thwart him, and rob him of his being. These powers are first of all the crushing outward forces that make of him physically the frailest reed of nature. The fortuitous play of circumstances, or chance, guides him more than he guides himself. "One would have to be able to account for fortune in order to be able to account for what one does," writes La Rochefoucauld.[1] Pascal says the same thing: "The most important thing in life is the choice of a calling; and chance decides it."[2] Consequently man is mistaken when he believes that he finds in himself the explanation of his destiny. If it is there, it is rather in the part of his being that is imposed on him and on which he cannot act.

We know the importance Pascal gives to custom, whose power he judges so great that the very shape of man has become difficult to perceive. "I am very much afraid that nature

[1] La Rochefoucauld, maxim 574. We will follow the numbering used in the Grands Écrivains edition.

[2] *Pensées,* Brunschvicg edition, 97.

is itself only a first habit, as habit is a second nature."[3] Habit even encroaches on the mind: "Habit influences the automaton, which in turn influences the mind without the mind's being aware of it."[4] In this deliberate attempt to dissolve human autonomy, the final step is to invoke the influence of the physical organism on the moral life. The automaton can influence the mind only because there is constant contact between the bodily "machine" and thought. Tendentially materialistic statements with respect to man abound in Pascal as they do in La Rochefoucauld. "The strength and weakness of the mind," says the latter, "are misnamed; indeed, they are only the good or poor disposition of the bodily organs."[5] And Pascal says, "(Illnesses) spoil our judgment and our senses; and if serious maladies change them perceptibly, I do not doubt for a moment that minor ills have a proportionate effect."[6]

The theory of "temperament"[7] springs from the same source, as does that of the "humours" by which La Rochefoucauld so often explains man's behavior. The organism as automaton does not merely act on the soul by transmitting the enduring tendencies it has itself acquired; it incessantly undergoes myriad changing influences, and they too are unfailingly communicated to the mind. Pascal says, "I have my foggy weather and my good weather within me, whether my affairs go well or ill makes little difference."[8] And La Rochefoucauld writes, "The caprice of our humour is even stranger than that of fortune."[9] Again and again both come back to

[3] *Pensées,* Brunschvicg edition, 93. Elsewhere Pascal gives the theological explanation of this state of affairs: *"True nature being lost,* everything becomes his nature." *Pensées,* Brunschvicg edition, 426.

[4] *Pensées,* Brunschvicg edition, 252.

[5] Maxim 44.

[6] *Pensées,* Brunschvicg edition, 82.

[7] Note particularly the maxims concerning young people, women, and the aged, and the admirable thoughts on sloth–above all, Maxim 630.

[8] *Pensées,* Brunschvicg edition, 107.

[9] Maxim 45.

man's fickleness, to what Pascal calls his "inconstancy," his "oddity," his "contradiction." Just as man's imagination makes him cling to a chimera, it also gives him a distaste for it, and judgment takes no part in any of his whims. "In dealing with man we think we are dealing with common organ pipes. They are organ pipes, in point of fact, but strange, changing, and variable ones . . . Those who know how to play only ordinary ones would produce no harmonies on these."[10] In the same vein La Rochefoucauld says, "Imagination could not invent as many different contradictions as exist by nature in the heart of every man."[11]

These contradictions are the final word on human nature, the most profound definition of man; what one ultimately finds in man is a kind of undifferentiated affectivity that can manifest itself in contradictory behavior. "Man is by nature credulous, incredulous, timid, and foolhardy," says Pascal.[12] La Rochefoucauld goes even further, saying, "Avarice sometimes produces extravagance and extravagance, avarice; we are often resolute out of weakness and bold out of fear."[13] Finally man's nature consists in an emotional flux whose capricious manifestations are all of equal value, in a "constant production of passions"–the expression is La Rochefoucauld's–whose course gives rational thought or free will no real foothold. The constant exclusion of these two faculties is explained principally by the fact that they establish man's autonomy in the world and that through them man thinks that he manifests an indomitable power in all his acts. With their help human action feels itself to be more than a simple given. It confers on itself an independent virtue; by means of those faculties the hero boasts of going beyond the realm of brute facts. What Pascal insistently refers to as the "detestable" ego is precisely the one that does not consider itself a thing or an effect in nature, but that lays claim to a

10 *Pensées,* Brunschvicg edition, 111.
11 Maxim 478.
12 *Pensées,* Brunschvicg edition, 125.
13 Maxim 11.

unique place, apart—"I detest it because it is unjust, and makes itself the center of all things."[14] Pascal is determined to demolish this claim and finally, after having broken the individual down into variable qualities extraneous to his will and judgment, he asks touchingly, "Where, then, is this ego?"[15] By reducing man to a blind and dependent sensibility, absolutely irreconcilable with our notions of liberty and reason, and by making him once more whole and entire, a part of brute nature, where his life, his desires, and his actions are but fragments tied to other fragments, the Jansenist moralists or their sympathizers end up with a dissolution of that very self that was to be the basis of all values, a self which is itself dispersed and fragmented.

Yet the glory of the self, thus negated by man's frailty at the center of the universe, could find refuge in the very desire glory inspires if it were proven that this desire was noble. That is what aristocratic ethics seeks to do when it portrays the love of glory as an impulse toward an immaterial good by means of which the soul escapes the harmful dependence on things, as a spontaneously ideal move on the part of human nature. And as the desire for glory can accompany and ennoble all our natural impulses, it is our being as a whole that rejects the weight of nature and assumes meaning and value. On the contrary, the writers who aspire to humble man always present this desire under its most slavish, least subtle, and most selfish aspect. For them instinct is first and foremost the instinct of appropriation, of jealous absorption. When they define human nature they replace the movement from within to without and the gift of generosity with a movement in the opposite direction, an acquisitive and possessive tendency. The main point of the discussion is that they link the very desire for glory to human instinct conceived in this way and stripped of all prestige. "If we were to take away from strength of soul the desire to keep and the fear of los-

[14] *Pensées,* Brunschvicg edition, 455.
[15] *Pensées,* Brunschvicg edition, 323.

ing, there would not be much left of that strength," we read in certain texts of the *Maximes*.[16] In aristocratic thought, the moral quality attributed to the desire for glory was self-evident. Christianity, if one takes it in its strict form, contained the opposite assumption–all desire is base, impulse and good are by definition antithetical terms; the desire for glory is only a form of self-interest, a touch of *libido dominandi*; glorious assertion of oneself is no better than cupidity. Between these two attitudes there could be no real discussion; one chooses one or the other. How can anyone refute one of Corneille's characters who is convinced that he is naming the highest values when he utters the words "glory" and "pride"? How can anyone convince him that his ambition is base? Now that is just what Pascal, La Rochefoucauld, and Esprit say. They desanctify the notion of glory and call it by the very name of egoism, *amour-propre*[17] or self-love. They destroy the ideal pretensions of pride and remove the fragile halo clinging to the desire for domination. Pascal writes, "Only command and sovereign authority are glorious, and only servitude is shameful."[18] The apologists of glory would not deny that; they would only ask whether the horror of servitude is not the source of every virtue in a great soul, and they would not be able to understand why the soul's debate between command and dependence should be considered despicable. Similarly one reads in Pascal, "Curiosity is nothing but vanity. More often than not we only want to know something so that we can talk about it."[19] Thus without argument, we see the glory of knowledge, of discovery, and of brilliance–the prestige of the Muses–reduced to nothing. Or again, "We are so presumptuous that we would like to be

[16] This *pensée* is found in the four manuscript copies of 1663 and in the Dutch edition of 1664. See the appendix to Vol. I of the Grands Ecrivains edition, p. 51.

[17] By a strange chance, this expression survived only with an ideal and "glorious" meaning; today *amour-propre* is something like dignity.

[18] *Pensées,* Brunschvicg edition, 160.

[19] *Pensées,* Brunschvicg edition, 152.

known by the whole world, and even by those who come after us."[20] A turn of phrase sufficed to make a concern with immortality, so often extolled as a source of virtue, seem an absurd desire. La Rochefoucauld is almost ambiguous when he writes, "The desire to merit the praise people give us strengthens our virtue,"[21] and if we did not know the rest of his work we could ask ourselves if by linking glory with virtue he wanted to speak in defense of the former or to repudiate the latter. The fact is that praise or glory, grandeur, ambition, and pride are understood in an ideal sense by one group and in a selfish sense by the other. The endless debate on La Rochefoucauld and his ethical system too often rests on erroneous premises because no one has perceived the double meaning of certain important words. "The restraint of men in their highest state," we read in the *Maximes* (with reference to the famous virtue of clemency or magnanimity) "is a desire to appear greater than their fortune."[22] And we immediately ask ourselves if magnanimity is really nothing but this desire, whereas we should ask ourselves quite simply if such a desire in itself deserves reproach or not. The real debate revolves not simply around facts but around values. For Corneille's Auguste as for Abbé Esprit, magnanimity is indeed "the highest degree of ambition,"[23] but they have two different notions of ambition. That is the whole difference, and it is a world of difference.[24]

[20] Ibid., 148.

[21] Maxim 150.

[22] Maxim 18.

[23] Esprit, *Fausseté des vertus humaines,* Part II, Chapter XIV.

[24] In their desire to deprive glory of all its ideal prestige, La Rochefoucauld and Pascal stress the fact that it can be attached to vice as well as to virtue. "A certain type of evil is as difficult to find as what we call virtue, and on these grounds this particular evil is often passed off as virtue. An extraordinary greatness of soul is needed to achieve this evil as well as to achieve the good." (*Pensées,* Brunschvicg edition, 408.) "There are heroes in evil as well as in virtue." (Maxim 185). But the hero would not deny this either; we have seen Corneille define his great evil-doers almost in these same terms.

Thus disaffection with heroic ideals manifests itself in a profound misunderstanding. Still one should notice that the champions of aristocratic idealism do not deny that glory, the thirst for approbation and the desire to eclipse rivals, has its absurd or base side. The misunderstanding lies elsewhere. It seems completely natural to them to distinguish between good and evil ambition, that which scorns selfish interests and that which is itself selfish interest, that which gives and that which covets, that which wins freedom and that which enslaves. They recognize two levels of human nature. And it is this distinction that their adversaries do not want to acknowledge and do not even conceive.

It is here, perhaps, that one can see most clearly the human import and the practical implications of the misunderstanding. If the desire for glory can sometimes be base and sometimes sublime, if it is sometimes turned toward selfish interest and sometimes toward the highest virtue, what makes it orient itself toward one of these directions rather than the other? The choice is going to depend essentially on the *quality* of each soul. All things considered, the duality introduced into moral nature comes down to a duality of well-born souls and common souls.[25] And noble *nature* in ethics is simply a transposed form of noble *birth* in society. When writers like La Rochefoucauld and Pascal discuss man they are setting out to destroy this duality at the heart of nature, to tie to the baser part of man's nature the tendencies that others aspire to emancipate, to show that they are tightly bound to their most worldly end. For them the word nature has only one meaning–it is the sphere of crude and morally indifferent necessity and they extend its borders to include everything that exists, with the exception of God and the order of grace. But when they unify nature at the expense of the moral sublime, they also unify mankind at the expense of the privileges of birth. In his *Traité de l'éducation d'un*

[25] Cf. Brémond, with respect to Nicole's theory on *amour-propre* concealed in the impulses of prayer, "The devout humanists would answer him by saying that there are two kinds of *amour-propre,* one of which is that of noble souls."

prince, Nicole censures great men "for forgetting what they have in common with all other men and tending to think only in terms of what distinguishes them from other men."[26] In the first of his *Trois discours sur la condition des grands,* addressed to a young prince, Pascal writes, "If public opinion raises you above the level of ordinary men, let your private opinion humble you and keep you on a level with all men, *because that is your natural state.*" Still more boldly he makes fun of the common people who "think that aristocracy is true greatness and consider the nobles as almost having a different nature from other men." The same opinion is expressed in almost identical terms by Abbé d'Ailly, according to whom "most nobles cherish the illusion that their nobility is a trait of nature."[27] Here the philosophical struggle against man's pretensions is carried to its logical conclusion, or rather it rediscovers its living source in the struggle against aristocratic pretension: the refusal to acknowledge a qualitative hierarchy among sentiments is aimed at the traditional doctrine that sets up differences of quality between men.[28]

In their attempt to obliterate the distinctions between the different levels of the human soul and reduce all to the lowest plane, the Jansenists had at their disposal a key argument by which they hoped to make their adversaries acknowledge their own defeat. Their method consisted in proving that the friends of glory are mistaken about themselves, and that if they could see themselves as they are they would see that they conform to the Jansenists' low image of man. In the last analysis all their confidence rests on their feeling of loving and searching for an ideal good, and this feeling is er-

[26] Part I, XXIV; published in 1670.

[27] *Pensées diverses,* 82.

[28] At times the cloak of Christian pessimism covers some remarkable audacity. For instance, in Abbé d'Ailly's *Pensée* 85, "Every day we are shocked to see individuals from the dregs of the people raising and ennobling themselves and we speak about them contemptuously: as if the greatest families of the world had not had a similar beginning if we were to search into their most distant origins."

roneous. Like all the intuitions one has concerning his nature or his inclinations, this sentiment is found on the surface of the soul, which would be disabused if it could sound its own depths. Everything uplifting that one seems to perceive in himself is but a mirage of his consciousness. Nothing could be more unwise than to make one's inner feelings the criterion of human truth. We have seen Nicole raise this objection against the mystics, but it could be applied generally to all cases in which man feels that his own impulses are sublime; we must then show him that his real impulses are radically different from what he feels they are, and explain this very feeling in terms of a hidden impulse of selfish interest. Consequently one reaches the point where the adversary's argument no longer has to be considered as an argument in itself, but becomes in its turn a simple fact to be explained like the others and, in short, is absorbed like the others into nature. Nothing is left of the hero.

In the psychology of the naturalistic writers of the seventeenth century there has never been enough importance given to the central role of the critique of the testimony of consciousness, and to how they are lead to assert that man does not really know himself because he sees himself as too noble for their taste. We generally admire their psychological penetration and their keen sense of moral analysis, but we imagine them above all devoted to a kind of introspective search illumined only by an abstract sense of the universal. The truth is that their attachment to common sense, which has so often been commended, taught them to mistrust subjective analysis and to judge man by some yardstick other than his inner sight. They revived the common idea that each of us labors under a delusion with respect to himself, and they deepened and embellished this idea to the point that their psychological work is principally distinguished by a mistrust of inner feelings. Their very realism explains this critical attitude, for it suggests to them the notion of a natural causality that transcends consciousness and envelops it. For them the unconscious is only the margin that separates man as he is from man as he sees himself; and the errors of the inner eye show the distance between the two. "We fall far short of knowing all our desires,"[29] writes La Rochefoucauld, who believes that our *amour-propre* dupes us as much as we dupe others and even more. His whole work rests on this central idea, which is explicitly stated a number of times.[30] The skills of *amour-propre,* far from being conscious calculations, are woven out of our own blindness, and their prodigious stage-settings are built in shadows without the knowledge of the actor who plays the leading role. Let us refer to the admirable reflection on *amour-propre* that opens the 1665 edition—". . . Nothing is so impetuous as its desires, so well-concealed as its intentions, so cunning as its ways; its flexibility cannot be described, its transformations surpass those of metamorphoses, and its subtleties those of chemical change. We cannot sound the depths nor pierce the darkness of its abysses. There it hides itself from the most penetrating eyes and makes a thousand imperceptible twists and turns. There *amour-propre is often invisible to itself; there it unconsciously conceives, nourishes, and rears a great number of loves and hatreds; it fashions some so monstrous that when they are exposed it repudiates them or cannot bring itself to acknowledge them. The absurd notions amour-propre has of itself are born of this night that envelops it; this is the source of its errors, its ignorance, its vulgarity, and the foolishness of its self-knowledge. . . ."*[31]

These views form the basis of a psychological method which perceives beneath the ethical sublime those appetites considered the lowest and the most shameful. The disguising of these sentiments is explained by a natural and unconscious need in man to avoid facing the truth about himself, which is always a humiliating one.[32] This new psychology calls for

[29] Maxim 295.

[30] See Maxims 119, 233, 373, etc.

[31] Maxim 563.

[32] Cf. Pascal, *Pensées,* Brunschvicg edition, 100, ". . . this human *ego* . . . wants to be great and is aware that it is insignificant," etc.; from this springs "a mortal hatred for this truth," an "aversion for the truth . . . inseparable from *amour-propre.*"

a complete reversal of ideas on the relation of brute instinct to intelligence and of the heart to the mind. The mind, or reason, instead of accompanying and illuminating the purification of the emotions, is useful now only to conceal their shameful nature. The intellect, no longer a conscious servant of glory, becomes the blind instrument of egoism. The brilliant subtlety of *bel-esprit*[33] is changed into a deceitful sleight of hand in which reason has surrendered all dignity; the mind becomes nothing but the "dupe of the heart," to use La Rochefoucauld's very expressive phrase.[34] In a similar vein the Jansenist Domat, a friend of Pascal, said, "All the deference the heart has for the mind consists in the fact that if the heart is not governed by reason it must at least convince the mind that it is."[35] But it can do this only by deceiving the mind, which is the seat of belief, so that this deference could more properly be called corruption and enslavement. Pascal, always stronger and more striking than the others, makes the same disqualification of intelligence emerge from a play of arguments that overtake and surpass one another—"M. de Roannez used to say, 'The reasons come to me later, but at first a thing pleases or offends me without my knowing why, and yet it offends me for that very reason I will only later discover.' But I do not believe that the thing offended for reasons that were discovered later, but rather that we find these reasons only because it offends."[36] For Pascal it is not enough

[33] The only work of Pascal in which we find *bel-esprit*, although quite erratically, is the *Discours des passions de l'amour*; but without raising the question of authenticity we can agree that the inspiration of passages like the following is completely different from that of the *Pensées*—"In a great soul everything is great. . . . A great, clear-eyed intelligence loves ardently and sees clearly what it loves." Nor does one find much of the spirit of the *Maximes* in these lines from the author's self-portrait—"I approve wholeheartedly of the noble passions; they are the mark of greatness of soul. . . ."

[34] Maxim 102.

[35] Domat, *Pensées* published by V. Cousin in *Jacqueline Pascal*, Appendix No. 3.

[36] *Pensées*, Brunschvicg edition, 276.

that intelligence be preceded by blind instinct; when intelligence acts it must act neither on its own initiative nor in search of truth, but to fulfill an evil task that is demanded of it without its knowledge.[37]

Man is not great. His desire to exalt himself does not exalt him. These are the two truths destined to destroy the ethics of glory. But how, then, can one explain that direct consciousness of the great and the sublime common to all men, that intuition of spiritual nobility that always accompanies glory and virtue? It is not enough, one might say, to expose the error if there is one; we must explain it, especially when it so generally assumes the nature of evidence.–I feel that I am pursuing an ideal good in glory, a good independent of my own selfish interest, which you cannot convince me to identify with. Besides, everyone knows how to distinguish in life between selfish and noble men; they are very different. Can you in good faith claim that we are wrong to distinguish them?

[37] These remarks on the role played by the idea of the unconscious in the naturalistic writers of the seventeenth century are of necessity very brief. In this inversion of the usual relationship between brute instinct and the highest faculties of man (the sense of the sublime, conscience, and intelligence) we again have one aspect of what might be called Jansenist materialism. Let us add that the writers of whom we are speaking are apt to base this notion of the unconscious, which might seem an ungrounded assumption, on the observation of human *behavior* and the differences between that behavior and the inner feelings of the subject and their articulation, however sincere. Without this recourse to the objective criterion of behavior, the distinction between the surface and the depths of the human soul would be in danger of falling into mythology. See La Rochefoucauld, Maxim 43, "Man often thinks he is leading himself when he is being led, and while his mind makes him incline to one end, his heart imperceptibly draws him towards another." Here it is clearly a question of what man ultimately *does* that permits one to make a sound judgment on what he has said or thought. All these writers, moreover, have the habit of judging virtues by their effects; with respect to friendship, for example, when the person we think we care for faces ruin, etc.

And if we are right, then you must be wrong.–The objection is an important one, and those against whom it is directed are very careful not to forget it. They must indeed admit the distinction that is pressed upon them. La Rochefoucauld does so very clearly when he writes that by *intérêt* he does not always mean material interest, but more often an interest of honor and glory.[38] But with him and those like him, even this distinction serves only to discredit honor and glory still further. Because if one feels that what is only an interest of honor is "unselfish" it is simply because, contrary to material interests, it has no real object but only pursues a smoke. As selfish in its impulses as other desires, it is superior to them only in its absurdity. All desires of man tend toward pleasure and to domination, and glory is no exception to the rule. All its absurd prestige springs from the fact that it aims at a shadow, so that folly is added to egoism. In the critique of glory the notion of *vanity* has been added to that of self-interest. And vanity does not justify self-interest, it merely empties it of reality.

This idea is as rooted as its contrary in common sense, which easily admits such inconsistencies. Vanity of birth, of glory, and of valor–underneath the admiration of the people, whether official or sincere, there had always smoldered a secret resentment toward the nobles. Christianity in its strict form traditionally struck this note. Consequently the idea of human vanity comes up again and again among the Jansenist writers. Pascal writes, "We are not satisfied with the life we have within us, and our own existence; we would like to live an imaginary life in the mind of others, and because of that we do our utmost to seem to be what we are not. We work unceasingly to embellish and preserve our imaginary self, and neglect the true one. . . . A great sign of the worthlessness of our being, not to be satisfied with the one without the other, and often to exchange one for the other."[39] Far from saving man's honor, the value instinctively attached to glory is here the most striking sign of his wretched state.

[38] *Avis au lecteur* in the 1668 edition of the *Maximes*.
[39] *Pensées,* Brunschvicg edition, 147.

The reduction of glory to a false and unreal idea played a central role in the disintegration of heroic ethics. "Glory and dishonor," according to Abbé d'Ailly, "are vain and imaginary if one does not relate them to the good and evil realities that accompany them."[40] And he offers as an example valiant men, "whose glory is limited to their imagination."[41] Similarly, their contempt for death is "folly rather than greatness and steadfastness of soul."[42] In this sense all of Jansenist thought seems to be, and is, an attack on moral idealism. Undoubtedly the worship of divine sovereignty is the final and most important end of this critique; but before we reach that goal, which reverses all the terms of the discussion, we see only the effort to extend the power and the limits of nature. When Jansenism, for the greater glory of God, clears away from the heart of things and of man everything that might compete with God, it really banishes God from the world and concedes reality, in a blind universe, only to a mankind that is devoid of glory and devoid of virtue.

By acknowledging the greed in instinct, by challenging the testimony of consciousness, and by denouncing the emptiness of glory, one attacked the very foundations of human greatness and submerged its highest peaks. And the waves that battered and submerged human grandeur are those with which a new period was to overwhelm the aristocratic hero. To become aware of this one has only to notice the virtues that foundered along with Pascal's "detestable" ego. They are all those virtues that had always comprised the aristocrat's ideal. The writers cited were perhaps unaware of this; they undoubtedly believed they were attacking only a perennial illusion of man, and their criticism can be appreciated on this level. One would misinterpret their true inspiration, however, if he were to isolate from the start the real conditions in which it was elaborated. We are speaking of ten or twenty years after the defeat of the Fronde, at the time of the greatest

[40] *Pensée* 5.
[41] *Pensée* 6.
[42] *Pensée* 56.

political weakness the nobility had as yet experienced. The monarchy had never been so strong, nor the individual noble so powerless. This is the profound meaning of the moral controversy examined above—it is an abridgment of a long episode in the history of society. One senses clearly that behind these aggressive volumes of *pensées* there are the half-sketched lineaments of an already outdated figure whose battered silhouette can still be discerned.

The quotations alone in this chapter are enough to allow us to identify this victim. La Rochefoucauld's enumeration of the disguises of *amour-propre* is identical with the list of chivalric virtues: illustrious grandeur, love of glory, unselfishness, magnanimity or "restraint" in success, loyalty, sincerity, friendship, gratitude, faithfulness, stoic "constancy," contempt for death, courage, and a purified and spiritual love. One alters the real meaning of the *Maximes* by speaking of them principally in terms of the existence or non-existence of altruism in man. Certainly this too is of some importance in La Rochefoucauld, but it is not the main point. The *Maximes* are concerned much more with the heroic magnification of the human figure, the sovereign power of the ego, and the nobility of desire, than with goodness. In this period it could not be otherwise because these were the principal forms in which one was then accustomed to conceive or deny the sublime. Abbé Esprit concludes his book with the portrait that in most of its features bears a striking resemblance to aristocratic virtue as we know it: "Human virtue would like to have a great number of witnesses and approving observers. . . . Human virtue is presumptuous. . . . Human virtue is haughty and arrogant, it never wants either to yield or to humble itself or to tolerate anything that rivals it. . . ."[43] The aristocratic sublime, essentially personal, was based on the brilliant triumphs of the ego. The more strongly socialized notion of the sublime current today rests more on goodness, capacity for self-sacrifice, and the ability to act for something other than oneself. Because of this, modern controversies over the *Maximes* invariably invoke the example of

[43] *Fausseté des vertus humaines,* Part II, Chapter XXVII.

the Good Samaritan. In effect, this is to substitute for the debate that preoccupied their author and his entire age another debate that he neither conceived of nor engaged in.

A consideration of the aristocratic public reaction on reading the *Maximes* provides one of the more interesting contributions to the study of the current of pessimist ethics. Among the papers of the Marquise de Sablé[44] one finds a dozen letters, mostly from her friends, which are unanimous in their protestations, except for two anonymous letters that are Jansenist in tone. Madame de Guéméné considers what she has read of the *Maximes* to be "based more on the author's temperament than on truth." Madame de Liancourt asks that "one do away with the ambiguity that confuses the true virtues with the false," naïvely invoking the traditional distinction of the two planes of the soul against a book that sets out to deny that distinction. Madame de La Fayette does not believe in the "general corruption." Madame de Schomberg judges the *Maximes* "dangerous" since they do away with moral responsibility. Madame de Sablé herself expressed a similar opinion in a draft of an article for the *Journal des Savants*. Furthermore, one reads in her *Maximes,* "When the nobles hope to make others believe that they have some great quality they do not possess, it is dangerous to show that we are not convinced; because when we deprive them of the hope of deceiving the world, we deprive them also of the desire to perform worthy acts in conformity with the role they are playing."[45] In this remark one can see a general refutation of La Rochefoucauld, a very meaningful refutation both for the social allusion it contains and for its modest tone. Madame de Sablé argues from expediency, like someone who timidly defends an almost hopeless cause. As far as La Rochefoucauld himself is concerned, his aristocratic status does not affect the meaning of his work; personal motives, his personality, his setbacks, and perhaps the desire to raise himself above common illusions may explain how an aristocrat such as he is

[44] They can be found in the Grands Écrivains edition of La Rochefoucauld, Vol. I, pp. 371–99.

[45] Madame de Sablé, *Maximes,* 75.

among the most relentless destroyers of the aristocratic ideal. This kind of individual defection, common in the history of ideas, does not alter the course of things. The fact remains that moral pessimism as it appeared in the seventeenth century and the theology on which it was based were generally hostile to the moral tradition of the aristocratic milieu.

The Jansenist Party

Up to this point we have concerned ourselves principally with defining what Jansenism sought to destroy; we have seen in it a varied but unwavering determination to attack the prerogatives of the aristocratic ego. We still have to describe the positive goals of the movement and its achievements and failures in history. We should not forget that Jansenism was not only a doctrine but a milieu and a party. Now Jansenism as a party or a sect failed. At no moment was its history auspicious; it is the long abortion of an innovation in an environment that, we are forced to conclude, was strongly inimical to it. Corneille has behind him all of heroic chivalry. Molière's thought is in harmony with his times and with times to come. Port-Royal, instead, begins with great men who were immediately condemned and exiled, and ends with the *convulsionnaires*[1] of the following century. The tragedy of its history seems to be prefigured in its initial convictions, rather vague and indefensible, a confusion of bold advances and retreats.

Yet to judge from all we have seen up to this point, Port-Royal was indeed moving in the direction of history and should have been favored by fortune. Indeed at the time of Louis XIV, the heroic sublime was in general disrepute, and all the great writers of the period–Racine, Molière, Boileau –were, each in his own way, the witnesses and the artisans of this fall from favor, the outcome of an irresistible evolution. A political evolution that augmented the power of the monarchy and the state was among the first forces that rendered the chivalric ego and its ethos anachronistic. Now it is interesting to note that the Jansenist notion of instinct implies an

[1] *Convulsionnaires* were the Jansenist religious fanatics who claimed to perpetrate miracles (*Tr. note*).

extreme mistrust of the impulses of the ego; ultimately it leads to an ethics of coercion, a strict regulation of the inner life and of behavior in which the ego and its impulses are enemies that must be eliminated. The economic evolution was another factor, still more inimical to the nobles' code of behavior. If ostentation and more or less wanton spending can be virtues in the aristocracy, it is because the accumulation of wealth would be meaningless in that social class, composed of old-style landowners or courtiers. It is only in the bourgeoisie that the amount saved from income is the prerequisite of all growth. As this practice became more and more widespread in economic life, the condemnation of squandering and extravagant spending was inevitable. For a long time the bourgeoisie had created luxuries only for aristocratic consumption. Much could be said on the role of glorious spending in the genesis of aristocratic ideology; in any case one can see that since the accumulation of wealth was not considered important, this spending was the principal sign of social superiority. An analogous situation could explain the unselfish character attributed to the natural impulses of the noble, his trust in the sublimation of desires and his optimistic ethics. The idealist notion of instinct so dear to the aristocracy was conceived at a time in which a certain liberal attitude with respect to money prevailed. Along with the middle class need to save, there appeared a new concept of instinct, more closely tied to reality and more concrete in its aim—how can instinct be sublimated if it aspires above all to acquire, to keep, and to amass material goods, to accumulate all things in order to continue to grow? This tendency, according to Jansenism, is the very definition of *amour-propre.* In the idealizing of instinct, the Jansenists then perceive the danger of self-diminution, of an outward gesture which is absurd and impossible. The only thing that truly exists, and that is called nature, is an impulse to self-satisfaction at the expense of the world. This impulse of necessity overcomes all attempts to embellish it. It is a necessary law of mankind, irresistible and lacking prestige. But in middle-class circumstances the tendency to yield completely to this law is counterbalanced by a spirit of constant calculation, a bookkeeping of gains and expectations, which presupposes the existence of a general principle of restraint that maintains order among the unruly powers of the emotions. The victory of nature consequently goes hand in hand with its condemnation, with recourse to an authority different from that of instinct and destined to check its impulses; bourgeois naturalism is thus tied quite naturally to an ethics of repression.

The sympathy of the nineteenth century *bien-pensants* critics for Jansenism springs from this twofold truth,[2] because Jansenism did much to lend credence to the two postulates, both eminently bourgeois, of the omnipotence of nature and the need to keep it under strict control. As a consequence Jansenism created a very different ideal from that of the impulsive, ostentatious, and spendthrift aristocrat; it proposed a type both realistic and constrained, conscious of his desires and prepared to wage war against their disorderliness. The influence and the strength of Jansenism can be measured by the fact that as soon as the French bourgeois dominated society he imposed this ideal on it, a classic ideal that combines a down-to-earth understanding of things with a measured dignity.[3]

Sainte-Beuve, to whom the idea of defining Jansenism in social terms seemed neither out of place nor preposterous, repeatedly recognizes therein the preponderant action of the upper middle class and especially that rich and cultured elite of lawyers within the Third Estate. "Port-Royal," he wrote without circumlocution, "was the religious undertaking of the aristocracy of the middle class in France."[4] In addition he observes that almost all the great figures in the Jansenist movement came out of that bourgeois aristocracy–Le Maître, Arnauld, Sainte-Marthe, Pascal, Nicole, and Domat, to men-

[2] It is true that this sympathy is mitigated and often destroyed by an aversion for Jansenism's insubordination to authority.

[3] We too often overlook one whole side of the bourgeoisie that is present from its beginnings–the side of dull and dreary contention. We imagine the rising middle class too exclusively as smiling, fearless, and naturalistic in the fullest sense of the word. This is not the case, especially in the seventeenth century.

[4] *Port-Royal,* preliminary discourse.

tion only the best known. Naturally the bourgeoisie had as its interpreters its most cultured and most respected elements, those closest to the nobility; the others were of almost no consequence. Undoubtedly the lawyers already enjoyed some privileges; but they made up a social category still clearly distinct from the aristocracy in the eyes of the public and in its own view. Disillusioned by the Fronde, this group met the aristocracy's customary contempt with a heightened sense of its own worth, its own dignity.[5] Bourgeois in spite of everything, they strove to be such with as much splendor as possible. From which we have the stately aspect of their refutation, reinforced by the majesty of Christianity, of the whole moral code that judged them, the bourgeois, inferior.

It follows clearly from all of this that Port-Royal was expressing a profound change in French society that had its roots in a relatively new and robust group. If this is true, why did it fail at this point? This seems even more surprising, considering that as a naturalistic and repressive philosophy, it thoroughly permeated the spirit of the age of Louis XIV. Given these conditions, how can one explain that as a sect it remained on the fringe of society, exposed to persecution by the legal authorities and unable to get the better of them, and that it functioned as a short-lived catalyst on all of society while it was itself eliminated? There must have been a profound incompatibility between Jansenism and the direction of history; this contrast, as one can see at every moment of the history of Port-Royal, touches the question of authority and obedience. Jansenism was considered suspect because it was not docile; it represented the only form of the bourgeois or modern mind not acceptable in the France of Louis XIV—that which asserted the rights of conscience against outward authority. The entire history of Jansenism is the history of this conflict.

[5] In the *pensées* of Domat, magistrate and jurist, a known Jansenist and friend of Pascal, we read the following reflection—"the *gens d'épée* [the aristocrats], call the *officiers* [officeholders and lawyers] desk people; they should be called brain people and the aristocrats should be called hand people."

The social heresy of Jansenism consisted principally in the affirmation of a certain freedom of conscience, which Port-Royal linked indissolubly with moral rigor. Jansenism exhibits the same tendency as does the Reformation to distinguish inner moral rigor from external coercion, though in a much weaker and more subdued way. In the Reformation the tightening of self-imposed moral rule tends to make for a more immediate relationship between man and God; man, more severe with himself, is also harder to control from the outside since the pledge of morality lies within the conscience. Port-Royal reproduces the same attitude, in spite of its denials and in spite of the extreme restraint of its moves. In this respect Jansenism can be considered as the last manifestation of a great current of thought that cuts across the beginnings of modern times and challenges the authoritarian ways of the Catholic Church. Port-Royal not only attacks laxity in Christianity and corruption in the government of the Church; it more or less openly blames Roman absolutism, to which it refuses or begrudges its submission.

The very theology of Port-Royal, while establishing a strict inner discipline, contains within it a principle, or rather expresses a desire for moral autonomy. Indeed, although the doctrine of efficacious grace seems to lead logically to fatalism and apathy by making God's help independent of man's merit, in reality it fulfills quite a different purpose. It attributes such superhuman and supernatural value to divine election that the chosen souls immediately feel themselves superior to all earthly fear and all servile submission. Efficacious grace formed robust natures, free of the fumes of glory and fortified with a divine force that increased their strength tenfold. The prestige of earthly institutions seemed to disappear before the idea of this investiture from on high, so rare and so direct. This fact explains the Jansenist propensity for "dissent" that in the Church ordinarily accompanies a strict doctrine of grace, dissent that is as evident in Port-Royal as in the Reformation.[6] At the same time that Jansenism reacted

[6] The theory of predestination, very close to that of efficacious grace, certainly played an important role in the bellicose vigor of puritanism and similar movements born of the Reformation.

against old-style individualism, it claimed to oppose the autocratic spirit that was triumphing more and more completely in the seventeenth century, in the Church as in secular society. That is what put Port-Royal on the fringe of its times, and that is what vanquished it.

For a long time the Catholic Church had been straining—and the great assault of the Reformation only accelerated the movement—to constitute itself into an absolute monarchy in which a single head, the pope, determined doctrine and ruled the hierarchy. Port-Royal tried to resist the trend and, almost alone in France, raised its muffled, unsubmissive voice. The problem of the respective rights of authority and conscience is one its writers posed most obstinately. Pascal already faces this problem, at least the intellectual aspects of it, in his *Fragment d'un traité du vide,* written several years before the properly Jansenist period of his life; and he resolves it by declaring beyond the reach of authority the knowledge of subjects that fall within the province of the senses or of reason. This is the same solution he reached ten years later in the eighteenth *Lettre provinciale*—"It was also in vain," he wrote to the Jesuits, "that you procured that decree from Rome against Galileo, condemning his opinion with respect to the movement of the earth. Decrees cannot prove that the earth stands still." This assertion of the rights of reason—strictly limited, moreover, to the knowledge of natural things, beyond which one must defer to the decisions of the Church—is certainly not exclusively Jansenist; this sharing of influence between reason and authority had long been generally accepted and the Church itself tolerated the idea. But in Jansenism this concept assumes a rather special character and the circumstances that surround it make it more dangerous. First of all, it is very difficult to say precisely where the sphere of natural things ends and that of revelation begins. Belief in revealed truths may at any given moment involve an assent with respect to matters more directly dependent on our judgment. A conciliatory spirit and a desire to avoid debate on delicate questions succeeded in smoothing over sleeping difficulties. But actually Port-Royal awakened this difficulty by demanding the freedom to evaluate all points of fact, including those raised by the supreme authority of the Church on the occasion of a decision with respect to dogma. Thus, for example, when some condemned proposition was attributed to an author, in this case Jansenius, his disciples considered themselves justified, in the name of the rights of natural reason, to dispute the existence in his writings of a heretical proposition that they recognize as such in the abstract. In this way the banal distinction between natural and supernatural objects of knowledge is transformed into a cunning weapon aimed against dogmatic authority. To this separation of fact and right, famous in the history of Jansenism, Desmarets de Saint-Sorlin, one of the most relentless enemies of Port-Royal to whom we have already been introduced, objected quite properly that the need to examine facts freely could continually lead to a refusal to respect authority, even recognized authority. Thus, who can guarantee that the host has been truly consecrated, and by a real priest? When the Blessed Sacrament passes, therefore, one would have the right to refuse the signs of veneration habitual with Catholics on this occasion by arguing that the facts are subject to doubt.[7] The argument is less sophistic than it seems. One must choose between the thought that is formulated from within, and that which yields to all-powerful suggestions from without and loses the habit of examining or controlling evidence. When reason surrenders its rights, Pascal wants it to do so willingly: "Nothing is so consonant with reason as this disavowal of reason."[8] "True Christianity consists in the surrender and the exercise of reason."[9] "We must know to doubt when necessary, confirm when necessary, and yield when necessary. He who does not act in this fashion does not understand the strength of reason."[10] Here it is no longer a question of a banal compromise between

[7] Desmarets de Saint-Sorlin, *Réponse à l'insolente apologie des religieuses de Port-Royal,* Part III, Chapter XVIII, 1666.

[8] *Pensées,* Brunschvicg edition, 272.

[9] *Pensées,* Brunschvicg edition, 269.

[10] *Pensées,* Brunschvicg edition, 268.

reason and faith in a purely speculative domain, but of a complete recasting of the relation of conscience to outward authority.[11]

One might be surprised to find in Jansenism, so strict with respect to natural man, such an attachment to the prerogatives of reason. The anomaly disappears if one considers that under the name of reason the Jansenists defended not the pre-eminence of man but the rights of his conscience such as they, as Christians, understood them. Pascal's dialectic, for example, blasts reason as the source of pride, but encourages and exalts it as a demand for truth. The exercise of reason is presented as a simple requirement of conscience, but in this guise it is indispensable for faith. "It is *amour-propre,*" writes Nicole, "that induces man to believe that one never sins by obeying, because by nature he loves security and because he would be overjoyed to see his path so clearly marked out as to eliminate all fear of losing his way. . . . God did not wish to encourage this inclination of man. . . . He willed that there might be snares and temptations everywhere. Consequently, the truly obedient never think that their path is completely out of danger nor that they can go forward with their eyes closed. . . . They do not consider themselves excused from the obligation to ask God's guidance to lead them." It is understood that one must appeal to God directly, over the heads of the established authorities; otherwise, Nicole continues in effect, they would be "not only the slaves but the worshippers of a mortal man. . . ."[12] The whole Jansenist rationale lies in this approach; it is a critique of blind obedience, a way of avoiding the injunctions of authority in one's relations with God. The exercise of reason, understood in this sense, is not simply tolerated; it is required as a safeguard for true faith, because servitude leads to superstition and both

[11] In all of this, leaving aside his own dialectic, Pascal echoes all of Port-Royal; see especially the *Apologie pour les religieuses de Port-Royal,* by Arnauld, Nicole and Sainte-Marthe (1665) and the tenth of Nicole's *Lettres imaginaires* (1665).

[12] Nicole, ninth *Lettre imaginaire.*

are the downfall of religion.[13] One can easily see that this new solution of the problem of reason and authority, less eclectic and more violent than the usual solution, presented also a greater danger to the Church's stability.

Moreover, as far as ecclesiastical government was concerned, the Jansenist spirit expressed itself by a more or less open opposition to the encroachment of papal absolutism and to the assertion—actually already triumphant—of papal infallibility.[14] The Jansenists rejected the idea of a Church organized along the lines of an absolute monarchy, whose head imposed his will from above on the members. They were apt to consider the Church as a community as well as a monarchy. "When we consider the Church in its unity," said Pascal, "the Pope, who is its head, is as it were the whole Church. When we consider it in its multiplicity, the Pope is but one of its members. . . . Multiplicity that is not reduced to unity is confusion; unity that does not depend on multiplicity is tyranny."[15] And again, "Unity and multiplicity. . . . It is a mistake to exclude either."[16]

By trying to swim against the irresistible current that was sweeping the Church along, Jansenism was bound to collide with the Society of Jesus, the pervasive embodiment of the growing authority of Rome. The two kinds of strength that animated Port-Royal and the Jesuits were opposed not only in their philosophical or ethical inspiration but also in their political essence. By and large, Port-Royal mistrusted the regular monastic orders. More often than not the rules of such religious orders imposed a passive discipline on their members. They were directly bound to the self-seeking authority of Rome, who used them to overthrow impeding traditions. The Jesuits were the most prominent, but these are the words

[13] See Pascal, *Pensées*, Brunschvicg edition, 254. The Jansenists' aversion for purely exterior and superstitious piety is well known; see the beginning of the ninth *Lettre Provinciale*.

[14] See *Pensées*, Brunschvicg edition, 871: "France is about the only place where one is allowed to say that the Council is superior to the Pope."

[15] *Pensées*, Brunschvicg edition, 871.

[16] *Pensées*, Brunschvicg edition, 874.

Pascal puts in the mouth of a Dominican who is asked why he agrees to ally himself with the Jesuits in spite of his profound conviction:[17] "We are subject to our superiors, they are subject to others. They have pledged our votes; what do you want me to do?" Pascal adds, "We knew how to read between the lines, and that reminded us of his *confrère* who was exiled to Abbeville because of similar difficulties."[18]

However, for all of their desire to instill new life into the Church to make it shake off the excessive tutelage of Rome, the Jansenists fell far short of advocating the idea of a democratic Church. They spoke admiringly of the primitive Church, in which the body of the faithful sometimes chose bishops; but this was simply an edifying and legendary memory. Jansenists, at least seventeenth-century Jansenists, were not very concerned even with the rights of the lower clergy. The group that they considered important and would have liked to see less dependent on Rome were the bishops.[19] Saint-Cyran lamented the fact that bishops were no longer chosen by chapters as they once had been, and that they were appointed by higher Church authorities. In the same way all of Port-Royal deplored the fact that the bishops, often residing far from their dioceses, no longer governed in a real and immediate way but drew their inspiration from the court or the Papal Nuncio. Thus, as Sainte-Beuve put it, Port-Royal's dream was to substitute for the papal monarchy "an aristocracy under the leadership of the bishops."[20] The "patricians of the upper bourgeoisie"—among whom Jansenism sank its roots, according to Sainte-Beuve—favored turning

[17] The trial and censure of Arnauld at the Sorbonne was at issue; the Dominicans had taken part in the condemnation.

[18] Second *Lettre provinciale.*

[19] Note, however, the action of the parish priests of Paris and Rouen who came to the defense of the *Provinciales* against the Jesuits in 1656; Pascal even put his pen at their service; but they were parish priests from great cities, relatively important and influential people.

[20] Sainte-Beuve, *Port-Royal,* Vol. I, p. 318, on the *Petrus Aurelius* of Saint-Cyran.

over the handling of religious matters to an ecclesiastical patrician class.

In secular society the same aspiration would have been more difficult to imagine and to express. The absolute power of the king was more to be feared and less open to question. For all kinds of reasons the upper echelons of the Third Estate made a timid opponent. But if the political loyalism of the Jansenists cannot be questioned, neither can it be doubted that their general state of mind or their views on discipline and obedience were out of tune in the France of Richelieu and Louis XIV. They were made to understand this clearly when certain distant aspirations toward independence were met with the same harsh measures that would have been meted out to avowed enemies of the Crown.

Opposed to autocracy as well as to the old feudal spirit, Jansenism was like a vague tendency of the upper bourgeoisie to found religious and social life on a discipline that was more demanding but more morally independent. This aspiration gives one an idea what a government of *notables* in France would have been like had it been possible to establish one there. With a government of such eminent men–important bourgeois, lawyers, nobles (if the nobles would have been able to forego their insolent and disorderly ways)–Port-Royal contained in germinal form, in the mixture of obedience and independence that characterizes it, a project of renewal and emancipation, in the obviously very moderate sense in which the notables understood the word. Jansenism might have succeeded if France had been capable of becoming a land of strict constitution and of rule by law with a solid and responsible patrician class.[21] But the strong imprint feudalism left on French society–the reactionary aspirations or the frivolity of the aristocracy and the profound moral cleavage between the nobles and the upper strata of the Third Estate–had long made evolution in this direction impossible. The upper bour-

[21] One should observe that the government of notables would have corresponded rather closely with the spirit of the French Reformation. Calvin, for example, prefers a regime he no doubt calls "aristocratic," but which he very broadly defines as being "rule governed by leaders and men of substance."

geoisie, with all its rancor, remained timid, whereas the aristocracy, with all its pride, was becoming powerless. Since the upper classes were incapable of coming to power, the monarchy—a force outside of and stronger than the upper classes, a power more and more beyond their control and feeding incessantly on their weakness—was able to gain a monopoly of political strength. At the time of Pascal, all spirit of independence and autonomy, even as timid and limited in scope as that of Port-Royal, was considered subversive and treated as such.

In this respect royal despotism and the despotism of Rome had the same basic interests. The period that followed the Reformation and the religious wars, the beginning of the seventeenth century, in which the French society regained a firmly established structure, had witnessed an entente between them. Rome, disavowing the doctrinal errors of the *Ligue* as errors resulting from specific conditions that were to be forgotten along with those conditions, provided the doctrine of divine right, which reminded men that God was behind political authority. In return the kings of France opened the realm to the Jesuits, who had become their regular confessors, and silenced the voice of the local churches in accord with Rome. The bishops, controlled by the court and the Holy See, clearly reflected this double despotism. More and more they demanded absolute obedience from their inferiors, and they themselves executed orders from above. This was the state of affairs when Port-Royal sketched the portrait of the ideal bishop and did its utmost to balance obedience and conscience. All the existing authorities opposed it; Rome and the Jesuits, the monarchy and the dignitaries of the French Church joined forces to crush it. By 1715 four popes had already condemned it in almost a dozen briefs, bulls, constitutions, and excommunications; while in the meantime three successive governments deployed against it the whole apparatus of ecclesiastical and police persecution. Richelieu put and kept Saint-Cyran in prison and dispersed the solitaries of Port-Royal; Mazarin and Anne of Austria saw to it that the Sorbonne condemned and expelled the great Arnauld, who was forced to live in hiding to escape prosecution; they dispersed the solitaries once again and initiated the great persecution of the *Formulaire*.[22] Louis XIV had scarcely begun to rule for himself when he renewed the persecution and had the *petites écoles* of Port-Royal destroyed, the students living there and the novices of the convent expelled, and the nuns who refused to comply questioned by the Archbishop of Paris, kept under surveillance, transferred, and excluded from the sacraments. After an interval of ten years the persecution picked up more intensely than ever in 1679 under a new archbishop. The *messieurs* were dispersed once more, Arnauld was forced to flee again, and the convent was once more forbidden to recruit. Finally in the last year of his reign, and anxious to bring the affair to a close, Louis XIV revived the *Formulaire* and demanded that all involved sign it; upon their refusal he obtained the excommunication of the nuns, dispersed them, appropriated the goods of the condemned convent, and finally had the abbey demolished and the remains of the solitaries exhumed. Such relentlessness against a relatively weak enemy can be explained only by the profound incompatibility that absolutism sensed between its own principles and the aspirations of Jansenism. Jansenism was wiped out inasmuch as it was inconsistent with the evolution of French society and the forces to which that society had given birth.

Jansenism's relations with official society are nonetheless extremely difficult to define, because while it contained a dangerous principle of insubordination, we have seen on the other hand that it introduced necessary changes in moral thought. A religion that was more indulgent toward man and more complacent toward the instincts undoubtedly contained a principle of moral laxity and consequently of compromise with the established authorities; and in the eyes of the monarchy this made it preferable to an intransigent and belligerent Christianity. Undoubtedly, too, optimistic Christianity, relatively sympathetic to the arts, to the sciences, and to civiliza-

[22] This was a document prepared by the Jesuits, adopted in 1656 by the Clerical Assembly, which the king enjoined all ecclesiastics to sign. It involved adherence to the bulls and a condemnation of the famous propositions of Jansenius.

tion, adapted itself better than Jansenism to all that made this period one of full bloom and brilliance to the profusion of luxury and progress in knowledge. This Christianity, less harsh in its principles, favorably disposed to the cult of the grandiose, and accommodating in its behavior, was much more in harmony with the culture of the Great Century, as it was with the politics of that century. But absolutism not only needed people who were tractable and easy to get along with; in a country as big and as relatively cultured as France was, it was difficult not to ground obedience on an inner tension, on habits of moral discipline. Though consonant with the spirit of despotism, the Jesuitical methods, which consisted of domesticating behavior by alleviating scruples, scandalized public opinion, which in spite of everything was influential and demanded something more serious, less blatantly deceitful. The casuists of the Society of Jesus did not have a good press. The general need of discipline and moral responsibility favored a certain strictness; in this respect Jansenism was only the spearhead of a movement of reform and recovery begun immediately after the religious wars. Furthermore, the monarchy itself could not look favorably on the scandal of the Jesuit maxims–laxity of conscience ultimately ran the risk of destroying obedience itself. The Jesuit Fathers who justified homocide in a duel must have been more displeasing to the monarchy than the Pascal of the fourteenth *Lettre provinciale,* who refused to make the life or death of a man dependent on a "phantasm of honor," and who reserved to "public figures" the right to demand punishment if need be "in the name of the King, or rather in the name of God."[23]

[23] Some elements of Jesuit theology had no better press than Jesuit ethics; certain members of the Society maintained that it was enough to fear hell in order to be saved. Richelieu had earlier used his authority to uphold an analogous doctrine, and it is said that Saint-Cyran was sent to Vincennes in part for having denied that doctrine. It met with a generally bad reception; common sense opposed it, to the extent one can speak of common sense in this sphere, and it aroused an indignation attested to in literature principally by the tenth *Lettre provinciale* and Boileau's *Épître XII,* one written forty years after the other.

In short the monarchy, and all official society as well, needed to reconcile seemly virtue and submissive behavior, orderly morals and tractable consciences. They needed an expurgated Jansenism with the poison of rebellion filtered out of it. The *bien-pensants* of the period, Bossuet for example, bent all their energies in this direction. It was a delicate task and one full of uncertainties that had repercussions in painful vicissitudes and contradictions in the fate of Jansenism itself, and mark it from its beginnings to its end. On the whole, however, the question was settled by condemning both the Jesuit casuists' "lax precepts" and the Jansenists' turbulent doctrine of efficacious grace. The propositions of Jansenius were quite naturally the first to be condemned, Rome's chief interest being centered there. But once public opinion and the French clergy had approved of this condemnation they obtained from Rome the condemnation of the casuists, which was taken up again with loud applause in France by the Clerical Assembly of 1700, whereas the *Lettres provinciales* were never condemned by the French ecclesiastical authorities.

We are in the habit of saying that Jansenism, defeated on theological grounds, triumphed with its ethics. Bossuet, who is always very cautious when he speaks of grace, and who approved the condemnation of the five propositions as marking the exact limits of heresy and orthodoxy in a delicate area,[24] was in close agreement with the ethics of the Jansenists and was one of the casuists' most relentless enemies, a driving force in their condemnation in France. There is a profound reason for this distinction between Jansenist theology and Jansenist ethics: the authorities could sympathize with Jansenism up to the point where Christian exigencies endangered the principle of authority. This point was the doctrine of efficacious grace, because this doctrine evinced a desire for striking innovations, for intellectual and emotional scandal, a desire to diminish the importance of everything in relation to divine election and those who might consider themselves favored by it. Short of this doctrine, rigors of conscience seemed compatible with obedience.

[24] Bossuet, *Oraison funèbre de N. Cornet,* 1663.

Thus purified of its dangerous elements, Jansenism thoroughly permeated the age of Louis XIV. However, one must not identify this diluted Jansenism with the one that arose on the fringes of official society, and that official society persecuted. What is properly called Jansenism draws its vigor from the fact that it represents a protest against the course of things and the established authorities, and the fact that it bases its very severity on thoughts that are carried to extremes and aspirations that are importunate to real society. Finally Jansenism has its place in the history of thought because of its restlessness and tenacity, and because it produced Pascal and the *Pensées*.

Nevertheless the fact remains that it was difficult for Jansenism to adhere to a position of strict intransigence in the midst of a society whose structure and whose established powers were opposed to it. Then too, all through its history Jansenism itself is dominated by a persistent timidity, a chronic dread of irremediable actions and of too violent ruptures. All those who have studied Jansenism have observed its frailty. Sainte-Beuve, who nonetheless does his utmost in his *Port-Royal* to emphasize all that is stately and strong in Jansenism, recognizes its basic weakness. "There was in Jansenism," he writes, "a principle that was concentrated and powerful but that rapidly lost its potency and shriveled up. There was nothing expansive about it."[25] Dragging the chain and ball of orthodoxy and caught in a morass of crippling disputes that were destined to reinforce that orthodoxy, Jansenism doomed itself before it was reduced to failure by its enemies.[26]

[25] Sainte-Beuve, *Port-Royal,* Vol. I, p. 294, note.

[26] It is useless to draw distinctions between different periods at Port-Royal—the Saint-Cyran period, the Arnauld period; the defect of timorousness and hesitation are common to all. Sainte-Beuve himself stresses that the destiny of Port-Royal always hangs on an "if" or a "perhaps." The author of *Port-Royal* points out as a striking coincidence that Jansenius, Saint-Cyran, and Pascal—the Jansenists who were in his opinion the most consistent and, judging by their character, those most capable of ultimately breaking with Rome—all died before reaching the decisive moment. The fact re-

Port-Royal could fight the relentless opposition of those in power only with the weapons of the weak: obstinacy, discussion, and theological hair-splitting. It never confronted the enemy and until the end it adhered to the irresolute psychology and contradictory thought of the dissident who claims to be more orthodox than his persecutors. Saint-Cyran and Jansenius, plotting together the reform of the Church, planned to win over the pope himself to their grandiose and hazy design. At the very moment Pascal comes very close to breaking with Rome—when with Arnauld and Nicole he advocates refusal to sign the *Formulaire* without qualification, when he writes the famous words of rebellion, "If my letters are condemned in Rome, what I condemn there is condemned in heaven"[27]—he is also attacking the anti-papist Huguenots "who destroy the unity"[28] of the Church. At the height of the anti-Jansenist persecution Arnauld and Nicole continued to fight the Protestants; in exile Arnauld, in the midst of Port-Royal's misfortunes, approved of the revocation of the Edict of Nantes. Both drew the distinction between fact and right that permitted them to declare themselves obedient to Rome in substance while refusing to admit that the condemned propositions were to be found in Jansenius. With them doctrinal rigor existed only potentially; it might have been the soul of the movement but it constantly lost itself in the swamp of their loyalism. Indeed as they proceeded through various

---

mains that they all hesitated until they died, in spite of great opportunities to act otherwise, at least for the latter two. The enemies of Port-Royal, when they do not yield to the temptation of exaggerating the monster's spitefulness and power, dwell even more cruelly on the congenital weakness in Jansenism; note particularly how Brémond does his utmost to destroy in an almost comical fashion Sainte-Beuve's hero, Saint-Cyran. (*Hist. litt. du sent. religieux en France*, Port-Royal, Chapters III, IV, V.) It is difficult, however, to accept his conclusion, which would make Jansenism a historical absurdity, an aberrant and inconsistent offshoot of Christianity. Jansenism existed, as tenacious as it was timid, and one is forced to believe that even in its defeat it represented something profound.

[27] *Pensées*, Brunschvicg edition, 920.

[28] *Pensées*, Brunschvicg edition, 874.

vicissitudes and fluctuations, they even modified the austerity of Jansenist theology by qualifying remarks destined to make it less shocking.[29] Confronted with the royal power their attitude was the same. One may cite some remarks of Saint-Cyran that clearly seem to express an instinctive hostility to despotism, but always in a tone of simple ill-humor.[30] As a matter of fact, contrary to a false legend Port-Royal never conspired in the political sense of the word, although it had every reason to succumb to the temptation.[31] Pascal, if we are to believe his sister, saw in the royal power "not only an image of God's power but a sharing in this same power."[32] And Racine asserts that they were convinced at Port-Royal "that a subject can never be justified in rising up against his prince."[33] These were the sentiments of the Jansenists at the very time when the monarchy was forcing them to go into hiding or into exile and when they themselves were daily transgressing the will of the monarchy by their gatherings, their projects, and their widespread clandestine publications.

Seventeenth-century Jansenism always remained torn between the force that urged it to separate itself from the prevalent currents and that which drew it along with that current.

[29] Nicole gave in completely at the end of his life. There were some at Port-Royal who had always been shocked at his lack of zeal, and not even Arnauld was beyond reproach.

[30] For example his remark to Mère Angélique Arnaud on the government that wants only slaves; see Sainte-Beuve, Vol. I, p. 486.

[31] The Jansenist sympathies of certain repentant Frondeurs (Mme. de Longueville, the Contis), though important in the history of Port-Royal's friendships and vicissitudes, are much less important for one who seeks to come to a judgment on its spirit and its direction. The Jansenists' intrigues with Retz come after the Fronde and have nothing to do with it; in opposition to the court they supported him as the titular archbishop of Paris, with the idea of winning over a power that would be sympathetic to them, and with no more elaborate design than that. Jansenism—and this is obviously in keeping with its character—always had the semblance and the disadvantages of conspiracy, and never had either the reality or the advantages.

[32] *Vie de Pascal* by Mme. Périer.

[33] Racine, *Abrégé de l'histoire de Port-Royal.*

The bourgeois elite's resistance to the spirit of absolute rule, and the awareness it may have had of its own importance, explain the movement's duration and obstinacy; the general trend of society, where the dice were loaded against Jansenism, explains the weakness of the movement and its habit of denying itself, of calling itself, in the words of its most persistent champions, the "phantasm of Jansenism."

Unlike Calvinism, Jansenism appears to be purely negative with respect to real life, even in its more impassioned aspects. There is nothing in it similar to that sense of duty or earthly vocation that went hand in hand with an inhuman theology in Calvinism. Though the Reformation pushed the anti-naturalist statements of Christianity to extremes it was careful not to belittle secular activity. While it exercised control in all areas it ennobled all things. This was in effect the rehabilitation of earthly life, although in a very peculiar form. By a kind of compensation that constitutes a modern aspect of the Reformation, the strengthening of morals banned asceticism and acts of mortification, and in part freed life from the curse to which it had been subject. On the contrary, when Catholicism is violent its violence is apt to be turned against life; all Catholic severity, when not practiced solely on the level of outward discipline, tends toward a sort of desperate protest against human nature. Jansenism, cut off from reality and from practical action, moved in this direction. There is a strong monastic flavor to it; having grown up around a convent–and a convent of nuns at that–it carried the opposition of heaven and earth to its logical conclusion. In spite of contrary tendencies that existed within it but lacked the strength to flower, it appears above all as an acute form of denial. If we consider Pascal's scruples in the world as his sister presents them, at the sight of this constant maceration we will easily comprehend the profound impotence bound up with Jansenism's fidelity to Catholicism.

There is a subversive element in Jansenism, however, and that is the aggressive turn it is apt to give to the negation of worldly values, particularly human justice and authority. On this point there existed a sort of Jansenist nihilism, more and more daring as real society offered less of a foothold to subversion. The passages in Pascal's *Pensées* that were corrected or deleted in the Port-Royal edition give one an idea of how far this boldness could go. We have now moved well beyond the naturalism that disqualifies magnanimity or glory. As long as it is only a question of ethical naturalism Port-Royal is based on a broader current drawn from all points on the modern horizon. Its originality is more apparent when it begins to deal with society and its justice in the same way it deals with man and his virtue, when the denial of human values attacks the prestige of authority and strips it of its halo. If La Rochefoucauld's *Maximes* seem to contribute to social disintegration, what can be said of Pascal's reflections on custom, high honors, justice, and authority? Sainte-Beuve, following Joseph de Maistre, compares Jansenius to Hobbes, and indeed one is forced to acknowledge a kinship between certain Jansenist views and the materialistic critiques of law and justice. Pascal cannot find the tiniest particle of justice in human institutions. Differences in laws and customs throughout the world, their contradictions, their inconsistency from the point of view of reason and justice, and their subjection to caprice or to chance–this is the picture Pascal sees every time he wants to define human society. For him there is only one unifying principle in this chaos–force. One thinks of his famous phrase, "Unable to arrange things so that what is just is strong, we have seen to it that what is strong is just."[34] Just as virtue in the individual is a disguise for his appetites, what poses as justice in human societies is but the mask of brute power. At the very most Pascal added to force "imagination" or "opinion," an accessory element, moreover, because "it is force that makes opinion."[35] Besides, "the sovereign authority founded on opinion and imagination rules for a while . . . that based on force rules forever."[36] When Pascal has interpreted order according to the truth, one will not be surprised to notice that, in keeping with the ways of Jansenism,

[34] *Pensées,* Brunschvicg edition, 298.
[35] *Pensées,* Brunschvicg edition, 304.
[36] *Pensées,* Brunschvicg edition, 311.

his nihilistic thought has in it something that leads to a paralysis of action. Because if it is absurd to believe that existing institutions are in accord with justice, the illusion that just institutions could replace them is no less visionary; and considering the radical corruption of the human race, that illusion draws its inspiration from a sacrilegious presumption. Consequently it is senseless to rise up against an unavoidable injustice in the name of an impossible justice; that is what the "half-clever" do and Pascal repeatedly takes the side of the common people against them. The "effects," simulacra of justice and grandeur to which the people yield, have their own justification (although it is not perceived by the people) in the futility of all human claims to justice and in the necessity of order and peace. All Pascal's nihilism, then, leads to submission and effective respect for the established order. The double nature of Jansenism, both shackled and rebellious, powerless and reforming, is evident in the tone of this respect which, however complete, wants to be free of all illusions as to the intrinsic value of those to whom respect is rendered. According to Pascal the truly "clever" are those who honor the great men of this world but without esteeming them for their greatness. In Pascal's obedience there is what he himself calls a *pensée de derrière*[37] a mental reservation, that distinguishes it from common obedience. If Pascal yields to force it is for reasons that place him morally above force. It is because of this that he describes tyranny not as the excessive exercise of power, because power holds all rights in its own sphere, but rather as the aspiration to hold dominion "outside of its own order," that is to say, to usurp a category of homage to which it has no right, for example to demand esteem simply because one is strong.[38] Pascal's dialectic, with its distinct orders and its constant gra-

[37] *Pensées,* Brunschvicg edition, 336 and 337.

[38] See the *Trois discours sur la condition des Grands,* and the whole of Section V of the Brunschvicg edition. Nicole took up Pascal's ideas again in the group of writings he entitled *De l'éducation d'un prince* (1671), to which he added Pascal's three discourses.

dations from pro to con, is used ingeniously here to couple contempt and obedience.

Moreover, one must be careful not to confuse the attitude of Pascal when he demands the right to recognize the powerful for what they are, with that of the philosopher who wants inner freedom once he has paid what is due to social necessity. Pascal, instead, speaks with the tone of a partisan whom unfortunate circumstances allow only the dissidence of contempt. For in his case it is clearly a matter of passionate contempt justified by Christian zeal, and not, as with others, a matter of a serene freedom of judgment. This blend of conformism and denial conceals a bitterness that can easily become aggressive, as this thought suggests: "When force attacks humbug, when a simple soldier takes the square hat of a first president and throws it out the window."[39] Violence, apart from the ultimate evaluation Pascal might have made of it, almost appears in this instance as the very voice of truth. Behind the seemingly balanced structure in which the dependence of social man and the liberty of the thinker appear to be reconciled, persist the bitter traces of the painful drama of Port-Royal, the drama of a rebellion doomed from the start. French society will never again experience this way of looking at the problem of politics–at once daring in principle, desperate in its design, and banal in its conclusions–because the history of Jansenism can never be repeated, the history, that is to say, of a reforming movement deprived both of tradition and of a future, drawing its inspiration neither from what it has been nor from what it will be, but from what it might have been were it not for the evolution of the monarchy, the rule of the emancipated notables and the ethics of constraint, the double triumph of conscience and law.

[39] *Pensées,* Brunschvicg edition, 310.

Racine

The tragedies of Racine can be considered as the fusion of a literary genre traditionally concerned with the sublime and a new naturalistic spirit resolutely hostile to the very idea of the sublime. There is more in question here than Racine's own ties with Port-Royal, which, as is well known, were very close throughout the first and last twenty years of his life. Racine's own temperament and the general spirit of his age, which goes beyond the influence of Port-Royal, were much more responsible for this character of his plays. The primary end of tragedy, in its revival in the first half of the seventeenth century, was to provoke an outburst of moral admiration in the audience. The usual forms, the very conventions of the genre, were all built around the idea of the grandiose. This was still the temper of tragedy in Racine's time; not even the vogue for tenderness had affected the primacy of the heroic personality. The theater audience was accustomed to admiring great actions, uncommon thoughts, and delicacy of sentiment; that is what the audience expected of these heroes, whether or not they were clothed in the guise of antiquity, of these great men and grandees, kings and princes who were the only characters worthy of tragedy according to the rules of the genre. Their glory was bound to that of the poet, who was all the more admirable in his sphere the more the heroes were in theirs. This explains why the attraction to heroic tragedy was so strong and so persistent in Racine himself, in spite of his natural leanings and the structure of his theater. It would be a mistake to think that Racine succeeded in infusing nature into tragedy on his first attempt, or that he saw clearly the radical changes he was imposing on the genre. Natural man slipped into tragic theater without changing either its framework or its appearance and without ever completely stripping the poet's creations of their thirst for the sublime. Racine's theater is made up of oscillations between the traditional sublime and a psychology that is inconsistent with it, of often delicate arrangements and gradations in the midst of which the newest elements do not always at first glance stand out clearly.

Racine began with tragedies tailored to the tastes of the time and it would be difficult to differentiate clearly the *Thébaïde* and *Alexandre* from the tragedies of Corneille and his successors. The *Thébaïde* is similar to *Rodogune* in the murderous megalomania of the principal characters, in their obsession with the throne, and in the cruelty and twisted pathos of certain scenes. The situation of the two hostile brothers who dispute a throne to which each has an equal claim gives rise to a long series of arguments and noble maxims on the value and the real meaning of royal dignity. Créon, the two brothers' uncle, a scoundrel who is also obsessed by desire for the throne, and a grandiloquent villain reminiscent of Corneille's villains, cries out after the death of his two sons,

> The name father, Attale, is a common one,
> It is a gift heaven rarely refuses us.
> So common a blessing gives me little pleasure:
> It is no blessing if it provokes no envy.
> But the throne is a good with which heaven is sparing;
> That high station separates us from other mortals.[1]

Jocaste, the mother of Étéocle and Polynice, realizing that she is helpless against their inhuman ambition, wants to die and says so with that violent and complicated bitterness that marks Corneille's heroines, Sabine or Rodelinde–

> For my own flesh and blood I no longer feel pity or
> tenderness.
> Your example teaches me to cherish it no longer,
> And I, cruel ones, will teach you how to die.[2]

So that nothing will be missing from the play, two elegiac

[1] *La Thébaïde,* V, 4.
[2] Ibid., IV, 3.

and *précieux* lovers Hémon and Antigone come to embellish its action, just as Corneille uses Thésée and Dircé to adorn the equally agonizing Oedipus legend.

The same conformity to prevalent taste is evident in *Alexandre.* This tragedy, less bloody, almost has the ring of an episode from *Cyrus.* In it we find glorious pride closely interwoven with love in King Porus and Queen Axiane, enemies of Alexandre determined to resist him and defend their independence. Porus satisfies the desires of this queen, who demands of her lovers enough courage to serve her "illustrious wrath" effectively. He almost exceeds his lady's demands and she is momentarily apprehensive of the dangers that surround him; but how could she urge him to yield?

> No, no, I do not believe it; I know too well, madam,
> The beautiful fire that glory kindles in your soul.[3]

For in this drama, famous for its tenderness, glory does not play the least important role. The uncompromising Axiane and Cléophile, the princess Alexandre loves and who urges submission, confront and taunt one another with all the haughty and glorious arrogance of Corneille's women. Face to face with the victorious Alexandre, Axiane speaks like Émilie in *Cinna* or Cornélie in *Pompée.* The great Alexandre acts toward his Cléophile as Corneille's César acts toward Cléopâtre; in the presence of his lady he is no longer the victor but the vanquished, he forgets all his glory for her, etc. And when he has pardoned his enemies, this perfect knight knows how to make his generosity count as virtue in Cléophile's eyes—

> Let me perform my whole design
> And display all my virtue before your lovely eyes.[4]

In Racine's first attempts, then, there seems to be nothing of that new psychology of instinct that later would be his main claim to originality. Passions run the usual gamut from

[3] *Alexandre,* II, 5.
[4] Ibid., V, 3.

the heroic to the tender. For it would not do to exaggerate the contrast between heroism and tenderness in the literature of those times. It is true that from 1650 on there is a tendency to exchange great interests and heroism for the cult of love, to replace the *généreux,* the nobles with lofty ideals, with the *mourants,* those who suffer the pangs of love. The names of Quinault and Thomas Corneille are identified with this transformation. One might ask himself, though, if this transformation had all the meaning and significance usually attributed to it. What was called tenderness at the time was a revived form of the old courtly religion and its traditional themes of absolute dedication to the beloved and the idealization of love. We have seen that the conflict between tenderness thus conceived and the highest virtues was very subdued. For it to burst out into the open, tenderness would have to rebel openly against the moral values accepted by society. But that is not usually the case, especially in the literature of the seventeenth century. Even in *L'Astrée* the most sublime forms of magnanimity always play their part. Consequently it can only be a question of nuance, of a blend of heroism and tenderness. And in that blend, emphasis can be placed on heroism, as in Corneille, or on tenderness, as in the romances or in certain tragedies at the time of Racine. The aged Corneille's recriminations against those authors carrying on his tradition who put too much stress on tenderness, and in turn the repeated charges of these authors (usually partisans of the great Corneille who is denouncing them) that there is too much tenderness in Racine,[5] who is being simultaneously accused by others of being too brutal, resulted in a confused tangle of controversy. In this controversy it appears ultimately that no one wants to be tender, that the cult of perfect love was ashamed of itself, and also that it was by and large implanted in literary custom. One should be careful, then, not to take this contradiction between avowed taste and real taste

[5] One understands how Saint-Évremond can criticize an excess of tenderness in *Alexandre,* since he is a rather consistent partisan of the heroic theater; but the *Mercure galant* and the *Gazette,* usually enthusiasts of Thomas Corneille and Quinault, make the same charge against *Bajazet.*

for a conflict between two clearly distinct schools.[6] Indeed, episodes from *L'Astrée* were staged long before Corneille's old age; and it would be easy to find in Corneille's dramas more than one *mourant* like Racine's Alexandre, and not only in his last tragedies as is usually claimed, but also in those of his heyday. César sighs at Cléopâtre's feet in 1641, and *Rodogune,* in which we see two princes willing to renounce the throne to marry a princess they love, was written in 1644. It is just as unusual to find a tragedy that is exclusively tender as to find one that is exclusively heroic. We have seen that there is a good deal of heroism and glory in *Alexandre*. This intermingling of the sublime and the tender is easy to understand if one remembers their common source. They are the two most important themes of aristocratic idealism. Heroism and tenderness are both tied to a certain quality of soul without which neither a true hero nor a true lover is conceivable. And as this quality of soul also requires clarity of thought and brilliant ideas, its matchless heroes and perfect lovers are willing logicians during their heights of heroism as well as those of tenderness. This peculiar characteristic can serve, if you wish, as their special individuating quality. By the same token, the absence of this distinctive trait in the truly Racinian heroes represents a revolutionary change in the psychology of tragedy. It matters little that the sublime had a tendency to become more tender in passing from Corneille to his followers; the real revolution will come only with the simultaneous rejections of heroism and tenderness in the name of nature. This is what Racine will attempt, and this constitutes his originality.

This attempt was initiated, and rather suddenly, in *Andromaque*. Not that it lacks the usual elements of the tragic

[6] In general, nothing could be more confused or tangled than the literary controversies of the seventeenth century. A dispute on a tragedy inevitably led to wrangling and quibbling over details having to do with the decency, credibility, historical truth, or grammatical correctness of one passage or another. It is usually extremely difficult to discern a central theme that runs through the discussion or any over-all view.

theater—a dispute between victorious Greece and what is left of Troy serves as the framework of the plot, in which interests of state and family obligations are not wanting. The rivalry of a hero's widow and a proud young princess, the opposition of a haughty and violent king to a long-rejected perfect suitor—all this, at least viewed from the outside, is the subject matter of traditional tragedy. Corneille had used almost identical materials in his *Pertharite,* without being unfaithful to his ideas and the natural bent of his genius. And even with Racine, the scope of the interests involved, the pride of Hermione, the devotion of Oreste, are more than a conventional façade concealing a brutal drama of instinct. These are springs of tragic emotion that attest to the strength of tradition in Racine. Nevertheless *Andromaque* is something completely new; instinct speaks there in an unfamiliar tongue, incompatible with the traditions of heroic ethics.

In *Andromaque,* a psychology of love takes shape that Racine will later pick up again and deepen, especially in *Bajazet* and in *Phèdre.* In Racine's theater, this psychology represents the element most openly and violently opposed to tradition. Everywhere else in the tragic theater of Racine's times and in the popular romances, the more or less modernized spirit of romantic chivalry triumphed. One might say that in France this spirit had never been banished altogether except in satire or comedy. The great literary genres were the province of that ideal of love. Racine shattered this tradition by introducing into tragedy a violent and murderous love, opposed in every respect to courtly custom. The dominant characteristic of courtly love is submission or devotion to the beloved. It permits itself to aspire to possess that loved one only when a previous sublimation of all its impulses has occurred. In the preface to *Andromaque,* Racine destroys this whole structure with one stroke of the pen when he writes, in response to those who found Pyrrhus too brutal, "I admit that he is not sufficiently resigned to the will of his mistress and that Céladon knew perfect love better than he. But what could I do? Pyrrhus hadn't read our romances." Indeed the love of the two principal characters in *Andromaque* no longer has anything in common with devotion. It is a jealous, greedy desire, clinging to the person loved as to its prey. No longer is worship offered to an ideal person, in whom all values reside. The most common behavior of this love, in which the passion to possess is linked with profound dissatisfaction to the point that it is difficult for us to imagine it happy and requited, is a violent aggressiveness toward the beloved as soon as he or she gives some sign of slipping away. The equivalence of love and hate, each constantly giving rise to the other—an axiom that is the very negation of chivalric devotion—is at the core of Racine's psychology of love. With Pyrrhus and Hermione one can still glimpse the possibility of another attitude, if their wishes were fulfilled. We could say the same of Atalide in *Bajazet,* torn between the desire to save the life of her beloved Bajazet by giving him up to appease Roxane, and the desire to cause his death rather than lose him, by proclaiming their love openly. On a conscious level the first desire triumphs, although the second is strong enough to dictate behavior at a decisive moment and to unleash the catastrophe;

> And when at times in my mind's eye
> I painfully pictured my happy rival,
> Your death (forgive the wrath of lovers)
> Seemed to me not the worst of torments,[7]

she says to Bajazet at the very moment she implores him to feign love for her rival; but she does plead with him to do so. Confident at least that he loves her, she will do everything to save him after she has ruined him. Racine went further with Roxane. In her, aggressiveness seems to be so constantly fused with love that one can scarcely imagine her happy. Right from the start threats are the natural expression of her love—

> At last Bajazet draws close to the sultan's throne:
> He need take but one step. But that is where I
> await him.[8]

[7] *Bajazet,* II, 5.
[8] Ibid., I, 3.

And to Bajazet himself she says,

> Do you realize that I control the gates of the Palace,
> That I can open them for you or close them forever,
> That I have supreme authority over your life,
> That you breathe only as long as I love you?[9]

Before *Bajazet,* Racine had portrayed in Néron—and in a more directly erotic form—the coupling of love and cruelty. Néron loves his victim, Junie, and his love springs from the spectacle of a distress he himself has caused; the amorous dream that follows this first impression is a dream of persecution. In such a man as this, the discernment of virtue in the beloved can intensify the attraction, but by inflaming desire, not by inspiring devotion—

> And it is this virtue, so new to the court,
> Whose steadfastness inflames my passion;[10]

This is the psychological mechanism of courtly love, but interpreted contrary to its usual meaning, and somewhat parodied.

Nowhere do the mingled roots of enmity and of love plunge as deeply as in the heart of Phèdre. In her the hatred of the one she loves borrows an extra measure of strength from the moral impediments that make it impossible for her to abandon herself to her desire. Because her love for Hippolyte torments her, she sees him as her tormenter—

> My peace of mind, my happiness seemed assured;
> Athens showed me my proud enemy. . . .
> Brought to Trézène by my husband himself,
> I saw again the enemy I had banished. . . .[11]

[9] Ibid., II, 1.

[10] *Britannicus,* II, 2.

[11] *Phèdre,* I, 3. In this same tragedy there is another character for whom love is also a cause of anxiety, and who surrenders himself to it with remorse; that is Hippolyte himself, in whom a sort of youthful misogyny plays more feebly, the role of censure that matrimonial and familial morality play for Phèdre; see II, 2:

This state of passive torture is waiting only for an opportunity to transform itself into aggression. The discovery of the love of Hippolyte and Aricie releases Phèdre's latent hatred; she denounces her innocent persecuter to Thésée by charging him with her own crime. *Phèdre,* then, shows us a veritable delirium of persecution, originating in a guilty love and leading to attempted murder. It should be added that the instinct for destruction that accompanies love in Racine's characters hardly ever spares even the lovers themselves, and leads Hermione, Atalide, and Phèdre to suicide. The brutal and possessive passion that Racine substituted for the ideal love of chivalry, while it expresses itself within the limits of nature, is powerless to find therein its strength or its equilibrium. That is the main link between Racine's psychology and the inhuman views of Port-Royal.[12]

Corneille's theater is not devoid of violence or of horror. And yet even in that respect it is still above nature. For there jealousy, crime, and vengeance are accompanied by a conscious assertion of the individual. There the transition from love to hate, and from entreaty to defiance, is clearly visible

---

After more than six months, ashamed, driven to despair,
Bearing everywhere I go the shaft that tears me asunder, etc. . . .

He is, as it were, the lesser counterpart of Phèdre, who contributes in no small degree to the atmosphere of remorse and self-disavowal that is the mood of the whole play.

[12] It is wrong to distinguish Racine's psychology, as is commonly done, simply by the fact that love dominates all other impulses. It is in the courtly works, in the romances, that love truly dominates. Céladon or any such perfect lover in Corneille effectively embodies the triumph of love. What distinguishes Racine's characters is not just the power of love but the form of that love, at once selfish in that it aims to possess the beloved at any price, and self-destructive, turned completely toward disaster. Racine's originality does not lie in the primacy he gives to love over the other instincts but in his general idea of instinct, stripped of all values and tragic, in short, *natural* in the Jansenist sense of the word.

and spectacular; with Racine, on the other hand, the sudden about-faces of instinct take control of the ego and toss it about instead of ennobling it. The characteristic feature of passion as Racine sees it is that it first tends to possess him who experiences it; love is the negation of liberty, the living refutation of pride. Those who speak of the selfish aspects of passion are usually the same people who judge its power and its impulses as fatal. La Rochefoucauld and Racine converge at this point in their desire to humble man to the level of nature.[13] And so that man's servitude may be total, Racine, like La Rochefoucauld or Pascal, submerges man's reason and his conscience along with his will and wants him to delude himself on the sources of his conduct.

It is at this point, perhaps, that we perceive most clearly the road traveled from Corneille to Racine and from *Alexandre* or the *Thébaïde* to *Andromaque.* Hermione's words are not, like those of Chimène or Émilie, in conformity with her actions and their real motives; her speech reveals the real Hermione only through a distortion that we must correct if we wish to grasp the true motives for her actions, motives which her utterances are designed to conceal from our eyes as from her own. This duplicity of the conscious and the unconscious is most commonly visible in what is generally called loving spite. Abandoned by Pyrrhus, Hermione pretends she no longer loves him, but she says she wants to stay near him so that she may hate him more. And when Cléone tries to enlighten her as to her true feelings, she retorts,

> Why, cruel one, do you want to aggravate my distress?
> I am afraid to know myself as I am.[14]

[13] La Rochefoucauld says, "If we judge love by most of its effects it is more like hatred than like friendship . . ." (Maxim 72). And on the other hand, "There is no passion in which self-love governs as powerfully as it does in love" (Maxim 272). And elsewhere, "The closest analogy we can find to love is that of a fever: we have no more power over one than over the other, either as to its violence or as to its duration" (Maxim 638).

[14] *Andromaque,* II, 1.

Passion as Racine portrays it wants to act in darkness, an when it pretends to explain or to justify its behavior one ha to look behind its false reasons for some all-powerful reaso of the heart. Faithful in this respect to the Jansenist spiri Racine depicts intelligence as a dupe. His characters are neve lower on the ladder of human greatness than when by chanc they argue: Hermione, for example, reasoning wildly in th disavowal with which she hopes to overwhelm Oreste afte the murder she herself commanded of him, or Atalide inte preting in a frenzied way Bajazet's submissiveness to Roxan whom she herself has entreated him to deceive.[15]

This false use of reason that Racine assigns his hero strongly suggests in certain cases a sort of caricature of her ism reduced to a verbal façade, whose real and seamy unde side we can glimpse. Hermione, for instance, incessantly i vokes her duty, her glory, and even the honor of Greece remain near the unfaithful Pyrrhus–

> . . . Think what dishonor would be ours
> If he became the husband of a Phrygian![16]

When Pyrrhus comes back to her the game continues; sh dismisses Oreste in terms reminiscent of Corneille–

> Love does not govern the destiny of a princess:
> Only the glory of obedience is left to us.[17]

When Pyrrhus again forsakes her, she invokes her wounde pride and a hatred of tyrants in order to convince Oreste

[15] Incoherence stemming from spite and jealousy were not u known in the literature of the romances; in *L'Astrée* the whole pl is based on the same type of incident. Here, as elsewhere, Raci seems to be picking up a romanesque tradition, although he uses for completely new ends.

[16] *Andromaque,* II, 2. Here the unconscious element is almo comical in the contrast between the reasons adduced and the re motives; cf. II, 5, Pyrrhus' boasts when he pretends to have co quered his love for Andromaque and wants to see her again, order "to defy her."

[17] Ibid., III, 2.

kill him. The language is Corneille's, but in a setting where everything proclaims it as false. The heroic tradition, seemingly faithful to itself, is found here only to be repudiated.

However, it would be a mistake to believe that in Racine the derangement of reason invariably accompanies the violence of passion. After *Andromaque* Racine seems to have increasingly preferred the portrayal of a lucid downfall that contemplates itself in despair and knows itself to be beyond help. The unconscious deterioration of judgment, if it perhaps marks a more advanced moment in the destruction of the heroic ego, is on the other hand accompanied by a state of irresponsibility that can weaken profound pathos—the most painful ruin is the one that can measure itself. Hermione and Roxane, the least crushed of Racine's heroines, still take pleasure in reflecting on their ill fortune, in recalling bitterly the contempt that their weakness accepts. Hermione complains bitterly,

> Cruel one! The look with which he dismissed me,
> Without pity, without the least sorrow, even feigned.
> Did I see him falter or lament for an instant?
> Was I able to draw from him a single moan? . . .
> And I pity him still? And to crown my woes,
> My heart, my cowardly heart still feels for him?[18]

Similarly Roxane, to whom the sudden revelation of defeat and misfortune exposes at the same time her own frailty—

> You won no great victory,
> Faithless one, by deceiving this anxious heart,
> Which was itself afraid of being undeceived.[19]

The tragic lament against fate, inherited from antiquity and clothed in the language of stoicism in Corneille and his contemporaries, reappears in Racine as a true lament burdened with the anguish of remorse and self contempt, for it

[18] Ibid., V, 1.
[19] *Bajazet*, IV, 5.

has been provoked not by a calamity from without, but rather by the passions. For the self-pride, guilty passion is a radical confession of wretchedness; and this confession, which changes man's very relation to the universe, can achieve the intensity of metaphysical anguish–

> And I, a sad outcast of all of nature,
> I hid myself from the light, I fled the clearness . . .[20]

Obviously so crushing a guilt can only be bound to instincts that were considered monstrous, but fundamentally every instinct falls into this category to some degree in the pessimism of Racine and Port-Royal.[21] The disturbing quality attributed to instinct justifies its strict repression, which in turn fosters a repugnance in man for his own being. One can easily see that this endless struggle between nature and ethics, with its antitheses and involutions, is different from the direct and sustained *élan* of heroic sublimation.

The revolution Racine brought about from *Alexandre* to *Andromaque,* then, is above all a revolution in the psychology of love; and this is understandable if one considers that, given the conventions of the time, a naturalistic representation of man could not have assumed tragic value in any other sphere. Moreover, its novelty was easier to perceive in this sphere–only love can link self-destruction and bewilderment with selfishness; ambition always retains some lucidity, some self-esteem, and it is not easy to distinguish in it that part of desire attributable to self-interest and that attributable to glory. At any rate this appears as a matter of nuance when

[20] *Phèdre,* IV, 6.

[21] If Racine's tragedies are Christian, it is only because of the guilt he attached to love. Arnauld's approval of *Phèdre* is well known. From the story of Phèdre, symbolic of the wretchedness of nature, Racine drew only a moderately edifying tragic portrait. But the prestige and attraction that evil-doing can enjoy in the theater and the boldness and the dangers involved in making use of sin for the purposes of literature did not weaken the meaning of the portrait, which was a profoundly disparaging view of man.

compared with the violent contrast that, for example, opposes a Pyrrhus to a Sévère in the sphere of love. Consequently, it is principally in the portrayal of love that Racine sought the renewal of tragedy. It was on this subject that he was better able to startle and surprise the audience. But other traditional aspects were too important; ambition and pride had enjoyed a privileged position in tragedy too long for him to avoid the need of adapting them to the new climate he had created. Moreover, in the opinion of his contemporaries one could not write great tragedies without portraying great personages and passions, and Racine was always anxious to prove that he could excel in this. So if it is in the portrayal of love that his peculiar genius had the most shattering impact, this portrayal is certainly not his only concern. More important for his contemporaries, and for Racine himself if not for us, was the part of the work in which he set out to portray ambitious heroes and great stakes. Yet in Racine greatness does not have the same ring it had in the tragedians of the preceding generation. It is interesting to study closely, in this difference, the change in the heroic sublime. Half-tones have a decisive role in Racine's dramas and are just as interesting as the brutal innovations.

Even in love Racine's characters are not always free from pride, and this lovers' pride is not always merely a façade, especially in his jealous and rejected heroines. Hermione is ashamed to let Oreste, whom she had previously abandoned, witness her own misfortune–

> What dishonor for me, what a triumph for him,
> To see my misfortune equal to his!
> "Is this," he will ask, "that proud Hermione? . . ."[22]

Similarly, Roxane resents Bajazet's indifference and treachery–

> Oh heavens, could you have sentenced
> me to this indignity?[23]

[22] *Andromaque,* II, 1.
[23] *Bajazet,* III, 7.

When her ill fortune is no longer in doubt the torments of pride grow more intense–

> At this peak of glory that I have reached,
> What shameful honor had you in store for me?
> Was I to drag out a hapless destiny here,
> The vile cast-off of an ingrate I would have crowned,
> Fallen from my station, equal to a thousand others,
> And the first slave of my rival?[24]

But what is new is that this pride is no longer uplifting. It is a wound of which the self is constantly aware, but which cannot be healed; through a cruel sense of shame that can be forgotten only in violence, pride serves to foster a consciousness of humiliation. Pride is no longer the spur of honor but the measure of dishonor. Comparable to other passions, as violent and wretched as they, it has reentered the realm of nature.

A change of tone, sometimes imperceptible, was enough to accomplish this, a change of nuance that Racine's contemporaries perhaps did not always clearly discern but that an ear accustomed to the language of glory could not fail to notice, even though it might not be able to explain it. "It approaches the grandiose," Saint-Évremond said of *Andromaque* . . . "yet, if one is looking for rich beauty he will find here something hard to define that will keep him from being completely satisfied."[25] This was the general feeling among Racine's enemies; in their eyes his tragedy was inadequate rather than poor.[26] If one wants to understand this change in more concrete terms, he will find that pride and ambition have ceased to express themselves sententiously, which is to say that they have ceased to know and describe themselves. They are no longer enlightened and sustained by self-knowledge and consequently they have ceased to ennoble. In this respect Vauvenargue's observation goes to the heart of

[24] Ibid., V, 4.
[25] In a letter to M. de Lionne.
[26] Cf. Mme. de Sévigné, letters of January 13, January 15, and March 16, 1672.

the matter—"Corneille's characters speak in order to make themselves known; Racine's characters make themselves known because they speak."[27] He means that Corneille's characters use language to project an image of themselves that they themselves recognize, whereas Racine's characters reveal themselves in their utterances, but do not always know themselves. This is the abyss that separates naturalistic psychology from heroic *bel-esprit,* and the power of reality from that of the sublime.

On several occasions in the course of his life, especially in *Britannicus* and in *Mithridate,* Racine tried to write tragedies in which great ambitions occupied the foreground. In *Britannicus* the portrayal of love is at least counterbalanced by the duel of ambition between Néron and his mother. One should not minimize the feelings stirred in Racine's contemporaries by Agrippine's proud apostrophes to Burrhus, or by the majestic speeches of Néron, contending with his mother for the rule of the universe. But one perceives how Agrippine differs from one of Corneille's ambitious heroines. With her, pride is like a sudden wild and offensive release of the ego, which bears with it more pain than satisfaction; it is a wounded part of the heart—

> What am I saying? They avoid me, and I am
> already forsaken. . . .
> Ah, Albine, I cannot bear the thought of it![28]

This pride is never expressed in glorious "maxims"; it bursts forth in rash moves, in ill-considered threats; it has misfortune and a bad conscience in its train. Néron, as greedy for power as his mother, loses his self-confidence in her presence —he admits it himself—just as quickly as she loses her composure in the face of danger. As a consequence their struggle, made up of instinctive impulses and actions, resembles a fit of passion rather than a contest of ambitions as Corneille would have depicted it. One could find the same naturalistic portrayal of ambition in the figure of Mithridate, although in

[27] Vauvenargues, *Réflexions critiques sur quelques poètes,* V, VI.
[28] *Britannicus,* III, 4.

delineation he reminds us more of Corneille than any other of Racine's heroes. In spite of all his arrogance, the boldness of his plans, and his reputation for being strong-willed, this great man does not achieve heroic stature. Mithridate is authoritarian, brutal, proud without a trace of the sublime, and great without a trace of chivalry. Forced to make moral speeches with Monime, he conceals the cynical ruses of the despot behind noble phrases. In love as well as in ambition (which Racine wanted to be stronger in him than love),[29] he is prey to a violent nature that he follows more blindly than is fitting for a hero. Whether intentionally or not, Racine always portrayed in the least edifying light those passions reputed as great.[30]

The boldness of Racine's naturalism was not noticed by the critics until quite late. The continuity of conventions and of externals in the genre of tragedy from Corneille to Racine and from Racine to his successors made it difficult to perceive the profound revolution Racine had brought about. And it is only at the end of the nineteenth century that the extreme violence of Racine's tragic theater became apparent. Many factors having nothing to do with a simple concern for truth contributed to this discovery. The definitive discred-

[29] Mithridate illustrates for us the possible relationship of love to great stakes; since neither escapes the naturalistic definition of instinct, the strongest impulse wins out without there being substance for an edifying conflict. Racine sacrifices love even more easily than Corneille, who is forced by the courtly rules of conduct to exercise greater caution and to justify the sacrifice. Kings and princes are willing to renounce their thrones or their ambition for love in Corneille more than in Racine. (Compare, for example, the figure of Titus to the corresponding figure in Corneille's *Tite et Bérénice.*)

[30] It is undoubtedly this aspect of Racine's genius that explains the fact that Saint-Évremond, so sympathetic to the somber aspects of tragedy and a defender of *Rodogune,* criticized *Britannicus* as too black and too horrible a play. Good champion of Corneille that he was, he demanded the sublime of glory, of bold designs, and even of evil-doing; in his eyes the characters in *Britannicus* are simply contemptible.

iting of the classical proprieties, and the growing fondness of the public for a literature free of prejudices, whether moral or mundane, forced the academic critic of this period to defend the age of Louis XIV on a different plane from that on which it had been defended up to that time, and to show that the great classical authors were not simply models of good taste but also pitiless portrayers of human truth. Brunetière, Jules Lemaître, and their followers are obviously anxious to find in classicism itself a substitute for the audacities of romanticism and naturalism. They point to the burning truth of the portraits of the Great Century to lessen the impact of the literary revolutions that followed. Consequently the rediscovery of the classics at the end of the nineteenth century was too quickly reduced to reactionary platitudes and has not always clarified the situation as well as might have been expected. This is even more true on the moral than on the literary plane, because the classics were presented again as edifying, no longer because of the nobility but because of the severity of their appraisal of man. Cruel truths were discerned in the classics merely to invest the prestige of their genius in the most tendentious dissertations on an eternally unworthy humanity, to make classical realism an antidote for the raptures of revolutionary humanism.

Yet the use made of this interpretation of classicism in the battle of ideas does not affect its intrinsic value. This interpretation marks an important moment in our knowledge of the age of Louis XIV and cannot be ignored. We ourselves are so imbued with it that it is difficult to imagine that another interpretation preceded it. However, there was an earlier interpretation, and it too had its proofs and its certainty. For almost two centuries no one was aware of Racine's boldness or his violence. Throughout the classical period and from that time up to the nineteenth century, Racine instead represented exquisite propriety, taste combined with truth, and the artistic temperament in control of the natural passions. Vauvenargues, Voltaire, Sainte-Beuve, and Taine all admired or criticized in his work something quite different from violence. And they were not completely wrong. For Racine did not always make the brutality of nature prevail over the ruins of the sublime.

He was often content with toning down and taming glory; he made heroism human, refined pride, and made glorious love tender. Wherever a touching sentiment is expressed in Racine, wherever a likable character appears, wherever violent and gloomy nature is not alone in making itself heard—that is to say in a very considerable part of his work—there reigns an elegant nobility quite as characteristic of him as the violence of certain portrayals. In the great theater of Racine, Andromaque, and Monime, Bérénice and Iphigénie, Britannicus, Bajazet, and Xipharès continue, in a more delicate and more natural form, the world and atmosphere of *Alexandre*.

The influence of Jansenist naturalism no longer plays much of a part in this new idea of moral nobility. This is no longer nature in the violent sense of Port-Royal, this is nature as it was understood at the court. The submission of the nobility was accompanied, in the moral order by a downgrading of the heroic values. But much of the old spirit persisted, and those elements that were least disturbing for authority and most compatible with the renunciation of the old pride were preserved. The aristocratic values were adapted to the times without being completely repudiated. The old idea of the morally beautiful still survived at the court, but as outward propriety, a touching ornament of real life.

We are acquainted with Taine's famous pages comparing custom and morality in Racine's theater with those at the court of Versailles. If we leave aside the purely esthetic aspect of the question and the undeniable agreement of Racine's work and its form with the etiquette, order, and ceremony of life at the court, and if we seek the profound moral evolution that accompanies and promotes the progress of classical esthetics, we can discern a general toning-down of the old heroic ideals beneath the triumph of literary conformism. In Corneille and his contemporaries the already tyrannical formalism and the still hardy hero-worship harmonize as best they can. In Racine, the progressive downgrading of the hero ends in the elegant and quiet victory of formalism.

Racine was certainly neither the first nor the only playwright to permeate noble, tragic sentiments with sweetness and tenderness. To a certain extent there was a general evolution in that direction. But the sweet and the tender authors Thomas Corneille and even Quinault, retained glorious tones and sentimental subtlety. Racine is truly the first to elaborate the heritage of the romances in a more natural and more modern way. His characters infuse heroism with a spontaneous reserve and a discretion of style that break with the usual articulations of glory and *bel-esprit*. In Racine's characters there is never a rupture between the heroic attitude and the very simple expression of heartfelt emotions. Compare the case of Andromaque, a traditional type of exemplary widow, with her literary predecessors such as Cornélie in *Pompée*. The contrast of the natural rancor and subdued pride of Andromaque with the shattering hatred and boastfulness of the same type of woman in the heroic theater gives one the measure of Racine's originality. Occasionally it happens that his characters are morally above ordinary nature, but the distance which separates them from it is never astounding or immodest. The good taste that Vauvenargues attributes to Racine and denies to Corneille, that "fine and faithful sentiment of beautiful nature,"[31] is not in Racine simply an esthetic gift, but a moral innovation; it is the accommodation of the heroic virtues to the restrained atmosphere of the court, where it was not fitting that anything in the individual should stand out above the ordinary in too striking a fashion.

Racine came back again and again to the theme, so common at that time, of the young girl whose love is thwarted by some authority or interest greater than she. This is the whole theme of *Iphigénie* and *Bérénice*, and for the most part it is the theme of *Mithridate*. But if it is true that in their worst trials Iphigénie, Bérénice, and Monime do not always refrain from invoking their "glory," as Corneille's Pauline does, they obey or rebel without proud exaltation, without subtlety, and without grandiloquence. When Bérénice is abandoned she begins by reproaches that contain more love than self-love, then more despair than anger, and finally, per-

[31] *Réflexions critiques sur quelques poètes,* V–VI.

ceiving that she is still loved and reluctant to spread unhappiness about her, she resigns herself in a way that Racine wanted to be simply touching:

> Bérénice, Lord, is not worth so much alarm.[32]

When Iphigénie asks the enraged Achilles to yield to Agamemnon's will, when she exhorts him to be more concerned with their common glory, and when he discusses her arguments, we are quite close to the *bel-esprit* of the romances, and would be completely within those limits if the impulses of the heart were less perceptible in this debate, and if the play of intellect were not overshadowed by the more profound play of tenderness and reproach, of reserve or surrender. One could say the same of Monime, perhaps closer to Corneille than any other of Racine's heroines–she banishes Xipharès after confessing to him that she shares his passion, hoping that he himself will help her to keep her glory unsullied. But the tone is one of saddened love, and the subtlety of the ideas, always brought into play discreetly, almost disappears in the gentle swell of the lament–

> I understand, you moan; but such is my wretchedness.
> I do not belong to you at all, I belong to your father.
> In this design you yourself must sustain me
> And help me to banish you from my feeble heart.
> I expect at least, I expect of your kindness
> That henceforth you will everywhere shun my presence.
> I have said enough to persuade you
> That I have too much reason to order you to do so.
> But from this moment if that generous heart
> With true love has burned for Monime,
> I will recognize the truth of what you have said
> Only by the care you take to avoid me.[33]

This delicate form of the sublime is more closely linked than one might think to the tragic use of violence; in Racine's

[32] *Bérénice,* V, 7.
[33] *Mithridate,* II, 6.

tragedy the lament is the counterpart of cruelty. By substituting for the type of the glib and haughty *heroine* that of the *victim* groaning in secret, Racine was blending together a cruel poetry, a veiled pathos, and an ultimately convincing portrayal of noble sentiments. In this completely new blend, heroism lost its old form even when its speech and behavior remained the same.

This change of tone brought its own problems. It is because of this that Racine's sympathetic portrayals of masculine heroes are invariably weak; what seems only softened in the heroines is insipid in the heroes. "Tender, gallant, gentle, and modest," as Voltaire put it; this description fits not only Racine's male protagonist but also the courtiers' ideal of a male protagonist. This ideal was in the air at the time; it was all that was able to survive of chivalry in a court from which all excessive self-assertion was banned. Racine certainly did all he could to keep alive in his suitors, in Britannicus, Bajazet, and Xipharès, some ambition, some courage, and some tenacity with respect to their royal pretensions. He tried to make them virile and at the same time touching, which does not mean that he succeeded in either direction. He was working within the limits his age set for him; the decline of the chivalric heritage and the attraction it still exerted were independent of his will, and for all of his genius he could not resolve this contradiction.

Outside of this ideal of the refined gentleman and the perfect lover, the court could conceive of no other types than that of the *honnête homme* and that of the intriguer, neither of much interest for tragedy, and finally that of the political man with great designs. But of course at the time Racine was writing the only politics that could give life to a play, that of *Cinna* or of *Nicomède,* was dead. The time of aristocratic rebellion had passed and the triumph of absolutism rendered obsolete, only twenty years later, the figure of the heroic conspirator and the maxims of noble politics. This is undoubtedly why political drama plays so small a part in Racine, in spite of Racine himself. He may have written *Britannicus* and *Mithridate*; but as soon as politics no longer fire anyone with enthusiasm, or turn into stirring appeals, or depict avenging heroes at grips with an injust power–and in this respect Racine did not want to follow practices he considered outmoded–politics are reduced to an interplay of ambitions barely rising above the level of private passions. Even when the view is much broader, when a great project is outlined or a plea is made for a great cause, when Racine opens for the spectator a wider view on public life and history, his scenes, his narratives, his eloquence always remain within the limits of nature. They are statements in which there is more meaning, more structure, and more naturalness than heroic inspiration. The great speeches of Agrippine and Mithridate or the arguments in the first act of *Iphigénie* fall into this category. It is positive politics, no longer glorious politics; it is the politics of the court and of the king's counselors, at once vast and calculated, imposing in its aspect and selfish in its ends.

It is not that Racine always avoided maxims and grandiloquence in his political scenes. Tradition and the desire to equal Corneille strongly suggested them to him. *Britannicus* is full of beautiful phrases on ancient Rome and *Mithridate* in part echoes the traditional tirades of kings against Roman servitude. But the evocation of republican Rome has become quite pale in *Britannicus*; Roman virtue is a memory, no longer a source of action, and the tirade in which Burrhus describes to Néron the ideal monarch he could be is more like a desperate petition than the arrogant remonstrances we find in similar situations in Corneille. It is not without significance that opposition to despotism is expressed in laments in Racine's tragedies; at the time they appeared it could hardly be otherwise. But one also feels clearly that something more than a conflict of the Néron-Burrhus variety was needed to sustain a tragedy, and we understand that political drama, weakened to such a degree, became more or less the important ornament of a weightier action. This is also the case in *Mithridate*. And what shall one say of the diplomatic debates in *Andromaque*, or the Moslem discussions in *Bajazet?* What do they contribute to the action other than a pretext? Perhaps politics has a truer place in *Esther* and *Athalie*, in which Racine earnestly and zealously comes back to the theme of the sovereign who is the victim of his wicked counselors. But the nuance is different–he is dealing with religious subjects, and religion was better able to sermonize royalty without creating a scandal than the nobles would have been. Religion was supposed to speak in the name of less violent and wider interests. It was the only source of guilt that henceforth remained to the absolute monarch. If there are rather bold maxims in the last two plays of Racine, for the most part they oppose the abuses of despotism in the name of Christian principles, the well-being of all the people, and justice–

> A good king, as God himself has proclaimed,
> Puts not his trust in riches and gold,
> Fears the Lord his God and keeps always before him
> His precepts, His laws and His strict judgments,
> And oppresses not his brothers with unjust burdens.[34]

The crime of sycophants is to say

> . . . That the most sacred laws,
> Masters of the lowly people, yield to kings;
> . . . That the people are condemned to tears and to toil
> And must be governed with an iron scepter.[35]

The tone is completely different from that of the Fronde; the criticism of despotism under the aging Louis XIV has a more solemn and already, in a sense, a more modern ring.

What tragic grandeur lost through the downgrading of heroism under the influence of the court and its spirit was compensated in part by a new prestige, less ennobling but perhaps more poetically compelling, that radiated from the court itself, from the court of Versailles with its festivities and its triumphs. All that was great resided in royalty, and the closer one was to royalty the more he shared in that greatness. The brilliance that came from on high was that of an

[34] *Athalie,* IV, 2.
[35] *Iphigénie,* IV, 4.

extraordinary power, above all unrest and all conflict. The idea of heroic greatness had yielded its place in people's minds to the idea of *majesty*. Man approached divinity not so much through valor as through power and success. This atmosphere is reflected in Racine, who often draws his pathos from the loss of and consequent longing for this kind of happiness. The lament of Clytemnestra when she thinks her daughter is doomed is an example–

> And I, who led her triumphant, adored,
> I will go back alone and despairing;
> I will see the roads still all perfumed
> From the flowers strewn under her feet.[36]

Iphigénie goes even further–

> Who knows even, who knows if the angered heavens
> Were able to endure the excess of my felicity?
> Alas! It seemed to me that so beautiful a passion
> Lifted me above the fate of mortals.[37]

In *Bérénice* one finds the same contrast between the expectation of supreme happiness and sudden disgrace. The picture the happy Bérénice gives of the night of the apotheosis of Vespasian, who will be succeeded by her beloved, is an indication of how much she has to lose and what is at stake in the tragedy. And this scene draws to a close with a eulogy of the royal charm of Louis XIV, under the name of Titus,[38] as if to link this poetry of happiness more closely in our eyes with the atmosphere of the court of Versailles in the early stages of his reign. The kingly station of heroes, indispensable in Corneille's theater to buttress the greatness of their actions, is put to a different use in Racine; foreign to any idea of moral superiority, it magnifies only the success and the misfortune of heroes, and it raises their triumph or their distress to the level of gods or of kings. If the value of the

[36] Ibid., IV, 4.
[37] Ibid., III, 6.
[38] *Bérénice,* I, 5.

hero, reduced by social evolution to the order of empty fantasy, is tragically denied in Racine, the majesty of his characters is not diminished. On the contrary, since it is not rationally justified, it is all the more striking. As long as the idea of greatness of soul obsesses the aristocrat, it never permits him to raise himself completely above all dependence, not even in evil-doing. He must always present himself to be judged and admired on the basis of that virtue which distinguishes him. In vain did the aristocrats pursue the dream of a superiority independent of personal merit. They were too close to the public; in spite of themselves they were too dependent on it and on its esteem. Hence the link constantly established in aristocratic tradition between noble birth and moral worth. The triumph of the absolute monarchy liberates the superhuman quality of the hero by detaching it from all moral judgment, whether in the case of the king or the nobles, who are nobles only insofar as they share to some degree in the brilliance of royalty. The more it is detached from the criterion of merit, the more the prestige of kings and princes derives from their condition, from their situation being above the common destiny of man. Their actions and their words, which are the same as those of others, have a different ring. The idea of a grandeur of this sort was not new; the poetic imagination had come under its spell during the great reigns of the preceding century. What was called poetry from the last Valois on is hard to separate from this sort of prestige. The very light of beauty is mingled with that of kingly station, and poetry conveys to all men the idea and in some way the enjoyment of that station. Here inspiration, themes, and style all evoke that living majesty of which royalty is the fountainhead.

Because Racine depicts for us royal figures who are morally the same as all men, we must not reduce his dramas to insignificant love intrigues as is sometimes done. Those who do so certainly contradict the sentiment of the audience for whom Racine was writing, and in whose eyes the projection of human actions on a royal or mythological plane was inseparable from tragedy. The situation of tragedy beyond the ordinary limits of life continued to be a strict requirement as long as royal grandeur and the prestige of the court endured. Moreover, the destiny of tragedy from the eighteenth century on was based on this convention, which was more than a convention, and whose downfall brought about that of the whole genre. With Racine, then, poetic grandeur is not an embellishment added by artifice to the truth of the passions. Each of the two elements is indispensable to the other and gives it its full meaning, in conformity with the very spirit of the pagan myth that was Racine's model for that gratuitous greatness, that fabulous world animated by the scandal of the instincts that is the soul of his theater. This fundamental agreement enabled Racine to revive with unequaled intensity in modern Europe the myths of ancient Greece. The sacrifice of Iphigénie, the bloody fate of Atrée's family, the legend of the Minotaur, and the aberrations of the daughters of Minos, inspire him only because he discerns in them the same fundamental elements that defined the destiny of the nobility since the decline of the chivalric idea—the grandeur of a privileged station, joined to the unveiled truth of nature.[39]

Racine himself makes tragic emotion dependent on the dimensions of the characters portrayed when he voices the hope that we will find in his Bérénice "that majestic sad-

[39] One could speak at length on the favor that the monarchic centuries displayed for the myths of pagan Greece. This favor is not limited to Racine. Too often we still see it explained as an artificial infatuation, due to the poverty of inspiration of poets who were only too happy to find in the storehouse of mythology the wherewithal to embellish their weakness in a stately fashion. This is to explain away in a very cavalier fashion a profound and tenacious taste without which two centuries of great European poetry would not be what they are. It would be better to try to discern the profound connections between the fundamental ideas of mythology and the spirit of the centuries that followed the Renaissance. One would then perceive in this period of European history evidence of an authentic sensitivity to the old myths, a sensitivity which could be accounted for historically. And the poetry of this period would take on new life; indeed of late the mere reading of these works has revealed this poetical vitality to the unprejudiced reader.

ness that is the source of all the pleasure we derive from tragedy."[40] As a matter of fact even outside of *Bérénice* and *Iphigénie,* which are the most striking examples, there are not many places where lamentation does not have for its object the loss of a wondrous grandeur. One might say that this very aspect is one of the most profound elements of Racine's poetry. This constant rapprochement, this near fusion of divinity and nothingness, this majesty which is unsteady and unwittingly threatened in times of happiness and true to itself in distress, this equal balance of joy and anguish—all this we may obviously consider and love in relation to mankind in general. Racine was great enough to give us the opportunity, to encourage us to do so. But it would be a mistake to believe that he was able to conceive and to feel "that majestic sadness"—in his opinion the source of all the enjoyment we derive from tragedy—independently of the prestige with which royal station was invested in his eyes and in the eyes of his contemporaries.

Certainly the fact that in Racine this prestige is extolled in terms of grief and disaster does not follow simply from the definition of tragedy. Here the demands of the genre correspond to a profound inclination of the poet. The king, close to divinity, is in the Christian and Jansenist view close to sacrilege. This explains the incessant threat of divine punishment which hangs over him. The obsession of the Christian veto, the new Nemesis, infuses the grandeur of royal figures with misgivings as to their own nothingness, though under the Sun King these misgivings are never strong enough to efface their royal quality. Phèdre's greatness, while it has less to do with virtue than does the greatness of Corneille's heroes, is more shot through with uncertainty. The debate between greatness and lowliness, between good and evil, took on a completely new aspect when its terms became a royal station freed from every obstacle and a concomittently intensified sense of guilt. When noble birth ceased to be at the center of all things, the fusion of social prestige and moral worth it represented was shattered. Unbound sovereignty of the mon-

[40] *Bérénice,* Preface.

archy and brute nature—the polar offshoots of this rupture—coexisted from that time on in a new synthesis, heavy with anguish, which looms up before our eyes in the tragedy of Racine.

Racine's tragedy is perhaps less representative than Corneille's in the sense that it is less spontaneously and less directly the expression of a social environment and a moral tendency. It is composed of elements that are not simply diverse but sometimes contradictory, and which can only be balanced by an astounding use of nuances. It is the triumph of a unique genius to have blended together Jansenist inspiration and the taste of the court of Versailles in its early days, and to have poured them into the same mold that Corneille had used. The pessimistic violence of Racine's portrayals of the human heart, inspired by Jansenist nihilism, would not have many imitators. This violence remained a solitary lesson, scarcely understood and quickly dismissed; like that of Pascal, and undoubtedly for the same reasons, it had no immediate successors. As for Racine the poet, the already ancient tradition he inherited becomes fixed in him, acquires a prodigious new depth and breadth, and dies with him. The eighteenth century will only admire and imitate in Racine his concern for the natural, his cunning perception of truth, his dramatic logic, and his sensitive elegance of style—all things that, without the rest, are merely the remains of the genre. Yet all that Racine had joined together, all the elements drawn from various sources that are harmonized in his theater—cruelty of the passions, plausibility of behavior, delicacy of sympathy, grandiose resonances of narration—everything, both substance and form, is obedient to the same law and the same impulse. Everything tends to bring tragedy into harmony with the bent of a new age, an age of disaffection with the old notion of the sublime. Consequently one may conclude that no one understood Racine better than Heine when he wrote, "Racine already appears as the herald of the modern age at the side of the great king with whom the modern age begins. Racine was the first modern poet, as Louis XIV was the first modern king. The Middle Ages are still alive in Corneille. The voice of the old chivalry gives its death rattle in his work and in the Fronde. . . . But in Racine the sentiments of the Middle Ages are completely extinguished; in him only new ideas awaken; he is the voice of a new society."[41] More precisely, perhaps, he is the voice of a new era, varied and contradictory in its innovations, in which an old society is finally dying and being transformed.

[41] H. Heine, *Die romantische Schule,* Hamburg, 1836, p. 131.

Molière

It may seem difficult to demand of comedy as it was understood in the past a precise view of human life and moral values. For by its very nature the comic genre, which is more concrete in a sense and closer to life and society than the other genres, may lead to some conclusions in practical ethics; but these conclusions are usually vague and platitudinous. The comic writer addresses the widest audience, and in spite of himself encourages in this audience the tendency to level everything through laughter, to measure everything that is new or unusual by the customary norms of life. Consequently comedy becomes the advocate of ordinary wisdom against any apparent absurdity. When one attempts to find in it a deeper moral inspiration, a more precise tendency, comedy rapidly becomes vague or obscure. That is certainly what has happened in the case of Molière; significantly, this champion of common sense and simplicity did not write a single great work whose meaning has not been bitterly disputed now for almost three centuries. There have been as many different interpretations as there have been readers of *Don Juan, Le Misanthrope, Tartuffe,* or even *Les Précieuses ridicules,* because while the law of comedy demands that it portray types drawn from life who bear with them on stage the debates they provoke in reality, the tone and the spirit of the genre prevent the comic author from presenting these debates with the needed intellectual clarity. Consequently, one might be tempted to see in works such as Molière's only a judicious and mild critique of all human excesses emerging from an unusually vivid portrait of those excesses. This accounts for the lasting value of these works, in which every period, even every individual, has been able to find some moral correction. This is the judgment of traditional criticism and for the most part that of Molière's admirers during his lifetime.

It is principally the nineteenth century, more interested than the preceding centuries in defining positions and discerning trends, that strove to give Molière more clearly defined and more individualistic features. Without rejecting the prevalent notion, nineteenth-century critics began adding to it more precise philosophical or sentimental interpretations–infinitely varied and contradictory interpretations from Musset to Brunetière which, through a host of editors and critics whose descendents have survived and developed up to the present, make Molière in turn a pessimist, a Romantic before his time, a precursor of the Encyclopedists, a good bourgeois, and a *précieux.* From the abundance of these interpretations, often fragile by virtue of their systematic character and often vitiated by anachronisms, a certain mistrust finally developed toward the very claim of "interpreting" Molière. Critics began to insist on the agreement between his works and the ideas prevalent in the polite society of his time. With the added assistance of all the tools of modern erudition and a more precise understanding of the seventeenth century, to a certain extent they ultimately returned to the traditional image of Molière the perceptive portraitist and sensible critic of social man.

It is indeed a waste of time to make a systematic thinker of Molière, or more precisely to look for a conscious purpose running through his work. From the fact that certain of his plays make fun of something ridiculous, we have been too quick to conclude that they illustrate a thesis. The custom of seeing things from a systematic point of view was not as common in the seventeenth century as it is today. With the exception of biased theologians or moralists, conflicts of ideas blended into a moral atmosphere that characterized society as a whole. Now, a comic author follows the general tendencies of the public for which he writes; he extends and embodies in the actions he depicts on the stage the thoughts of everyone; for his humor he seeks the widest possible audience, for his thought he chooses the paths trodden by his contemporaries. Consequently, Molière cannot be a "thinker," for he cannot be truly partisan; and one is building on air when he tries to expose as declarations of war what Molière meant only as the expression, in the frequently irresponsible language of comedy, of the already fixed judgments of his listeners. In Molière all thought is presented with an aura of public approbation, from which it cannot be separated without some distortion.

But even when a body of thought is not systematic, even when it is presented as comedy rather than as thought properly so-called, one cannot conclude that it lacks a definite tendency and direction. Methodic thought, fundamentally, is an exception, and society as a whole is guided by confused opinions which, for all of that, are not wanting in either practical coherence or direction. And every direction, even a unanimously adopted direction, implies a choice, a rejection, or an implicit debate. Those opinions that made up worldly wisdom at the time of Molière constitute, in spite of everything, a philosophy in the broad sense of the word, a particular and tendential way of looking at life. Indeed what is called common sense, even considered apart from time and place, constitutes a special philosophy that is a proper subject of debate, no matter how common it may be or how self-evident it might want to be. "Common sense" has its favorite targets, its weapons sharpened in a certain way, its victims and its enemies. It is upheld from one society to the other only because it seems to be useful in the preservation of all societies. Quite often eternal truths are only truths that are equally valid for the societies we have known up to now, the practical expression of social constants that have not yet been contradicted. But this constancy is itself only approximate. Whether one likes it or not the common sense of 1665 is not the common sense of 1865. To make Molière a wise man who can stand the test of time or one who suits our time (these two are quite often the same) we have occasionally blurred all his distinctive features, particularly those to which his audience was most sensitive. If, then, in studying Molière, one must beware of singular and systematic ideas which he excludes by temperament and by profession, one must be equally careful not to distort the proper meaning of his works by the use of excessive generalities. Even if his theater is the mirror of the common ideas of his time, it is still highly profitable to reconstruct those common ideas in their proper atmosphere, and to set them in their own light which is not the same as ours. His contemporaries did not expatiate on Moliere's thought only because there was a perfect sympathy between them and him. We do not perceive our own idiosyncrasies. At any rate, one cannot base any argument on the somewhat vague generalities that characterize the judgments of his contemporaries. Certainly we should not imitate them, and from the start attribute to Molière a universal human value which we do not perhaps understand as they did.

One of the most common tendencies of criticism, as soon as it tries to *situate* Molière's work precisely, is to discover there the average ideas of the *bourgeois.* How many times this word has been used, especially over the last sixty years, to describe his characters or his philosophy! Common sense and the bourgeoisie are two notions that have become so identified in our minds that everything in Molière that ridicules extremes is considered bourgeois today. A consideration of his work limited to a few of his plays—and one might question their interpretation besides, particularly the *Précieuses ridicules* and the *Femmes savantes*—confirms this feeling. The habit acquired since Brunetière of separating the first half of the seventeenth century, imaginative and idealistic, from the period ushered in by Molière, Racine, and Boileau, a period of naturalism and positivist ideas, has reinforced the notion of a bourgeois Molière, the interpreter of the well-balanced, sound, commoner aspects of the reign of Louis XIV. Although that was not the idea Brunetière had in mind, by setting Molière's work in opposition to the general current of aristocratic idealism—he saw Molière rather as someone who effected a revolution in morals, a link between Rabelais and Diderot—he did much to make him seem bourgeois. Faguet will go so far as to depict the author of *Don Juan* as the French Sancho Panza.[1] This notion is so widespread today, and has so eclipsed the too obviously erroneous idea of Molière as a pathetic and sorrowful Romantic, that it de-

[1] Faguet, *En lisant Molière,* 1914, p. 98.

serves to be the first consideration in any discussion on Molière.

No matter how generally accepted Molière's supposedly bourgeois inspiration may be, as soon as one reads the whole of his theater without preconceptions, that notion runs into unanswerable objections. One must not forget for whom in particular Molière was writing–without the court and the great lords his glory would not have amounted to much. And the bourgeois public fashioned its tastes in accordance with those of high society. This can be seen clearly in Molière's works, where the beautiful and the ugly, the brilliant and the mediocre are separated in anything but a bourgeois fashion. The characters and in general the style of life which Molière finds most to his liking unquestionably correspond to an aristocratic view of life. They bear the mark of *quality* in a very special way which should be clearly defined, but nonetheless they bear that mark almost without exception. The absurd or the odious are almost always colored with some bourgeois vulgarity. This fact, which is hardly surprising given the period and the circles in which Molière moved, and which was too obvious for anyone to notice in the age of aristocracy, was later so disguised by the need to adapt Molière to the reigning bourgeois morality and outlook that even today we have trouble recognizing its obvious quality. This adaptation, rather than pure considerations of literary merit, perhaps explains why an entire group of his comedies has been scorned. With the exception of Sainte-Beuve,[2] only recently have we stopped considering Molière's elegant or heroic plays, his pastorals, his "comedy-ballets" with musical interludes, as an offshoot of his real work and taken them into account in defining his genius. Yet it is in these plays that Molière is closest to his times and to his public; almost all of them were written for court entertainments and intended to please the taste of high society, and they reveal the connection between Molière and his contemporaries better than his masterpieces. Molière himself did not disdain these works. Everything leads us to believe that he did not by any means

[2] See *Portraits littéraires,* Vol. II.

write them unwillingly; he wrote them spontaneously and by preference, and he appreciated the success of these secondary comedies as much as that of his great works.

In several of his comedies there reigns a sort of showy *galanterie* that is common in the literature of the times but that may seem surprising in a writer who is supposedly the embodiment of bourgeois sentiment. The adversary of the *précieuses* and the *femmes savantes* often displayed a taste for the showy and the romanesque. In addition to his fondness as a comedian for heroic roles and his love of splendor there is evidence in his works that he was anything but unappreciative of the aristocratic ideal of his times. As proof of this, one notes early in his career that curious *Don Garcie,* whose failure was such a severe disappointment to Molière. This play, which like Corneille's *Don Sanche* bears the subtitle of "heroic comedy," is a collection of elegant debates on the possible relationships of perfect love, masculine jealousy, and the glory of woman.[3] There are similar debates again in the poetry and prose of the *Princesse d'Élide,* where one sees the glory of scorning love mingled and intertwined in a sentimental atmosphere with the pleasure of loving. In *Mélicerte,* a "heroic pastoral comedy," one finds once more the sentiments, the style, and even details of *L'Astrée.* In *Amphitryon* the conversations between Jupiter and Alcmène are filled with

[3] The same remarks, which are absurd when spoken by Armande in the *Femmes savantes,* originally had a serious meaning in *Don Garcie*–

> . . . And the first flames. . . .
> Have such inviolable rights on illustrious souls
> That one must lose greatness and renounce life
> Rather than incline toward a second love.

(Verses 912–15 of *Don Garcie,* used again almost word for word in the *Femmes savantes,* IV, 2.)

On a more purely literary plane we should compare the sonnet of Oronte, which, without being presented as ridiculous, is still made fun of, to the sonnet found in the first scene of the *Comtesse d'Escarbagnas,* which a congenial lover recites to his mistress without the slightest hint of ridicule, although it is much more clearly *précieux.*

the subtleties of gallantry and tenderness. Situations popular in the novels of the time, the conflict of love and dignity in a well-born young lady, pastoral or fanciful interludes, are the subject matter of the *Amants magnifiques* as well as of *Psyché* (with an added mythological dimension), which Molière wrote in collaboration with the two great authors of romanesque theater, Corneille and Quinault.

In all these plays Molière has yielded to a kind of sentiment that has nothing to do with the bourgeois spirit. He shares the taste of his contemporaries for tenderness and gallantry, and like them responds to the spectacular aspect of the theater. We cannot minimize in Molière the traits and qualities that betray the influence of sumptuous court festivities–a good number of his works were written for these festivities and conceived in their spirit. Molière was so far from looking on this part of his assigned work with disdain that to satisfy these demands he created the new literary genre of the comedy-ballet, a mixture of the old court ballet with comedy in the proper sense of the word, and he left about a dozen examples, from *Les Fâcheux* to *Le Malade imaginaire*. The age of Louis XIV loved spectacular *galanteries,* as had every period of courtly splendor, under Louis XIII as under the Valois kings. From the start the taste for splendor had been bound up with a *galante* type of literature. Festivals, tournaments, and royal entertainments reflected the easygoing and relaxed side of chivalry. The seventeenth century, with its court ballets and its "carrousels" did not discontinue this tradition. It simply accentuated the pleasant, imaginative, mythological element in it at the expense of the properly chivalric or heroic element. Seen from one perspective, Molière's theater is the culmination of this evolution.

The unfolding of the spectacle was not designed simply to delight the spectators' senses. If the courtiers of Louis XIV found it so pleasant to watch Olympian gods and goddesses in their entertainments it was because they were apt to look in these plays for the image of a world more brilliant, more irresponsible, and less fettered than the real world, and one that further magnified the idea they might have of their own position. The spectacle's prestige was not unrelated to the station attributed to the principal characters. The attraction exercised by this station is very obvious in Molière, and not only in his minor works. Two of his great comedies, *Amphitryon* and *Don Juan,* are replete from beginning to end with the contrast of gods and great lords with common humanity.

All the dramatic interest and all the peculiar poetry of *Amphitryon* are produced by grouping the characters in contrasting pairs, setting a greater against a lesser figure: Mercure-Sosie, Amphitryon-Sosie, Mercure-Amphitryon, Jupiter-Amphitryon. In this hierarchy the relationship of servant to master is extended mythologically by that of man to god. From the beginning of the play, before he even meets Mercury, Sosie is clearly portrayed with all the customary attributes of the socially inferior—cowardice and vanity, complaints about the demands made on him by his master, and an irresistible attachment to the honor of serving him—

> Reason in vain bids us to retire,
> In vain does our spite at times consent:
> Their glances have too powerful an influence
> on our ardor,
> And the least favor of an affectionate glance
> Ensnares us more tightly than ever.[4]

Here Sosie is simply describing a kind of relationship between manservant and master of which there are numerous examples in Molière's works. A servant is as it were a shadow of his master. Unruly and rebellious by fits and starts, he is compelled in spite of himself to follow his master and to serve him; he combines malice with ludicrous inferiority and submissiveness. In this sense he is a lesser counterpart of his master, whom he apes more often than he curses. The game of constantly juxtaposing the reactions of servants to those of masters in all possible situations—love, happiness, disaster—is more than a traditional technique of comedy. The rapprochement of the two conditions and their constant opposition were

[4] *Amphitryon,* I, 1.

a part of life—of social life governed daily by differences in station, as well as of moral and poetic life completely influenced by the image of the aristocratic demi-god. By developing the opposition in a playful, relaxed, and ultimately conservative tone, comedy fulfilled an important social function.[5]

The originality of *Amphitryon* lies in the form, borrowed from the old mythical motif of the alter ego, that the relationship between the inferior and the superior assumes in the two most important instances. Mercury took on the appearance of Sosie to harass him, and Jupiter assumed the appearance of Amphitryon to seduce his wife. The drama thereby acquires more intense human significance. The legendary theme of the double who persecutes, as it appears in Amphitryon's Greek legend can indeed pass for the metaphysical transposition of a feeling of personal rather than merely social inferiority. The double, with his supernatural powers, embodies the ambitions of the ego, and his overwhelming hostility reflects the inability of the ego to raise itself to the level of its desires. Mercury, identical with and superior to Sosie, keeps him from being himself, and rebuffs him even when Sosie entreats him to accept him as his reflection—

> S.: Oh cruel and tyrannical heart,
> Permit me at least to be your shadow. —M.: Never.
> S.: Let your soul be touched with a little human pity.
> In this capacity let me stay close to you:
> I will everywhere be to you so obedient a shadow
> That you will be happy with me.
> M.: I grant you no quarter. . . .[6]

[5] Voltaire displays a delicacy in sharp contrast with the traditional response when he writes, with respect to Corneille's *Suite du Menteur,* "These scenes in which servants make love in imitation of their masters have finally been banished from the theater for good reason. They are simply base and disgusting parodies of the principal characters." The same judgment could be applied just as easily to *Le Dépit amoureux,* to *Amphitryon,* etc., and in Voltaire's own century, to the comedies of Marivaux.

[6] Ibid., III, 6.

Thus Sosie expresses in comic fashion both a social inferiority proper to a class of men and a misery common to the human race. It is quite clear that Molière had no intention of injecting pathos into *Amphitryon* and that the themes taken from pagan mythology in his time served principally as a pretext for entertaining an imagination not prone to metaphysical anxiety. But one should not go too far in this direction, since the seventeenth century was inclined to be deeply affected by mythology for reasons that have to do with the very form of its sensitivity, which responded to the attraction of greatness. And the very habit of sporting with greatness that characterizes all the poetry of the period does not alter either the meaning or the hidden resonances of the themes evoked. However concealed it may be by the sort of brilliant play that envelops the entire work, the comedy of *Amphitryon* is shot through from beginning to end with the desire for divine freedom. This is easy to see if we leave Sosie and Mercury and go above the terrestrial Amphitryon: we will then recognize in his immortal rival the true moving force in the drama. Indeed all the action certainly proceeds from Jupiter, the master of seduction and mystification, and converges on Jupiter, who cuts the drama short by making its protagonists accept, along with his divine identity, the irresistible prerogatives he has just exercised once more among mortals. It is clearly Jupiter, rather than Mercury or Amphitryon, who represents the type that is the antithesis of Sosie. Mercury, a lesser god dressed as a manservant, and Amphitryon, *homme de qualité* tricked by a god who reduces him to the ridiculous condition of a second Sosie, each in his own way occupies a middle position between the manservant and the god who, situated at the true poles of the action, embody respectively the highest and lowest of states.

Jupiter's state is characterized at once by an excess of power over things and a diminution of the inner impediments created by timidity or scrupulousness. For him, everything that ordinarily limits desire (in other words, reality and moral prohibitions) do not exist. Transposed into human terms, a character of this type would distinguish himself from the common run of men not by the strength of his virtue but by the ease of his success. It is no longer a question of greatness of soul but of something newer, of a superhuman quality that is happy, free, and easy, in a word, pagan. This idea of a pre-eminence or a majesty bound up with the free enjoyment of pleasure is one of the principal lessons that the aristocracy of modern times thought it could draw from the revival of antiquity. All art, and poetry especially, was renewed by it. The flowering of poetic ambition in the rediscovered plentitude of life, a taste for the sumptuous blended with a taste for the natural, a mixture of pleasure and infinity–all the beautiful poetry of the seventeenth century, the work of poets like Maynard, Théophile, and Tristan, springs from these motifs. Majesty and desire speak with one voice in the works of the poets; the heavenly Olympus and the earthly ones, gods and kings alike repeat as their deepest secret the all-powerful law of pleasure.

It is worthy of note that the "commonplaces of lustful morals" Boileau speaks of are always described in his times in exalted language. Conversely, there is little poetic grandeur that does not have pleasure as its subject matter. Once *galante* poetry has broken this tie, once it has ceased to re-echo themes of grandeur, it will turn into pure and simple banter. But this is far from the case in Molière's time. One too often reads the poetry of his period with the mind and taste of the following century. The constant use of exalting symbols of mythology, the repeated appeal to themes as troubling for the imagination as those of the phoenix or the Sun King, the divinity attributed to the beloved woman, the habit of giving vent to the impulses of the human heart in the adventures and metamorphoses of myth–one might say that all this, under Louis XIII and Louis XIV, is hardly more than literature. But literature, if it does not involve belief, at least involves sentiment and imagination, and cannot be limited to simple "manners of speaking." Its function, in society and in the individual, is a more profound one. The truth is that in seventeenth-century France there was a mixture of playfulness and profundity, frivolity and poetic breadth, whose formula was lost along with the conditions that made it possible, and later was no longer recognized.

Such a formula suited an aristocracy that was always preoccupied with its greatness, but at the royal court that greatness could only consist in pleasure and royal favor. This was a rather unreal formula, and one that reveals a need to transpose and resolve poetically a problem that was harder to solve in life. In fact, in the domesticated aristocracy the pretension to greatness, spectacularly enlarged, becomes more and more unreal, more and more inclined to deny itself and to lose itself in the attractions of pleasure instead of ennobling itself. The superhuman state is dissolved in dissipation, the contempt for morality is dissolved in complacency. From the moment one ceases to consider *Amphitryon* as pure poetry the play is not free of this defect. There is a tradition according to which this comedy depicts the love affair of Louis XIV, the new Jupiter, with Mme. de Montespan, whose husband did not take his ill fortune in good grace. Whether this tradition is true or false, it is significant that under the pleasant trappings of poetry one can imagine the theme of a cynical *fabliau* transformed into court flattery. Certainly the great lords aspire to exercise in their sphere rights analogous to those they grant to the sovereign; seen from this angle, the fundamental ideas of the comedy, the off-handedness of the god, Amphitryon's comic fury, in short the irresistible precedence of the high-born lover over the lawful husband, echo a kind of relationship that could be observed throughout the society of those times, and which is summed up perfectly in the word privilege. The poetry of Molière's Jupiter is the poetry of privilege considered in general as a way of life. But the notion of privilege, of gratuitous superiority that one does not even try to justify, becomes important in the life of the nobles only to the degree that the aristocracy ceases to exercise an effective social function, to the degree that it feels itself powerless to vindicate its rights. The word privilege implies not only primacy but also social uselessness. Consequently the only deference that can be attached to privilege is of a servile nature—

> To share with Jupiter
> Is no dishonor,[7]

[7] *Amphitryon,* III, 10.

the god preaches to the husband he has supplanted. In this light the revival of pagan myths in the period we are studying can appear to be a rush of superstitious fancies come from far, far away to enhance disparity and arbitrariness with poetic prestige.

One will be convinced of the connection between the theme of *Amphitryon* and the social fact of privilege when he sees that the story told in *La Princesse d'Élide* is similar in all respects to that of Jupiter and the Greek general, except that in the former all the action takes place on a terrestrial plane, between a prince and a peasant. The buffoon Moron, the peasant's son, tells the story to the prince's son–

> My mother in her day was thought quite a beauty,
> And was not by nature very severe;
> Your late father, then, that generous prince
> Had very dangerous ways with the ladies,
> And I know that Elpénor, who was known as my father
> Since he was my mother's husband,
> Recounted to our shepherds as a great honor
> That the prince once came to his house
> And that at that time he enjoyed the advantage
> Of being bowed to by everyone in the village.[8]

This is the same situation as in *Amphitryon,* but kept to the scale of real life, where the god's right is no more than "the lord's right" and where, moreover, the victim himself is so deceived that he prides himself on his misfortune and almost proclaims, before Mercury does,

> That blows from the staff of a god
> Bring honor to the one who suffers them.[9]

Molière had already dealt with the main themes of *Amphitryon* in a more dramatic way in *Don Juan,* where the problems and conflicts created by aristocratic amorality are evoked more strongly than in any of his other plays. It is

[8] *La Princesse d'Élide,* I, 2.
[9] *Amphitryon,* III, 9.

strange that the kinship between this play and *Amphitryon* has gone unnoticed in general. Yet the two works invite comparison in many respects: in the behavior of Don Juan, as irresistible and as fleeting a seducer as the pagan god, in the ease of his conquests, and in the contrast between him and Sganarelle, a coarse and lowly counterpart. Because *Amphitryon* is a sprightly play in which all difficulties are resolved in pagan fancies, while they seem naked and unsolvable in *Don Juan,* we have looked at the two plays with different eyes. Both, however, are based on the idea of a sovereign hero who claims that his wishes are above censure and above restraint; and in both, real relationships are perceptible through the mythical world.

It is not difficult to see in Don Juan and Sganarelle the characters already observed in the mythical pairs of *Amphitryon.* Only in *Don Juan* we are closer to the real model, the gentleman-valet unit as Molière could observe it in real life. Certainly Sganarelle, who is constantly complaining about his master, claims, not without sincerity, to hate him and attests that he is bound to him by fear alone—"I must be faithful to him in spite of what I have against him; fear does the work of zeal in me, bridles my feelings, and often drives me to applaud what my soul detests."[10] But beneath this hatred a kind of helpless deference shows through, that makes the valet, whatever he says, the echo of his master. The irony with which Sganarelle repeats the attitudes of Don Juan is that of an inferior more bewildered than truly mocking. Thus when Don Juan tells him of a scheme to kidnap a young bride-to-be by boat he says, "That's all well and good for you, and you will go about it in a proper fashion: there is nothing like pleasing oneself."[11] One recognizes the same intonation in the reply that redoubles the derisive laughter of Don Juan when Elvire threatens him with God's wrath: "Really, we don't give a hoot about that, not us!"[12] One sees how Sganarelle, aping Don Juan, rids himself of M. Dimanche,

[10] *Don Juan,* I, 1.
[11] Ibid., I, 2.
[12] Ibid., I, 3.

who is a creditor of the servant as well as of the master; in this instance Sganarelle proves clearly that he admires his master enough to imitate him when he dares. His whole character has been conceived as a timid, pitiful, basically *inferior* embodiment of all those who might be scandalized by the impudence of Don Juan. Molière has been taken to task for having heaped ridicule on Sganarelle, the defender of morality and of the faith; but however he may have felt about Don Juan, if one considers the fact that the type of the manservant was already provided by tradition, he was compelled, by the very nature of his subject and the fundamental ideas of society that he could not change, to depict Sganarelle as he did, both scandalized and ridiculous, indignant and stammering, in a state of perpetual protest and perpetual defeat.

Toward him, as toward all the other lesser figures in the play, Don Juan's attitude is that of a lord to whom everything is due, who demands and takes what he likes, and owes nothing in return. The bourgeois from whom he borrows money, the peasant whose fiancée he seduces and whom he insults at the first protest, are all cut from the same cloth as Sganarelle, and their condition is clearly defined by Don Juan's banter with his servant: "I do you too much honor; happy is the servant who can have the glory of dying for his master."[13] That Don Juan is not stupid enough to believe in this edifying formula simply adds to his superiority. Furthermore, all those he holds in contempt are so constituted that the hero's overbearing attitude disconcerts them in spite of themselves, and is somehow justified by their inability to retort.

As for the mythological ramifications of the action, if they are less obvious here than in *Amphitryon,* they exist nonetheless. Don Juan's greatness is not simply an earthly one. It manifests itself just as clearly on the metaphysical plane by a pretension to share the same level as divinity which is scorned and defied, thus calling for a supernatural ending. Without a doubt there is in Don Juan something that goes beyond the usual limits of the human condition. It is not only that his desires are supreme and that they occupy the whole range of

[13] Ibid., II, 5.

his thought, flinging back into an almost unbelievable forgetfulness all that might impede them (as happens the moment after each of Elvire's importunate appearances); but their very object is without limits, it exceeds human bounds. In Don Juan inconstancy is not merely the effect of sensuality; it manifests a fundamental insatiability, a loathing for a limited pleasure, a constant ambition to go beyond victories already won. Consequently his profession of faith on this matter is always on the borderline between banter and grandeur. It is a tone we recognize; Don Juan excels in it—"However involved I may be, the love I feel for one lovely creature never commits my soul to doing injustice to the others; I still have eyes to see the merits of all and I render to each the homage and the tribute nature demands of us. Whatever may come of it, I cannot deny my heart to anything I see that is worthy of love, and as soon as a beautiful face asks it of me, if I had ten thousand hearts I would give them all. Fresh attachments, after all, have mysterious charms, and all the pleasure of love lies in change. . . . In short, there is nothing so sweet as the conquest of a beautiful woman, and in this sphere I am as ambitious as a great conqueror who flies perpetually from one victory to the next and cannot bring himself to set limits to his ambitions. There is nothing that can check the impetuosity of my desires. I feel I have a heart made to love the whole world, and like Alexander I wish there were other worlds so I could extend still further my amorous conquests."[14]

Thus conceived, the character of Don Juan would harmlessly enchant the imagination if he belonged to a mythological world. It is because he is a man, because he scandalously embodies the dreams of aristocratic paganism, and because in him privilege, instead of projecting and perfecting itself in the poetic sphere, is the object of a vital and limitless demand, that difficulties loom up before him and he is cursed. Heroism appears in him, with utter clarity, as the enemy of all moral restraint. Consequently he must render an account to the Christian God against whom he has declared war. Corneille's

[14] Ibid., I, 2.

hero, for all his pride, can be accommodated to Christianity, at least to a certain kind of Christianity. Racine's hero is no sooner outside the moral law than his own confusion destroys him and convicts him of error. Don Juan roams the world over defying God, who has no grip on his soul. There is no other solution to this open conflict than the final thunderbolt.

This supreme amorality, exempt from all feelings of guilt,[15] undoubtedly borrows its characteristics from a notion of the hero that long antedates Christianity. The supernatural elements in the story of Don Juan—the invitation to dine with the dead man, the statue come to life, the supernatural punishment of the hero—reveal an archaic legendary formation whose meaning certainly goes beyond the obvious moral of the drama. Consequently one could consider the legend of Don Juan as the point where the old notion of the sovereign hero who assumes the role of husbands, eclipses them, and sows the seed of life to his heart's content, confronts Christian ethics, which not only condemns all claims to being superhuman but is bound up with institutions in which the jealousy of men and the honor of women are in league against the seducer's adventures.[16]

This interpretation of Don Juan as a Christian rendition of a pagan hero who has been cursed has the advantage of taking into account both that aspect of Don Juan that re-

[15] It is impossible to put too much stress on this point—Molière's Don Juan feels no anxiety. Romanticism is responsible for blending anguish with Don Juan's ambitions and desires. For Molière and for the seventeenth and eighteenth centuries in general, Don Juan is Don Juan chiefly in that he knows no anguish; scandal and punishment originate outside of him; he is struck down from without. Don Juan as the Romantics see him is more attractive to his audience, who hardly ever condemn him any more for wanting to be like God, but he carries within him his own limit, which is his disquiet, and he finally proves himself (at least in most cases) inferior to his ambitions. In this sense one might say that Romanticism, while violating the Christian limitations on the ego, reconstructed them in the ego itself.

[16] This is the thesis that O. Rank seems to uphold in his often profound but unfortunately rather obscure study on *Don Juan* (French translation Paris, 1932).

mains obviously alien to Christianity and the aspect of the drama that assures Christianity's overwhelming victory. But it is not entirely satisfactory if we consider that the legend of Don Juan evolved only after long centuries of the Christian faith, and at the moment in which Christianity had undergone its first serious jolt, immediately after the Renaissance; the Spanish Burlador, literary prototype of Don Juan, dates from the beginning of the seventeenth century. It is equally worthy of note that the character only gradually disengages itself in the course of the seventeenth century from the residue of Christian psychology to take on the real form of a pagan hero. In Molière for the first time, forty years after his appearance on the scene, Don Juan holds his own from beginning to end against the Christian threat of punishment, truly free of scruples and of remorse. This clearly seems to indicate that the character of Don Juan is principally the fruit of a modern evolution in which pre-Christian memories were simply reactivated, an evolution that was, in short, born of a recent split between aristocratic mentality and religion. In fact his fortune is tied to that of religious disbelief as it developed in the noble class from the sixteenth century on in Italy, in France, and in England, because these are the adopted countries of Don Juan, who quickly forgot his too-Christian country of origin to settle and take on his real characteristics in the lands of aristocratic *libertinage*.

The whole problem of Don Juan, then, comes down to rendering an account of the modern intensification of the conflict between Christian law and the aristocratic aspirations to a kind of superhuman status. It is quite obvious that Christianity had to suffer, in this sphere as in all others, from the broadening of knowledge and of the human horizon that marked the beginnings of the modern age. The great men of this world took advantage of the occasion to violently reject a morality of abstinence and humility they had always impatiently endured. But they were not able to devote themselves so shamelessly to the cult of pleasure without losing to a certain degree their responsibility to society as a whole. Moral dissoluteness, which is a cynical disavowal of the old idea of *noblesse oblige,* with which Don Juan's father long and vainly confronts him,[17] ultimately drives its adherents out of all responsible positions in society, and consequently out of any sound and effective leadership. This great lord who is a demigod is at the same time a great lord who has fallen, and his place is clearly in the centuries in which the political decline of the aristocracy is unmistakable. Rodrigue or Nicomède are convincing human models and correspond to a working ideal that prevailed for centuries. It is impossible to hold Don Juan up as an example, and we must not forget that he is defeated in the end, as was aristocratic *libertinage* with its disdain and its scandals, which died without bequeathing anything to the future. From the *Importants* to the *Roués,* the type of the scandalous gentleman is to be found throughout the centuries that the monarchy was in power—great (and of a sort of empty greatness) only to the extent that he defies the timid stupidity of men and can choose pleasure over advantage, over life itself. Don Juan belongs to this class. He scorns death as much as he pursues pleasure, and preserves as traits inseparable from his semi-divinity contempt for men and forgetfulness of danger, the natural reflexes of pride and bravery.

Such a character's conflict with Christianity is merely a particularly clear-cut aspect of his general opposition to everything that exists—to the needs of society, to ordinary scruples, and to the laws of love, family, and society embodied in Elvire, his father, and in the Poor Man. Finally, *Don Juan* marks the point at which aristocratic ambition, virtually detached from social reality, becomes both subversive and vain. Molière, who was primarily interested in faithfully reproducing a certain state of affairs, does not seem to have given much thought to taking a position himself in the debate. The prestige he gave his hero was consonant with the thought, or at least with the secret feelings of the audience. But this prestige is clearly offset by a no less obvious endorsement of the reprobation attached to the character. There is no contradiction here. The "great lord who is evil" is both awesome and

[17] Cf. also Sganarelle's line, "Oh yes. His station! That's a fine reason. He would deny himself many things on that account." (I, 1).

revolting. And it cannot be denied that he is evil, or that Molière at certain moments made him more like Satan than like Jupiter.[18] Nevertheless, he brought to the stage the clearest, most unbearable portrayal of aristocratic pretension. This accounts for the enigmatic impression the play makes on the spectator, who can neither safely admire the demi-god, nor condemn him without feeling regret, nor forgive him without being inconsistent. *Don Juan* helps us to grasp more fully, by contrast, the balance, even though facile and superficial, of *Amphitryon,* and beyond *Amphitryon* of all the *galante* and mythological literature of the period. In any case the temptations and dangers of the aristocratic imagination, its all-powerful charms, in brief the whole complex of attractions that surrounded the consciousness of *qualité*[19] for a man of the seventeenth century, interested Molière enough to provide him not only with a good part of the embellishments of his theater but with material for several plays, two of which are among his greatest.

A cursory examination of Molière's plays suffices to show that the bourgeois is almost always second-rate or ridiculous. There is not one of Molière's bourgeois characters who as bourgeois displays some nobility or moral worth. It is useless to look through his plays for even the idea of a properly bourgeois virtue. A sense of proportion, or of the golden mean, is his mark of a gentleman, a man of the world, whether of noble birth or not, but molded according to the ideal of aristocratic courtesy, not the bourgeois as such. Even in those works that seem to be most hostile to aristocratic modes of living and thinking, in the *Précieuses* and the *Femmes savantes,* the type of the good bourgeois gets its share of ridicule. Gorgibus is no more of a model to imitate than are the *précieuses.* The contrast between his frankness and the pretension of his daughters makes us laugh and momentarily enlists our sympathy. But when Molière wanted to de-

[18] See Act I, Scene 3, Don Juan's account of his jealousy and the resentment he feels at the sight of a happy couple.

[19] "Social station" (*Tr. note*).

velop his subject further in the *Femmes savantes* he made distinction between two possible kinds of common sense b embodying it both in Chrysale, where it is bourgeois (that i to say, prosaic and ludicrous) and in Clitandre, where it is a integral part of good breeding; common sense, when it i worthy of polite society, has lost all traces of the bourgeois As for the *précieuses* or the *femmes savantes,* their absurdit originates largely from the disproportion that exists betwee their station and their ambitions. Gorgibus and Chrysale, de fining their true milieu, a completely commonplace one makes them seem like middle-class ladies mimicking thei noble counterparts. Here we have a comic element that wa even more obvious at that time than it is today. Not tha Molière did not ridicule in the *précieuses* certain traits bor rowed from an undeniably aristocratic philosophy, in particu lar the ethos of the romances. But he makes these idea bourgeois in order to make them ridiculous, he permeate them with the mediocrity of the common man, he presen them as obsolete fashions poorly imitated by an inferio world. He thus appears as the champion not of bourgeoi common sense but of aristocratic breeding.

The link established by Molière in the *Femmes savante* between *préciosité* and pedantry is no less worthy of note The pedant was one of the types most incompatible with th ways of fashionable society and according to writers of th period, a horror of pedantry is one of the marks of th *précieuse,* who, according to Abbé de Pure, is "perpetuall warring against the Pedant and the Provincial."[20] Similarly the *précieuse* in Boileau's *Satire X,* far from allowing hersel to be embraced "for the love of Greek,"

> Laughs at the vain amateurs of Greek and Latin.

Molière, then, multiplied the number of traits that could dis tinguish his *précieuses* from those of fashionable society. No that he admired the latter without reservation, but in any cas the way in which he caricatured their imitators betrays n

[20] Abbé de Pure, *La Précieuse,* Part I, Book I, p. 193.

bourgeois bias. The true spirit of the *Femmes savantes* can be found in the vehement defense of the tastes of the court that Clitandre, son of an aristocrat and the *honnête homme* of the play,[21] addresses to the pedants. Clitandre, who "agrees that a woman should have some knowledge of all things" but does not want her to have pretensions to learning or to flaunt her knowledge, has exactly the same opinions as Mlle. de Scudéry.[22] Consequently, Molière's *femmes savantes* are something less than the books they read, just as literary circles of the period, too given to priding themselves on *bel-esprit,* deviate from the ideals of good breeding.[23] The anonymous *Portrait de la Précieuse,* which appears in Mlle. de Montpensier's *Recueil,*[24] points out that the *précieuses* rarely go to the court "because they are not welcome there." However vague this information may be, it proves that *préciosité* could be repudiated from other than a bourgeois point of view.

Essentially the two plays most often used to move the bourgeois character of Molière's common sense are very close to the *Bourgeois gentilhomme* in inspiration. There ridicule strikes at the pretension of the commoner, the labored effort of common society to rise to the level of high society. If Molière sometimes seems to approve bourgeois common sense in these plays, it is in a very special way, not too flattering for

[21] *Les Femmes savantes,* IV, 3.

[22] This similarity, already pointed out by Victor Cousin, who quotes several passages from Part 10 of *Cyrus,* becomes immediately obvious if we compare Clitandre's comments (I, 3) with the portrait of Alcionide in Part 3, Book 3, pp. 1111–12, of the same romance—"She speaks equally well on all subjects and yet remains so admirably within the proper limits that custom and propriety prescribe for women so that they may not seem too erudite that when one hears her speak of the loftiest things one would say that it is only through simple common sense that she has some knowledge of them."

[23] Boileau has his interlocutor in *Satire X* say,

> Bourgeois admirer of books and writings,
> Am I going to marry an apprentice author?

This is good breeding contemning *bel-esprit.*

[24] Published in 1659.

the bourgeoisie. Indeed the proposals of Chrysale or Gorgibus are considered valid only insofar as they are meant to preach modesty and acceptance of a modest station to the bourgeoisie. It is bourgeois common sense, if you will, but one that acquiesces to the inferiority of the bourgeois.[25] And that common sense is not very attractive in Molière except in this form, as is borne out above all by the *Bourgeois gentilhomme*. This play has no other meaning but that, and the absurdity of the merchant who aspires to a higher station is not counterbalanced but heightened by the wisdom of his wife, who is a sort of female copy of Chrysale. The misfortunes of George Dandin suggest the same lesson as the extravagances of the *bourgeois gentilhomme*. Certainly the aristocracy is not always favorably portrayed in these plays—the Sotenvilles are not likable, nor is Dorante in the *Bourgeois*. But that is not the point. What matters is the emphasis Molière puts on the social inferiority of the bourgeois, and the fact that at no time does he dream of stirring us up against those who draw unfair advantage from differences in social station. This indifference verges on scandal in the case of *George Dandin*. The conjugal misfortune of a commoner married to a noble lady and eclipsed by a young courtier is presented there as something natural and highly amusing. One could find the fact deplorable and immoral, but Molière is apparently not interested in this aspect of the question.

We must not forget that in the seventeenth century the bourgeoisie did not yet enjoy much prestige in society. The leveling process was more advanced in the following century; but under Louis XIV the bourgeois, in the common view, was above all the draper, the small lawyer, the shopkeeper, and in fashionable circles he was hardly ever mentioned without disdain. It would be inconceivable that Molière, who so often was writing for the audience of Versailles, could have thought of preaching a Place Maubert philosophy there. A bourgeois intonation and spirit were disastrous in an author. There were

[25] Note the ease with which Chrysale fraternizes with a peasant girl as coarse as Martine. He represents a bourgeoisie without ambition that still feels close to the people.

others who were censured on these grounds. Boileau, for example, was justifiably open to this charge because it was he who really introduced the spirit and the ethical maxims of the bourgeoisie into the mainstream of literature by attempting to give them dignity. And consequently for twenty years he became the butt of sarcastic jibes and humiliating attacks from the wits of high society.[26] There is nothing like this in the many criticisms aimed at Molière. He made too much fun of the bourgeoisie to be reproached for having been born in that class or accused of resembling them. Moreover, however ill-informed we may be as to his mode of life, his tastes, and his sympathies, it is in any case certain that in choosing from his youth the profession of comedian when he could have laid claim to a comfortable bourgeois inheritance, he did not manifest too high an esteem for the milieu in which he was born, a milieu that is often erroneously evoked to explain his work.

Caricature of the bourgeoisie was traditional in comic literature. The bourgeoisie provided comedy with a clearly defined type with its defects and its absurdities—avarice, lack of courage, jealousy, a usually thwarted propensity for domestic tyranny, a mirth-provoking self-sufficiency, egoism, and naïveté. From the beginning Molière frequently used this type, distinct both from the gentleman (or more generally the man

[26] One should compare the *Satire V, Sur la noblesse,* and the sarcastic violence that erupts here and there in that work, to the conformism of the *Bourgeois gentilhomme.* Not one of Boileau's numerous enemies failed to reproach him for his bourgeois origins, inspiration, and spirit. See Coras, *Le Satirique berné,* 1668 (in particular the epigram on *Satire V*); Carel de Sainte-Garde, *Défense des beaux-esprits de ce temps contre un satirique,* 1675 (articles III and XVII); Desmarets, *Remarques sur les oeuvres satiriques de sieur D . . . ,* 1675 (especially the remarks concerning the *Discours au Roi* and the first *Épître*; Pradon, *Le triomphe de Pradon,* 1684 (a study of *Satire III*); *Nouvelle remarques sur les ouvrages du sieur D . . . ,* 1695 (remarks on *Satires VI* and *IX,* on *Épître VI*); *Réponse à la Satire X du sieur D . . . ,* (preface and *passim*).

of breeding), and from the manservant, and it occupies a place of considerable—perhaps first—importance in his theater. The Sganarelle of the *Cocu imaginaire,* that of the *École des Maris,* Arnolphe, the Sganarelle of the *Mariage forcé,* a last portrayal of Sganarelle in *L'Amour médecin,* and finally Harpagon, form as it were a long line of descendants among whom, to the great embarrassment of the bourgeoisie, we find time after time the same unattractive or comical family likeness resulting from a basic mélange of possessive passion and pusillanimity. These are clearly the two initial traits that delineate the character, diversified and mingled in different proportions, but present in all varieties of the type, which is thus found congenitally decked out in the defects that the most thorough aristocratic cynicism still rejected as unworthy of it: greed and cowardice. In the common opinion of the times these two defects doubtlessly constituted the dividing line between two social classes.

If it is mostly in love that Molière's bourgeois reveals his inferiority, this is not simply due to the fact that the domain of love and of pleasure is that in which Molière preferred to make values confront one another. There was a traditional incompatibility between the bourgeois character and *galanterie.* The bourgeois manner and *bel-amour* did not go together very well. To return, for example, to the meaningful case of Boileau, it is all the same to reproach him for his low birth and bourgeois spirit and to accuse him of being unfit to write *galante* poetry.[27] The typical traits of the merchant's mentality were considered fatal in love, since courtly tradition, even when reduced to simple *galanterie* attributed to love a nobility or an excellence to which common souls could never attain. Not that the bourgeois is not susceptible to love:

[27] See Coras, loc. cit., parody of Épître IX; Bonnecorse, *Lutrigot,* 1686, up to the second canto and note; similarly, Perrault, in his *Apologie des Femmes,* 1694, written in reply to Boileau's *Satire X,* paints a portrait of the *loupgarou,* who hates women; a portrait which, while applying to Boileau, certainly echoes in some of their traits Molière's *barbons,* or stuffy old men. Lastly, see the beginning of Pradon's *Réponse à la Satire X du sieur D . . . ,* 1694.

Molière likes to depict his Sganarelles and his Arnolphes in love, even to attribute to them a passionate earnestness in their desire, a cruel susceptibility to pain in failure. But they do not know how to love. They infuse love with the same jealousy, the same possessive instinct they display in all other spheres. They speak to their beloved as Harpagon speaks to his money box, like proprietors—"You will no longer have the right to refuse me anything, and I can do with you whatever I please without scandalizing anyone. You will belong to me from your head down to your toes, and I will be master of the whole."[28] This artless egoism, so unlike the methods employed in aristocratic and knowing *galanterie,* is ridiculous in direct proportion with the self-assurance that accompanies it—

> Hai! hai! my little nose, poor little mouth,
> You will not pine for long, take my word for it:
> Hush, now! You can see, I am not putting words in her mouth:
> It is only for me that her soul sighs.[29]

The proprietor's mentality has its illusions and its blindness, which are no less tenacious, no less ludicrous than his anxieties; this explains the frequency of the comic theme of mocked jealousy. The Sganarelle of the *École des maris,* as he delivers the preceding lines, is unknowingly engaged in promoting a meeting between his beloved and his rival.

Yet underneath the selfishness and the conceit, pusillanimity is quickly discernible. It is not simply a question of that form of cowardice that paralyzes the hero of the *Cocu* in the presence of his rival. The dread of having to take up arms to fight for the object of one's affections is accompanied by just as striking a weakness in the presence of the woman herself. For in all of these characters there is a bitter feeling of inferiority, ill-disguised under an apparent well-being. For example in the *École des maris,* Sganarelle's failure reveals a

[28] Sganarelle in *Le Mariage forcé,* Scene II.
[29] Sganarelle in *L'École des maris,* II, 9.

deep-seated fear of women, barely distinguishable from his inability to love—

> Unhappy the man who trusts a woman after that!
> The best of them is always full of malice;
> It is a sex begotten to damn the whole world
> I renounce it forever, this deceitful sex,
> And I give it all gladly to the devil.[30]

Deep down, these characters do not feel they were made for love and success, and that is why they seek their assurances in a tyrannical notion of married life. Conversely, their boundless egoism, which does not permit them any real communication with those they love and constantly deprives them of the certitude they demand, makes them apprehensive and fearful of failure.

Arnolphe in the *École des femmes* is doubtlessly Molière's most complete portrait of the enamored bourgeois. A whole play is dedicated to him, and not a commonplace play at that. One would have to quote everything he says to show him by turns a solemn bugaboo, a licentious old man, and above all a jealous proprietor—

> I am rich enough, I believe,
> To choose a partner who gets everything from me,
> And whose obedient and complete subordination
> Could not boast of any wealth or high birth.[31]

[30] Ibid., III, 9.

[31] *L'École des femmes,* I, 1. That the spirit of domination can stem, in the relations between the sexes as elsewhere, from the dread of being dominated, goes without saying. The glittering characters of aristocratic literature know nothing of obsessive jealousy, which is reserved for lovers little suited for inspiring love. But on the other hand, just as *bel-amour* cannot be imagined without exclusive rights, a certain confusion results in *galante* literature, which nevertheless lays down very clearly the rules for aristocratic jealousy. This jealousy, which originates in an excess of love, may be touchy and painful but it is never really aggressive. The main point is that the "object" not be treated as property that one possesses but rather as a person, and a person loved. Subtle discus-

As the accomplished final form of several characters previously sketched by Molière, Arnolphe combines confidence and uneasiness in perfectly equal proportions. These two traits, which characterize this type, are contradictory only in appearance. The idea of humiliation, instead of being conveyed from the start as in *Le Cocu,* or only coming out at the end as in *L'École des maris,* is here elaborated slowly in the course of a gradual stripping of the character until it finally appears in its true light in inferiority and defeat. In itself the obsession of cuckoldry already betrays a deep fear of women which, moreover, Arnolphe expresses naïvely from the very first scene. When his disgrace has gradually stripped him of his false air of despotic superiority, there is nothing left of him but helpless rage and vain supplications. In the last two acts, Molière painstakingly and cruelly explored the twists and turns of that despair.

All these portraits of the bourgeois lover that fill Molière's plays simply transpose into the sphere of love the characteristics attributed by common sense to the bourgeois considered as a social being. Insofar as Harpagon embodies bourgeois behavior in its economic form, almost chemically pure, he is the type who engenders the other characters of this lineage and in whom they are resolved. In him the acquisitive passion finds its true object, money, and its perfect form, delirium. One of his strongest lines, and the one which best betrays this temperament in which instinct feeds on its object, desires it to be palpable, and wants to *grasp* it, is that concerning the so-

---

sions on jealousy abound in the literature of the romances and in *galante* literature. What has often been called *préciosité* but in reality is usually nothing more than the *galanterie* common to the whole period, rejects possessive jealousy as something odious. Molière himself, who had already taken note of that perennial debate in a scene of *Les Fâcheux* (II, 4) gave very different colorations to jealousy in the two successive portrayals (the second of which, however, is patterned on the first and echoes it in long passages of dialogue) of Don Garcie, unjustly but respectfully jealous, and of Alceste, a violently jealous man with despotic pretensions. The first succeeds, the other fails. On this subject, see in particular Baumal's work, *Molière auteur précieux.*

called dowry that Frosine has allotted to Marianne–"It is a mockery to expect me to consider as her dowry all the expenditures she will never make. I am not going to give a receipt for what I do not get, and I must have something substantial in hand."[32] This desire for grasping possession is the foundation but also the unsubstantial dream of all avarice. True certitude and enjoyment lie only in reciprocal relationships and exchanges with the living world. In the end Harpagon gets no enjoyment from the things he *grasps*. Arnolphe, too, is so anxious to hold on to Agnès that he does not allow her to think of love. The wretchedness of such an attitude perverts reason. Everywhere Arnolphe looks he sees cuckolds and diabolical women; Harpagon imagines himself surrounded by enemies. In the latter Molière has pushed this trait to the very borders of madness–he says himself that everything he sees seems to be the thief that robbed him. Harpagon thus combines the extreme stylization of caricature with a most direct psychological truth. In him Molière has given the abstract formula of a real mentality, which one might call bourgeois, designating by this term (in tune with the whole seventeenth century) an inferior moral nature incapable of realizing the highest human ideals.

Thus revived from the outside, Molière's theater is far from constituting a defense of the bourgeois. In the immediately apparent distribution of its values, in the manner in which from the very beginning it alternates the attractive and the dismal, the brilliant and the mediocre, it rather makes all prestige reside in forms of life and sentiment typical of aristocratic society. Molière did not pursue this end systematically; he simply portrayed the bourgeois and the gentlemen as they were conceived by popular opinion, dominated as always by the habits of thought of the highest social class. And it is this fact that makes his work meaningful–it gives evidence of a certain state of accepted ideas.

But these ideas did not exclude all criticism of the aristocratic character. Good breeding censured certain aristocratic absurdities, which Molière depicted freely among country

[32] *L'Avare,* II, 5.

squires and their ladies. Characters like the Sotenvilles, Pourceaugnac, and Mme. d'Escarbagnas were considered comical in Paris and Versailles, where it was not even shocking to satirize ludicrous courtiers. Molière's enemies constantly tried to prod courtiers into being angry at his portrayals of the marquis. But they confess with some bitterness that Molière's victims seem to enjoy his attacks, and in any case with the exception of a single incident, completely personal and not based on the soundest testimony, they never succeeded in turning the important people at the court against Molière.[33] The fact is that Molière attacked the marquis in the name of the very principles of *honnêteté* as conceived by the court; when he made them look ridiculous he did not hurt their class–quite the contrary. The testimony of the audience in the gallery, which he invokes against the marquis' poor taste in the *Critique*, does not question the prestige of the court. The courtier Dorante, *honnête homme* and spokesman for Molière, speaks in defense of it when he denounces "a half-dozen gentlemen who dishonor the members of the court by their extravagant ways and convince the people that we are all like that."[34] A man of high birth is not necessarily an "honnête homme," and sometimes the people are good judges in that respect. There is no evidence to show that an axiom like this was considered subversive under Louis XIV, nor that it obliged the one who expressed it to renounce commonly accepted ideas on the categories of noble and bourgeois and on their respective value.

Theater is primarily spectacle, and as such, it can influence morals and suggest one behavior or another. This consideration throws some light on the "maxims" of Molière. By

[33] Cf. in particular Donneau de Visé in *Zélinde* (1663); Boursault in *Portrait du Peintre* (1663). The same year Visé also wrote a comedy entitled *La Vengeance des Marquis,* and in his *Lettre sur les affaires du théâtre,* arguing the matter on a higher level, he declared that those marquis whom Molière treated so shabbily were the intimates of the king, "the support and glory of the State."

[34] *Critique de L'École des femmes,* Scene 5.

choice we have restricted ourselves to the level of "spectacle," that sphere where prestigious or brilliant values are immediately recognizable. If we want to enter into what could properly be called a discussion of moral values and to define not the poetry of Molière but his wisdom, we will find there a compound of sound and shrewd virtues where the equilibrium of courtly civilization is expressed. This wisdom, originating at the court, is held up as a model to all of polite society. The court is merely the center and the epitome of the monarchic world.

The influence of royal courts in the ethical history of the nobility does not begin with the absolutist period. The *courtly* spirit owes its name and its birth to them. It was in court circles that the great medieval attempt to fuse the religion of love with heroism, the heart with virtue, developed. And there is not the slightest doubt that this orientation according to sentiment which was taken by the aristocratic mentality bears the mark of those already appreciable temptations offered to feudal barons by the brilliant life of the courts. The memory of amorous chivalry remained quite closely tied to the ideas of love and spectacle, to a sumptuous magic, to wonder. In the seventeenth century as in the twelfth, there are no romances of chivalric inspiration in which the adventures are not related to the life of some particularly famous court. But the compromise the courtly spirit represents between heroism and pleasure could not survive changing circumstances indefinitely; the increase of royal wealth and splendor in the course of the monarchic centuries, the ever-stronger attraction of life at the court, finally weakened it. At the expense of the traditions of courtly chivalry, the monarchy encouraged an easygoing philosophy centered on pleasure.[35] In a general way the seventeenth-century records

[35] It is in this respect that the old monarchy differs most profoundly from modern dictatorships, which are the fruit of a regression toward poverty. The architecture, arts, and painting of those earlier times express an ebullient ideal (all the more freely expressed since it was conceived only for a minority). Modern dictatorships, born of a relative narrowing and not a broadening of the general well-being, and more concerned about mass movements,

an appreciable advancement of the philosophy of pleasure in the aristocratic spirit, which professes to be the philosophy of fashionable society and of the new era. Not only do the *honnêtes gens* break their spears against the old severity, which is now evoked only in its always ludicrous bourgeois form, but the very conquests of courtly morality seem to be the fruits of an obsolete idealism. Molière attacks not only parents or tyrannical *barbons* but also the *précieuses.*

This raises a very difficult question. Molière's true relationship to *préciosité* has been remarkably clouded by the fact that to describe it we have most often consulted only the two plays he dedicated entirely to this subject, namely the *Précieuses ridicules* and the *Femmes savantes.* When isolated from the rest of his works, these plays merely show Molière as the champion of common sense against the wild fancies of the literature of the romances. Reacting against this ill-considered interpretation, others have tried to demonstrate on the contrary that Molière himself was completely *précieux.* This discussion is complicated by the absence of any clear definition of that *préciosité* that Molière is supposed to have fought or defended. Indeed, partisans of one hypothesis or the other list the most contrary things under the name of *préciosité.* To begin with, since the *précieuse* is fond of *belles-lettres,* some define *préciosité* on a literary plane, by a preference for a polished style and by a certain bent toward *galanterie* and ingeniousness. But these are attributes common to all poetry of the period. If *préciosité* is defined in these terms the whole period is *précieux,* and one would have to be blind to claim that Molière was not. If we read him we can see that in his poetic passages his style is that of his times. The entire period certainly joined him in censuring a certain exaggerated and ludicrous affectation of *bel-esprit,* but the

---

make virtue out of necessity, simulate a Spartan style, pass retroactive judgment on pleasure, and know no other splendor than warlike splendor, the mirror of all poverty. Nevertheless the conflict between the repressive and expansive tendencies within the monarchy was to prove fatal to it. The friends of luxury and of progress were ultimately to become the enemies of respect.

existence of a special sect that made this affectation their rule of life is pure legend. Victor Cousin rightly observes that "all women who had a bit of culture and charm were called *précieuses.*"[36] The *Grand Dictionnaire des précieuses* of Somaize (1661) or the *Cercle des femmes savantes* of La Forge (1663) are as it were lists of all the ladies of fashionable society, just as the list of those called *précieux* poets or writers would include almost all the authors of the times. It follows that in literature *préciosité* is neither an organized party nor a special doctrine. It is the taste of cultivated society, fond of *galanterie* and *bel-esprit.* Once the unlikely and exaggerated aspects inherent in all caricature have been discarded, ludicrous *préciosité* seems no more than a complex of universally condemned failings that everyone adamantly refuses to recognize in himself since they only exaggerate the habits common to all—that is, a search for the pleasant and the brilliant, the beautiful, and the clever. Ludicrous *préciosité* is further defined by an overevaluation of literature and of intellectualism in general, an overevaluation that falsifies one's values. This is strikingly clear in Abbé de Pure's romance *La Précieuse,* which abounds in definitions that depict the *précieuse* as a pure intelligence. For example, "She is the epitome of mind and an essence of human intelligence."[37] But here we are leaving the domain of literature for that of morals. And there the discussion becomes clearer. There are certainly in this field specific attitudes which are ordinarily attributed to the *précieuses,* and which in a sense constitute their proper philosophy. It would be advisable to distinguish these attitudes before we ask ourselves what Molière could have thought of them.

Ethical discussions pertaining to *préciosité* in the seventeenth century have love as their principal object, for they seek to determine the true nature of love and its place in life. In the *Cercle,* in Vol. I of his *Oeuvres melées,* Saint-Évremond defines the *précieuse* in a line,

[36] V. Cousin, *La société française au XVIIe siècle d'après le Grand Cyrus,* ch. XII.

[37] Part I, Book 1, p. 177.

Intent on studying the ethics of love.

Even the mania for intellectualism attributed to the *précieuses* is the result of a certain attitude with respect to the amorous instinct–it is in order to purify this instinct that one invokes lofty thoughts. This is almost as obvious in the *Précieuses ridicules* as in the *Femmes savantes,* where the whole first scene, with the parallel drawn by Armande between the joys of marriage and those of philosophy, is amply indicative. But as soon as one tries to define the *précieuse*'s notion of love, taking into account all the relevant testimony, he is struck by a surprising ambiguity. We notice that contemporaries reproached the *précieuses* sometimes for wanting to abolish love, and sometimes for giving it too much importance. Thus, in the *Déroute des précieuses,* a *mascarade*[38] written about the same time as Molière's *Précieuses* we read for example–

> *Précieuses,* your maxims
> Destroy all our pleasures;
> You label as crimes
> Our most innocent desires. . . .

Or again–

> Ye gods, what a silly beast a *précieuse* is!
> What a hard time writers had
> While these old maids
> Dominated literary circles!
> As for me, I did not dare give birth
> Either to stanzas or to a single rondeau on the
> subject of Love.

Boileau says just the opposite in his *Satire X* when he warns the prospective bridegroom how the *précieux* romances can corrupt women–

> At first you will see her, as in *Clélie,*
> Receiving her lovers under the gentle name of friends,

[38] A *mascarade* is a ballet where dancing and recitations are intermingled (*Tr. note*).

Confining herself to the little attentions that are allowed;
Then soon, in deep water, on the river of Tenderness,
Sailing as she pleases, saying everything and listening to everything.
And do not presume that Venus, or Satan,
Will allow her to remain within the limits set by the romance:
In crime it is enough to begin;
One fall is always followed by another;
Honor is like a steep-cliffed island without a shore,
One cannot return once one is outside.
Perhaps before two years are out, eager to offend you,
In love with a younger man, drunk with love of a musketeer,
We will see her frequent the most shameful gaming houses,
Arranging to meet her lovers in Mrs. Cornu's house. . . .

Yet these two exactly opposite critiques, which in turn see in *préciosité* an excess of austerity and an encouragement to dissolute living, can be found again and again in the polemics of the times, whether they are concerned with the *précieuses* in particular or more generally with the morality of the romances, which is always identified with the morality of the *précieuses*. And indeed *préciosité* merely reaffirms the traditional attitudes of the romances and courtly literature, and it is because these positions constitute a compromise between the defense of the amorous instinct and its condemnation, because they insist on upholding the rights of love while purifying it, that they are subjected to attacks from both sides. Saint-Évremond, who, somewhat like Molière, condemned the *précieuse* philosophy of love as fanciful, defined it accurately enough in both of its aspects when he writes, "For the *précieuses* love is still a god. It arouses no passion in their souls; it creates there a sort of religion. They have intellectualized a completely emotional passion of the heart, and converted emotions into ideas."[39] All of *préciosité* is in this definition: the religion of love, the disavowal of natural in-

[39] Saint-Évremond, *Le Cercle*.

stinct, and the appeal to intelligence to sublimate it. Abbé de Pure, whose romance is the most far-reaching and the most valuable document on the ethical ideas popular among the *précieuses*, writes in a similar vein. One of his heroines gives a remarkable definition of perfect love, which according to her is found only in the prude, whose character reconciles the demands of duty with those of the heart–"I think . . . that duty helps and strengthens passion. Because then the soul acts with greater freedom and can use its reason, with all the understanding of which it is capable, as well as its heart, with all the fervor of which it is capable. The soul is not divided; neither judgment nor shame attenuates any of its desires or its concerns, and it is brought whole and entire to its object, with the pleasant advantage that it satisfies both the tenderness of its sentiments and the strictness of its duty."[40]

It is to be expected that such a concept, which is nothing but the modern development of old courtly ideas, should be met with opposition both from rigorous moralists and from the partisans of freedom and nature. Austere moralists and the friends of pleasure, though they start from opposite points of view, were both traditional enemies of the courtly doctrine. But it can also happen that the defenders of pleasure and those of perfect love find themselves in league against rigid moralists who condemn them both, even mistaking one for the other. There we have the secret of the common ground between Molière and *préciosité*. If he condemns as an illusion and as an evil the attempt of the *précieuses* to purify and intellectualize desire, he finds himself joined with them in a common effort to break the old bonds of restraint and assert the rights of love.

All things considered, Molière's satires are aimed less at women who read romances than at the pompous old men who persecute such women. Alongside of the ludicrous romanesque lines Molière puts in the mouths of the *précieuses*, and the

[40] Part III, Book 1, second conversation, see pp. 288 to 290. It is worth noting that this is not so much a portrait of a prude in love (that is to say, a hypocrite) as one of the heroine of a romance enjoying the perfection of "honorable love."

final imprecations Gorgibus calls down on romances, which might almost seem persuasive, one could cite the comical sermonizing of his namesake in the *Cocu,* who would like to give his daughter in marriage against her will–

> There, there we have the fruit of that eagerness
> With which we see you night and day reading
> your romances:
> Your head is filled with *quolibets* of love,
> And you speak less well of God than of Clélie.
> Throw into the fire all these wicked writings,
> That every day spoil so many young minds.
> Instead of this nonsense read, as you should,
> The *Quatrains* of Pibrac, and the learned *Tablettes*
> Of Counselor Mathieu, a worthy work
> And full of beautiful maxims to learn by heart.
> *La Guide des Pécheurs,* too, is a good book.
> It is there that one soon learns to live well,
> And if you had read only these moral lessons
> You would be better able to conform to my wishes.[41]

Similarly, in *L'École des femmes,* where Molière obviously sets out to ridicule a hateful notion of life and love, Arnolphe is a declared enemy of *préciosité*–

> As for me, am I going to be burdened with an
> intellectual woman
> Who speaks only of clubs and literary cliques,
> Who would write sweet notes in prose and in verse
> And who would visit marquis and *beaux-esprits,*
> While under the name of Madame's husband
> I would be like a saint that no one invokes?
> No, no, I want no cerebral type;
> A wife who writes knows more than she should.[42]

These are almost the same words Chrysale uses in the *Femmes savantes,* but they have a completely different ring. Moreover,

[41] *Le Cocu imaginaire,* Scene 1.
[42] *L'École des femmes,* I, 1.

Arnolphe's aversion for the *précieuses* is expressed on several occasions and always in a ludicrous way–

> Heroines of the times, Learned Ladies,
> Champions of tenderness and beautiful sentiments,
> I defy all your verses, your romances,
> Your letters, your love notes, all your knowledge,
> To be worth as much as this honest and modest
> ignorance.[43]

He has no sooner uttered these words than he is cruelly disillusioned. It is the same later on, when Agnès rebels against him–

> See how the wicked girl reasons and replies!
> May the plague take me! Would a *précieuse* say more?[44]

All these examples are proof enough that the enemies of the *précieuses*, who are the enemies of love, find Molière blocking their path.

The moral problems that are characteristic of *préciosité*, and which Molière up to a certain point solves does assume the aspect of social problems in his plays. The preceding texts all draw on situations that debate the place of women in society. But this is nothing new. The rights of love and those of woman were already identified in the Middle Ages, when one either recognized or rejected them together. The enemies of *bel-amour*, those who criticized instinct, are from this time on the enemies of women. In parallel fashion, the idealization of love in the literature of the romances goes hand in hand with an attitude of respect toward woman, now the source of the principal values in life. From this time until our own, and for many reasons, the male sex has become the exclusive embodiment of the strictest virtues–severity, self-denial, insensitivity. At the very least it is in these virtues that man thinks he displays his own excellence. Man claims as his privilege the

[43] Ibid., I, 3.
[44] Ibid., V, 4.

ability to scorn pleasure, especially the pleasures of love, which is considered the principal enemy of duty. Since this conflict between manly virtue and love tends to take on the aspect of a struggle against womanhood itself, it is natural for any loosening of moral rigor, any increase of happiness and of culture, to be reflected on the contrary in a greater prestige for women. The civilized and rich Middle Ages were the courtly Middle Ages. And there is no period in which the image of womanhood, in all its clearly discernible power and attraction, held a higher place than in the three great centuries during and following the Renaissance.

The entire seventeenth century evidenced as much interest in the social aspect of the question of women as in its moral aspect. The discussions of the *précieux* circles, as they are portrayed for example in Abbé de Pure's romance, touch as often on the subject of the authority of fathers and husbands as on the subject of love–basically it was one subject. The struggle of young women and men against family control, represented by some old man, a father or a ridiculous suitor, is found again and again in Molière. It is the mainspring of the action in all his plays. The young always triumph over the old, as does inclination over restraint and freedom of love over old family precepts. In order to place these ideas, common to Molière and the *précieuses,* back in their own atmosphere one should keep in mind the centuries-old precepts about the place of women. From the Middle Ages on we see right-thinking moralists striving to combat the influence of courtly literature by outlining for woman her real duties–absolute submission to man and systematic renunciation of her instincts and her intelligence. They condemn finery, flirtations, social calls, readings, and correspondence; they make chastity, or even an almost total absence of spontaneous desire in every sphere, the sole womanly virtue. They advocate complete obedience to the husband, even a servile behavior when confronted with his fits of anger and ill-humor.[45] They

[45] Thus, Philippe de Novaire, in *Quatre tens d'aage d'Ome* (thirteenth century) counsels, "Our Lord commanded that woman be always under authority and in subjection. During her childhood she should obey those who rear her, and when she is married she

were still writing this way in the sixteenth century, and in all seriousness. In his *Institution de la femme chrétienne,* the erudite Vivès confirms at the height of the Renaissance the rigorous teachings of earlier times. He wants women to avoid conversations and social calls, to busy themselves exclusively with their housekeeping and their children, to know nothing of romances or of any works that deal with love, and above all to be entirely subject to their lords and masters. These traditional ideas, forced into retreat by the advances of social life, were nevertheless still very much alive in the seventeenth century. In spite of the opposition of women and of *beaux-esprits,* they still held sway in ordinary education as it was received at home or in the convents, and they governed everyday morals. This oppression was attenuated only—as any oppression—by the natural sociability of human beings. It is to these ideas that Abbé de Pure's *précieuses* are alluding when they call to mind "those tiresome maxims of our fathers, who only approved of women at home."[46] These are the ideas that Molière, with a fidelity that extends to the very language they use, attributes to his *"barbons."*[47] The book Arnolphe gives to Agnès, entitled *Maximes de mariage,* which is to teach her her duties, repeats the traditional prohibitions: no dressing up, no make-up, no social calls, no gifts, no letter-writing, no entertaining, no games, and no outings.

Molière obviously makes common cause with the *précieuses* when he upholds their objections against this oppres-

---

owes complete submission to her husband, as her lord" (Paragraph 21). Even Christine de Pisan defines the relationship between wife and husband in this way—"She will yield humbly to him in act, in respect, and in speech, she will obey him without complaining and with all possible solicitude" (*Le livre des trois vertus*). And Anne de France advises her daughter, "You must be especially humble with your lord and husband, to whom, after God, you owe perfect love and obedience, and you cannot in that respect humble yourself too much" (*Les enseignements d'Anne de France à sa fille Suzanne de Bourbon,* Ch. XVI).

[46] *La Précieuse,* Part I, Book 2, p. 314.

[47] See especially *L'École des maris,* I, 2; *L'École des femmes,* I, 1; III, 2.

sive moral code. And we must certainly take note of the fact that ideas of emancipation in this sphere were not very attractive to the bourgeoisie, unquestionably more backward in this respect than the upper classes. It is impossible, too, to pass off as protests of bourgeois common sense what in Molière are rather protests of the new spirit against prejudices and customs especially deep-rooted in the bourgeoisie. Some critics thought they could extricate themselves from this difficulty by suggesting that Molière had all the ideas of the average bourgeois *except* that he advocated the emancipation of women and marrying for love. But this is too important a reservation; it destroys the whole thesis. In any case it is certainly in members of the bourgeoisie that Molière embodied the moral code that condemned love and women. And he fought against that morality they embodied. He made them the victims of womanly spontaneity and guile. The authoritarian ethics of characters like Sganarelle and Arnolphe is nothing but an easily recognizable transposition of that greedy and anxious lust for possession that became the characteristic feature of the man of common birth. The old men's maxims almost always betray traces of inferior social status. When Molière attacks the authority of fathers and husbands, in general he has the court and the salons on his side. To defend *galanterie* and lavishness, to declare war on the past, had always been the task of fashionable society; it had always claimed to civilize life, to rescue it from the old primitive ways. This called for a broad mind, a taste for beautiful things. That is why Molière, in the midst of all his daring critique, and even when he attacks strong and widespread prejudices, gives the impression of being supported by the evidence against a ridiculous opponent. He would have been less confident in his attack on established ideas if the progress of civilized life had not enlisted the most brilliant part of society against these ideas, leaving them no other champions but a Sganarelle or an Arnolphe.

The strength of the new modes in French society is sufficiently attested to by the widespread opinion that considered France pre-eminently the land of feminine freedom. In their conversations, polite society not only evidenced a universal hatred for the cruelty of "Turkish" customs, but prided itself on not imitating the jealousy of Spaniards and Italians. In *L'Amour peintre,* Molière turned the struggle of French *galanterie* and Sicilian jealousy to the glory of the former and the confusion of the latter. "One of the most pleasant aspects of our France," says one of Abbé de Pure's *précieuses,* "is that of the freedom of women. . . . Jealousy is just as shameful to a husband as the licentiousness of his wife; and whether it be taught by fashion or by custom, this is the first lesson to be drilled into those who marry, to shield themselves from suspicion and jealousy."[48] There is an abundance of similar evidence to prove the point. Pradon, in his *Réponse à la Satire X,* an indictment of Boileau's misogyny, which he claims is one of his bourgeois traits, argues in the same vein—

> The honest freedom that is allowed in France
> Far from increasing vice, banishes licentiousness;
> Without using here, as in other climes,
> Iron bars, bolts, keys, padlocks,
> Which often only embolden the most timid,
> Honor and virtue serve here as guides.

We find it quite indicative of the state of public opinion that none of the many detractors of the *École des femmes* questions Molière's basic ideas on the subject. Agnès was considered "disquieting" only in the nineteenth century. Indeed, the jealous persecutor who kept his wife or daughter under lock and key was a type that was generally held up to ridicule, especially in high society, where women, accustomed to luxury and amusement, had to a certain degree acquired the right to govern themselves. All *belle galanterie* was based on this custom of "entertainments" in which the two sexes took part, free of excessively strict family control. The romances and *précieuse* literature in general are filled with these *galantes* gatherings, balls, outings and "gifts," serenades, readings of poems and letters, discussions on love, and entertainments involving dancing and singing. These are the pleasures Molière's wives and young girls demand, and the husbands

[48] *La Précieuse,* Part I, Book 2, p. 309.

or suitors who refuse them these pleasures are without exception depicted as ludicrous and incapable of inspiring love. "I love the games, the visits, the gatherings, the gifts, and the outings, in short all kinds of pleasure,"[49] Dorimène says to her husband-to-be Sganarelle, in *Le Mariage forcé*. And far from contenting herself with "honest freedom," she asks that her suitor, after rescuing her from her father's tyranny, live with her in "a mutual accommodation," an absolute mockery of the marital bond as it is usually conceived. To be sure, nowhere does Molière imply that he is holding her up as an example, but the whole play demonstrates clearly enough that if he has indulged in comical exaggeration it is in order to ridicule more effectively the hapless Sganarelle, who a moment before had completely abandoned himself to the naïve joy of possession. The same situation is picked up again and treated in the same amusing way in *George Dandin*,[50] with the more serious complication that here the heroine, Angélique, is speaking to her husband, not to her fiancé. Here, too, it is perfectly obvious that Molière had no intention of holding her up as a model, but Angélique adequately justifies her conduct by reminding her husband that she was given to him against her will; and above all, whatever reflections Angélique may suggest, it remains no less true that the whole play is conceived in such a way as to amuse the audience at the expense of her husband.

As soon as we set Molière back in his own century, nothing seems more debatable than the notion, which began to circulate two hundred years after his death, that he is the defender of the bourgeois family. It is all too clear, on the contrary, that Molière's true sentiments on love and marriage became awkward for society as soon as it became entirely bourgeois and the old bourgeois outlook took on the status of an official philosophy. Since one could not send Molière to the devil, one adapted him to the times. Thus gradually the idea gained credence that Molière's often shocking or scandalous portraits

[49] *Le Mariage forcé*, Scene 2.
[50] *George Dandin*, II, 2.

of the family circle were drawn for purposes of edification, and that he wanted to make the excesses or failings he denounced all the more odious by showing them more fatal to an institution sacred among all institutions. Following this line of thought, Angélique proves by her example the deplorable effects of marriages in which there is no proportion between the contracting parties in social standing, age, or intelligence; Agnès illustrates the dangers that poorly educated innocence encounters, and so on. Consequently, all the feminine protests against restraint are misrepresented as so many disturbing manifestations, solemnly denounced by Molière himself.[51] It is certainly acknowledged that Molière condemned restraint, but that was to maintain order. The truth is rather that Molière, by temperament, defends order only insofar as it is free of restraint. In his works likable women are almost always in revolt against some odious authority, flouted at the end of the play. Everything in his comedies betokens the triumph of youth and pleasure over respectability and family conventions. Their scandalous aspects are at times so strong that they have withstood all attempts at compromise. Agnès in particular has a fairly bad press, and Brunetière, who generally stresses the subversive character of Molière's ethics, openly admits that he is particularly shocked by Molière's young girls. The playwright, in fact, concerned himself very little with the family as an institution. He accepts as a basic assumption the fact of the family, the family as the natural framework for the problems posed between individuals and between the sexes. In the seventeenth century no one was yet either for or against the family. Only Molière, by natural preference, was apt to consider as an ideal family that which would exercise the feeblest restraints on its members,

[51] One cannot imagine how far the delicacy of some modern critics goes in this area. The conduct of Elmire in *Tartuffe*, for example, generally passes for "suspicious" or "ambiguous." Yet no one disputes the fact that her obliging ways with Tartuffe are pure politics, but those critics would like her honesty to make the role she is playing more difficult. Some of our contemporary moral views have the same characteristics as a jealous husband. In Molière's time Elmire did not provoke misgivings.

that in which the parents, joined by mutual agreement, would not infringe on those of their children. We are certainly forced to observe that on every occasion Molière urges the relaxation of family ties and the weakening of that authority that is meant to make this tie prevail over the inclinations of the individual. When Molière suggests the liberalism of fathers and husbands as the best means for them to win affection or fidelity for themselves, we should not attribute to him a concern with "preserving the family," any more than we should consider him the defender of religion when he implies in *Tartuffe* that an excessive zeal destroys piety. In both instances it is less a question of safeguarding an institution than making it tolerable, opening it to the higher demands of life.

Molière's final word on the philosophy of marriage is that trust encourages faithfulness and that restraint, on the contrary, provokes hatred and revolt. But if we seek to place such a notion in a seventeenth-century context, we find that it is the central idea of all *galante* literature and that *préciosité* made it one of its articles of faith. In Abbé de Pure, likable husbands have the same moral principles as Ariste. Convinced, like Climène in *Le Sicilien,* that "a jealous man is a monster everyone detests,"[52] they do all they can to avoid the reproach of belonging to this discredited species; they do not dare express the least sign of jealousy without couching it in phrases of extraordinary tact. Like Polyeucte after Sévère's return, they are determined never to seem uneasy or distrustful.[53] Feminine opinion carefully fosters this tradition of deferential *galanterie* and Molière is faithful to that tradition when he has one of his heroines say, "The great mark of love is to be subject to the wishes of the woman one loves."[54] The morality Molière has his bourgeois young heroines preach comes straight from the romances.

Molière's only originality lies in the fact that the wisdom

[52] *Le Sicilien,* Scene 18.

[53] *La Précieuse,* especially Part I, Book 2, pp. 331, 339; Part II, Book 1, third conversation, *Histoire de Caliste.*

[54] *Le Malade imaginaire,* II, 6.

of the romances is rarely found in his works without a hint of mockery or of scandal, as if he were bent not on enlightening the mind by setting forth a sensible doctrine, but on destroying its self-confidence by unceremoniously stripping it of its prejudices. This is certainly the tone of Dorimène and of Angélique; it is that of Ariste, that *honnête homme* in the *École des maris* who takes pleasure in dumfounding his brother with his broadmindedness.[55] The scene is well known; in it the new code of behavior permits itself the heartening luxury of provoking scandal instead of trying to quiet it.

It is true that there is more than this in Molière's attitude. The comic treatment of cuckoldry, the consistently frivolous way in which the subject is handled, the mockeries that ultimately transform the pseudo-tragedies of marital infidelity into inconsequential farces—all these things served to strengthen the maxims of *galant* or courtly liberalism, but by expressing them with a new accent. It will suffice to compare Ariste, a man of the world and a well-bred philosopher, to Chrysalde in *L'École des femmes,* when he urges Arnolphe not to exaggerate the importance of cuckoldry.[56] Chrysalde, who at the beginning of the comedy joked about Arnolphe's "itch" to acquire an aristocratic name, is not simply a good, unpretentious bourgeois. In his carefree ways, his good nature, his lack of inclination for the solemn principles that are ordinarily the sign of respectability in his class, this imaginary sage is a link with the popular tradition. And indeed if there is something in Molière's wisdom that strengthens and gives body to the elegant liberalism of the *honnêtes gens* it is not bourgeois reason but rather the completely natural frankness and impudence of the common people. This is made clear in the important roles he gives to valets and maidservants in discussions of matrimonial philosophy. The maidservants in particular are permitted to express the rebellion of women with a freedom that would ill-suit their mistresses. While the women or young girls of higher station assert their rights with a delicacy proper to fictional heroines, their maidservants, who are

[55] *L'École des maris,* I, 2.
[56] *L'École des femmes,* IV, 8.

always made use of in their love affairs, draw from popular wisdom a more energetic and more amusing variant of their mistresses' complaints and threats. They transpose into an aggressive style the impulses of women's pride against the injustice of men. For example, Sosie's wife, Cléanthis, says,

> Why is my heart not resolute enough
> To punish this infamous wretch?
> Ah, how maddening it is at a time like this
> To be an honest woman![57]

In Molière, maidservants carry more weight than manservants; it is from the women that we hear the plain wisdom of the people. While the valets put only their wits at their masters' service, the maidservants truly represent common sense and truth coming to the rescue of the unrecognized rights of women. A threat to the despotism of the male, since propriety does not have much of a hold on them, they hurl the menacing truths of instinct and justice in the face of the authorities:—

> All these precautions are the visions of idiots;
> The surest, indeed, is to trust us:
> Anyone who stands in our way puts himself in dire peril,
> Our honor always wants to look out for itself.
> To go to such pains to keep us from sinning
> Almost awakens in us a desire to sin,
> And if I felt hemmed in by a husband,
> I would be sorely tempted to confirm his fears.[58]

Or again, "That's the way to act if one wants never to be deceived. When a husband puts himself at our mercy we only take such liberties as we must, and we act as we would with those who open their purses and tell us, 'Take what you need.' We do not take advantage, and are content with what is reasonable. But we do our best to fleece those who wrangle with us, and we show them no mercy."[59]

[57] *Amphitryon,* I, 4.
[58] *L'École des maris,* I, 2.
[59] *George Dandin,* II, 1.

Molière's "feminism," then, appears to be an accord be-
ween aristocratic *galanterie* and plebeian candor or humor,
and this accord is reached by jumping over the zone of bourgeois respectability. One might even say that the blend of aris-
ocratic charm with popular banter generally defines Mo-
ière's tone. We will have occasion to come back to the
mportance of this fusion of elements, which, by setting a
free and natural Molière alongside of a *galant* Molière, forces
us to clarify the nature of his disagreements with *la galanterie
précieuse.*

It is a fact that twice, at the beginning and at the end of
his career, Molière attacked the *galanterie* of the romances.
Les Précieuses contains explicit allusions to *Cyrus,* to *Clélie,*
to the *carte de Tendre,* and at least two of the three heroines
of the *Femmes savantes,* Armande and Bélise, are infatuated
with the philosophy of love they find in the romances. It is
generally felt that the apparent contradiction that makes Mo-
ière both the advocate and the opponent of the feminist
cause can be resolved by saying that he sides with the demands of *préciosité* up to a certain point, and condemns its
extremes, that once again he adopts the golden mean between
the philosophy of the *barbons* and that of the *femmes savantes.* The truth will not seem so simple if we consider that
in many instances Molière's boldness does not fall short of
that of the *précieuses,* but goes even further. His philosophy
of love, less "purified" than theirs, more open to instinct and
to pleasure, is more free of moral preconceptions. It is the
philosophy of the romances, instead, in its attempt to idealize
love, that seems to be an ingeniously mapped-out middle
ground between traditional prohibitions and a wider freedom,
a freedom of which Molière's comedies give us some idea.
Thus, to clarify Molière's double judgment with respect to
préciosité, one would have to say rather that they part company at that point in the road where *préciosité,* too timid,
draws to a halt. Yet this explanation is not completely satisfying either, since from another point of view it is Molière who
first draws to a halt. When for example Philaminte aspires
to raise women to the level of men in the intellectual order,

or refuses to take an interest in running a house, Molière laughs at her expense, and in this instance there is no doubt that his is the laugh of a conservative.

Yet before the contradiction ever manifested itself in Molière, it could be discerned in the very concrete historical conditions in which women's desire for emancipation asserted itself. Such a desire can come to light in two ways, and a powerful tradition shows us how different the two can be. In opposition to the repressive morality imposed upon them, women can demand the right to live and to enjoy themselves according to the inclinations of nature, and they can also demand that they be accorded a dignity and a station equal to those of man. Molière accedes as far as possible to the first demand and enjoys making fun of the second. He becomes indignant when instinct is outraged, and is much less indignant if pride or a sense of justice is attacked. The whole absurdity of the *femmes savantes* lies in their obsession with equality, in their rebellion against the attribution of a higher value and prestige to men, because in the final analysis that is what the problem of intellectual ambition in women can be reduced to. If they demanded, even with some scandal, the right to behave and to love as they pleased, Molière would be willing to listen to them, but the problem is that they feel themselves bound to scorn love in order to shake off the inferior status of women. Molière indissolubly linked their prudishness and their rebellion, and condemned both with a single stroke. And he did not arbitrarily create this antinomy of happiness and dignity. He found it in our condition, as that condition had been molded by centuries of wretchedness and a long, incurable divorce between greatness and pleasure. The divorce is especially profound in woman, since the common view embodies in her every weakness of the emotions and the senses, the better to relieve man of them. Consequently, as soon as she aspires to some greatness she must completely repudiate herself. It follows that the most boldly ambitious women are rarely capable of happiness and fulfillment in love. Here, then, is the cause of the extreme difficulty we encounter in defining, in a social milieu that has scarcely changed in this respect since Molière's time, an absolute feminine ideal which does not in some way feel the ill-effects of woman's real condition. This explains the defects of *précieux* feminism, its constantly unreal and affected aspect, the extravagant spirituality on whose shoals it is shipwrecked.

To try to repudiate one's own nature is a fanciful enterprise doomed to all possible contradictions. Molière saw clearly the principal difficulty in feminine idealism—the unsolvable problem of a doctrine that disapproves of love without ceasing to exalt it, that extends its sway to all areas to make woman prevail everywhere, and at the same time denounces it as a danger to feminine independence. The result was a type of woman obsessed by love and in revolt against it, both a coquette and a prude—precisely the type of the *précieuse*. And in this sense the *précieuse* is a universal type. Now it is just this contradiction, and the useless efforts at spiritualistic synthesis by which the *précieuse* attempted to resolve it,

> That Molière, with a stroke of his art, defamed,

to use Boileau's words; or, to be more precise, that Molière meant to defame. Molière never missed a chance to expose the emotional weakness that the platonism of the *précieuses* ill-concealed. In place of the absurdity of a love

> In which one is never aware of having a body,[60]

Molière offers not a golden mean but the undiluted force of instinct—

> I love with my whole self, and the love I receive
> Is addressed, I admit, to all of me, body and soul.[61]

To this defense of instinct is added a sharp critique of ethical idealism; the sublimation of desires is an illusion—what sen-

[60] *Les Femmes savantes,* IV, 2.
[61] Ibid., IV, 2.

suality loses, pride gains. Feminine idealism conceals and fosters the ambition of woman to dominate man, to bind him without conceding him a thing. Not only

> This dominion that reason holds over the senses
> Does not make us renounce the sweetness of flattery,[62]

but prudishness and the thirst for adoration strengthen each other. In fact, the indifference of the coquette turns into violent resentment as soon as compliments are lacking. Armande's whole role in the *Femmes savantes* is meant to illustrate these truths.

Among all the elements of the *précieuse* neurosis, Molière gives a privileged place to the tactics of war and domination that women unsatisfied with their lot constantly direct against man. Armande would like to rule over her suitor, and Philaminte rules over her husband, who confesses that he trembles in her presence. When they speak of equality they mean revenge, and inordinate revenge, fruitless and endless agitation. The war of wives against husbands—that is the concrete, half-scandalous, half-ludicrous form in which common sense conceives the protest of women. And there is a basis for this, because women themselves think and feel according to the usual norms, and react to oppression with a desire to oppress. But hostility toward man so impedes woman from living that instead of a broadening there results a profound moral narrowing, a distortion of the whole of life. We can understand that under these conditions, after having rejected the oppressive maxims of the past, one might have been tempted to begin reform in the easiest way, that of pleasure and well-being, without raising deeper and more thorny problems that the complex of social conditions made it difficult to solve. That is clearly the case with Molière, in whom a taste for the *obvious* is at once the beginning and the limit of daring.

The rebellion of women against the prohibition to love is a relatively easy thing to unravel, because the hatred of dep-

[62] Ibid., I, 1.

rivation implies a desire that is already fully formed. Nature, then, triumphs by itself, and in addition, nature and society can come to terms in this sphere without too much backwash. On the contrary, the revolt against the inequality of the sexes, which calls into question the traditional social structure, is not as easy to solve even in theory. It moves in the realm of the uncertain, the unreal, and the difficult. Anxious to find "remedies for the evils of marriage," Abbé de Pure's *précieuses* devise the most contradictory, the most outlandish solutions ranging from complete emancipation through polyandry or systematic inconstancy to apathy and deliberate coldness toward one's marriage partner, passing through divorce, provisional marriage broken off at the birth of a child, a system where authority would alternate between husband and wife, an ideal state in which nature itself would be charged with punishing unfaithful husbands by turning their pleasure into pain or transferring that pleasure to the abandoned wife.[63] This atmosphere of dissatisfaction, wild fancy, unsurmountable difficulties, is obviously not the atmosphere we find in Molière. Worst of all, this feverish quest, which aspires to establish fairer relations between the sexes, succeeds only in setting them hopelessly at odds. One touches off a war between the sexes out of horror of a false peace, but one is powerless to create a true peace. One upsets life and disturbs love to no purpose. Furthermore, this mute revolt on the part of women, this touchy pride, these complaints, this ambition, are not traits found only in the *précieuse*. One finds their imprint throughout the literature of the romances with its demanding and sensitive heroines, thirsting both for love and dominion. Abbé de Pure simply de-

[63] *La Précieuse,* Part III, Book 1, first conversation: *Des remèdes aux maux de mariage.* On the subject of marriage see also, in the same book, the second conversation: *Des ragoûts pour les dégoûtés du mariage*; in Part III, Book 2, the *Raisonnements de la précieuse sur le mariage.* Likewise, Part II, Book 1, fourth conversation, the story of Eulalie, married against her will; fifth conversation (if a woman forced to marry has the right to go on loving the man she loved). Finally, Part IV, Book 1, especially at the beginning and the end, the proclamation of the reign of women.

veloped more frankly than others the thoughts and discussions that come up among women of this type and their circles. "We marry in order to hate and to suffer," he has one of them say.[64] Another, telling her own story, describes in these candid terms the coldness of the woman married against her will—"She is obliged to accept at her icy breast the ardor of her husband, to endure the caresses of a man she does not care for, who is repugnant to her senses and to her heart. She finds herself in his arms, she accepts his kisses, and whatever defense her aversion and her distress might be able to devise, she is forced to submit and to accept the law of the conqueror."[65] In another passage of the novel the same heroine sees no other solution but a profound insubordination to the husband, carefully cultivated beneath a semblance of resignation—"The *précieuse* does not marry like common people. In yielding she elevates herself; the more she humbles herself the greater her pride. . . . She is married as though she were not. . . . She makes distinctions and sorts things; she knows how to observe differences and degrees between love and friendship."[66] In conclusion, the war between the sexes properly so-called is declared with a great display of imagination and irony in the last part of the romance, where we see an old astrologer study the heavens on the day of an eclipse amidst general confusion and predict the revenge of women and the imminent establishment of their empire.[67] "The longer the reign of injustice," one *précieuse* cries out, "the longer will our sex reign in its turn."[68]

It would be surprising if the seventeenth century had been much more capable than succeeding centuries of conceiving

[64] *La Précieuse,* Part III, Book 2, p. 411.

[65] Ibid., II, 1, p. 274.

[66] Ibid., III, 1, p. 129.

[67] Ibid., IV, 1, p. 14.

[68] The whole account of the project is remarkable for the violence with which the inferior status of women is denounced, especially the tendency of the majority of women to envy and to discredit those who shake off the yoke (p. 231). Note, too, a general criticism of custom in the name of reason.

the natural and peaceful equality of men and women, without hatred or prejudice on either side. But such a conception was not completely beyond its reach, at least if one is to accept the testimony of Poulain de la Barre's work on *L'Égalité des deux sexes,* published in 1673, which may still seem astonishing today. The author, explicitly refusing to state his argument in terms of *galanterie* (which obviously has nothing to do with true equality), bases his assertion of perfect equality, especially intellectual equality, on a Cartesian critique of prejudice. In a tone reminiscent of Perrault in *Les Paralleles,* he takes great care in his preface to rule out the idea of feminine revenge. The war between the sexes is the actuality, not the ideal; equality should bring that war to a close—"Only injudicious women could make use of this work to rise up against the men who would treat them as equals or companions."[69]

On the contrary, for Molière, as for the majority of his contemporaries, the equality of the sexes assumes an aspect of war and dissension. And since he loves innovations only when they are easy and lead to pleasure, he never alludes to woman's desire for equality without drawing comic effects from it at the expense of the innovators. For him, where women are concerned, laughter is as often the weapon of prejudice as the revenge of nature.

Molière's hostility toward nascent feminism, and his intervention from the beginning of the dispute in favor of traditional notions cannot, however, conceal his daring in the direction he chose to take. Many heroines in his comedies still scandalize bourgeois families tolerably well. They would find Armande mad, but Agnès "depraved," and there is no one who is not aware that the second offense is much more serious than the first. When the *précieuse* rebels against the servitude of marriage, she objects to pleasure as well, and this is an undeniable advantage in the eyes of moralists. Agnès,

[69] The same author later published a work on the *Excellence des hommes,* in which, in the guise of a retraction, the same ideas are found as in the preceding work, and they are as vigorously defended.

fundamentally less rebellious and not so quick to take offense, heads straight for what she likes with a spontaneity that defies all ethics–

How can I banish what gives me pleasure?

This is where Arnolphe is wrong to confuse her with a *précieuse*. When she justifies herself for the last time to Arnolphe, she so calmly embodies instinct's defiance of all restraint, her ingenuousness is so redoubtable, that we have seldom dared to look this "disquieting" creature in the face. Her seductiveness is all the more scandalous in that it overcomes so easily and dispels from the outset the specters with which morality surrounds desire–danger, sin, and perdition. It is this obvious beauty, which the impulses of nature assume in her, and the very absence of perversity in desire that make the spiritual descendants of Arnolphe cry out against her perversity. She does not rebel against morality, she is unaware of its existence, and she demonstrates that it is useless.

What sets Molière apart is not so much his portrayal of instinct as all-powerful, but his willing acceptance of this omnipotence. That the commands of nature are not easily ignored is a traditional objection to moral idealism that in itself has no subversive meaning. To the extent that he believes that natural instinct governs life, Molière is no different from the *barbons* he ridicules. Far from denying the strength of temptation, Arnolphe and his kind are literally obsessed with it; "The flesh is weak" is their main axiom. But a sense of realism in ethics can just as easily lead to strictness as to laxity. It is this realism that can create a completely illusory semblance of harmony between a certain bourgeois wisdom and Molière's, as far apart from one another as mistrust is from sympathy. This sums up the whole question of Molière's "naturalism."

There is a kind of naturalism that exposes the omnipotence of evil in the recognized omnipotence of instinct, and believes that it is enough to demonstrate that man is subject to nature in order to degrade humanity. This attitude is a curious blend of an austere morality and a taste for scandal.

Already in the Middle Ages the criticism of courtly sublimations involves not only a wish to edify but also a cynical bias with respect to love and to women. The woman who is curious about love is the object of contemptuous satires in which a mocking tone and a hypersensitive morality are on a par with one another. In any case this attitude is very popular in anti-romance literature of the seventeenth century. The *barbons* are apt to appear cynical in their remarks; they pretend to see only adultery and debauchery everywhere they look. If they are strict with respect to instinct, their greatest pleasure lies in pointing out the havoc it plays in someone else's home. All of Arnolphe lies in this attitude. In the same way, Boileau's *Satire X* is nothing but a constant mixture of cynical jokes about marital fidelity and ultra-strict moral axioms. For him, as for Arnolphe, the honest woman knows nothing of love, and the world is full of cuckolds. It is not surprising that this poem provoked attacks from the defenders of *bel-amour*. It was as if the core doctrine of the *barbons* was suddenly introduced into great literature. But if polemics like that of Perrault and Pradon against *Satire X* aspire to avenge *galant* idealism for the assaults of a certain naturalism, Molière's work delineates a third position. Though his philosophy of nature exposes as illusory the moral pretensions of the romances, it remains free of any spirit of disparagement, of any peevish notion of good and evil.[70] It is accompanied by an impulse favorable to desire, and in that way gives us a glimpse not of a golden mean between the bourgeois spirit and *galanterie précieuse*, but rather of another attitude that goes beyond both.

[70] The idealist tradition in literature well-disposed to love was so strong that it was possible, without seeming ridiculous, to misunderstand Molière's meaning, or to pretend that one did not understand it. From the mere fact that he had portrayed the triumph of desire in Agnès without idealizing it, some of his enemies thought they could discern in his play an attempt to degrade woman and, as surprising as that might seem, to make Arnolphe speak for the author. See Donneau de Visé, *Zélinde*; Robinet, *Panégyrique de L'École des femmes*; see also the sentiment Molière has the *précieuse* Climène express, in the *Critique*, Scene 6.

As soon as one spells out the quality of Molière's naturalism he is forced to pose the question of his attitude to religion. One need not demonstrate that any lax morality poses a threat to Christianity. Compromises in this sphere are risky and presuppose a great many explicit precautions and accommodations in which Molière showed but little interest. Though his theater is not distinctly anti-Christian, either in intention or in fact, it does represent a current that after a long period of coexistence with the Christian tradition was finally to free itself from and combat that tradition. All the discussions on *Tartuffe,* whether or not they have been distorted by the fear of too openly sowing discord between Molière and religion, or by the obviously anachronistic hope of discovering a militant *philosophe* in him, do not alter this eloquent fact—the most diverse spokesmen of Christianity in the seventeenth century, whatever their character or that of their sect, believed *Tartuffe* was dangerous. One can go on forever discussing Molière's intentions, but the fact is that he brought together in common opposition to him Jesuits like Bourdaloue, Jansenists like Baillet, militant spies of the Compagnie du Saint-Sacrement, which was neither particularly Jesuit nor particularly Jansenist, and men like Bossuet and Lamoignon, who represented in its broadest form a rigorous Christianity. To be sure one must take into account the protests of Molière, who was not necessarily as aware as we are of the contrast between his morality and the precepts of Christianity. Even if there is a logical incompatibility between Molière's wisdom and the "foolishness of the cross," that is not to say that one must always be aware of this incompatibility. Logical inconsistencies often burst out into the open only much later, after a long period of incubation, during which incompatible elements can get along quite well together. The seventeenth century, and Molière with it, may very well not have seen clearly that the wisdom of *honnêtes gens* and the law of Christianity were hostile to one another. There was, however, a clear awareness of the dilemma at least among the more exacting Christians, who ruled out all compromise. And then, to appreciate the full implications of *Tartuffe,* one should be concerned not so much with Molière's intentions as with the role his work played in the history of popular feeling. From this point of view the vicissitudes of the text of *Tartuffe* and of its author's intentions lessen in importance when compared with the dispute raised by the work. This dispute seems much less the result of a misunderstanding than an episode in the gradual decline in prestige of Christian ethics from the Renaissance to the Encyclopedists.

Tartuffe was written at a time when the strength of the Christian veto had diminished but this disaffection had not yet been expressed in open philosophical boldness. One began by distinguishing superstition from religion before one called religion itself superstition. Sganarelle's "surly monk" and even the much more venerable tradition of the "boiling caldrons" of hell, with which Arnolphe still tries to terrorize his ward, began to seem ludicrous before dogma did. People laughed at all this gear, which was good for terrifying the ignorant, they laughed at these solemn tricks designed to frighten the foolish, at these already limp bolts of lightning in the hands of grumpy Jupiters of the old family Olympus. Perhaps they laughed at them without any thought of blasphemy in the back of their minds, and yet Molière's enemies thought it necessary to denounce as sacrilegious any encouragement given to that sort of laughter.[71] Laughter that strikes a blow at superstition has a disagreeable ring in the ears of the devout, even the most philosophic of them, whether they feel painfully the offense to any belief, even the crassest, in the supernatural, or whether they dread seeing faith identified with simplicity of mind, to which they do not like to confess their indebtedness. More than once the anathemas Christians hurled at Molière were inspired by this motive, which is tied to other more serious motives; the same laughter that strikes a blow at terrifying superstitions also at-

[71] For the protests stirred up by Arnolphe's sermon (*École des femmes,* III, 2), see Scene 5 of the *Critique.* Devout critics expressed the same indignation with respect to Sganarelle's absurd remonstrances to his master (*Don Juan,* III, 1; V, 2); see Rochemont's *Observations* on this play (1665) and the Preface to *Les Sentiments des pères de l'Église,* a posthumous work of the Prince of Conti.

tacks excesses of religious scrupulousness, and in a general way the whole strained and anti-natural side of religion. The facile philosophy of fashionable society was allied with the common sense of the people to ridicule prudishness, whether real or affected, penitent miens, and the aggressive zeal of the devout. When Dorine scolds Tartuffe in the language of a servant she provokes the laughter of the well-bred audience. Of course ridiculing a pious man who is shocked at a plunging neckline or who upbraids himself for having killed a flea while saying his prayers was not something entirely new, but the reactions aroused by Molière's plays suggest that satire of the bigot was beginning to assume a subversive character; it is because religion already felt itself threatened that it no longer enjoyed the joke. The time was not far off in which laughter would be philosophic naturalism's standard weapon against religion.

Whatever Molière's intention may have been, the portrait he drew of the "holy person" heralds at more than one point the ideas and the tone of the following century. It is not unusual for a work to go beyond the intentions of its author and to borrow from the whole historic unity of which it is a part an actual meaning that is more real than its intentional meaning. In several passages *Tartuffe* is a hundred years ahead of its times–

> The love that binds us to beauties that are eternal
> Does not snuff out in us the love of those that are
> temporal.[72]

This is Voltaire's thought and approach. How can we express surprise that the Christians of those times raised their voices in shrill protest at the portrait, which *philosophes* will trace again and again, of those ambitious and evil bigots

> Who know how to fit their zeal to their vices,
> Are hasty, vindictive, unfaithful, full of guile,
> And to ruin someone insolently cloak
> Spiteful resentment with the judgments of heaven;

[72] *Le Tartuffe,* III, 3.

All the more dangerous in their bitter wrath.
Because they turn against us weapons that are held
in reverence,
And because their passion, which people admire in them,
Sets out to slay us with a consecrated sword.[73]

These lines lost their virulence only when devotion had ceased to be a privileged means of plotting to dominate and to do harm.

Even if we do not assume that Molière wanted to attack some specific militantly devout group like the Compagnie du Saint-Sacrement, and if we make Tartuffe a more general type, the type of the devout man restless and greedy for domination, it is quite obvious that this type existed and that Molière's portrait reminded the audience of real people. Outside of the special cliques, the more or less secret societies that set themselves the task of spying on morals and governing the actions of the faithful, what was in a general way called the devout "*cabale*" designated a broader group, a fellowship of tendencies, of interests, and of behavior rather than a party properly so-called. "This character," writes the author of the *Lettre sur l'Imposteur* with respect to M. Loyal, "is an admirable clarification of the nature of the bigot and shows how there are some in every walk of life and that they are more closely bound together than honest folk because, being more covetous, they consider more carefully and know more clearly how they can be of use to one another when the opportunity arises, which is the essence of the *cabale*."[74] The *cabale* in this sense was neither Jesuit nor Jansenist. It was inspired by everything in Christianity that was capable of permitting censorship, persecution, and encroachment. In this mixture of zeal and self-interest, the rigors of Jansenism were allied with Jesuitical diplomacy. Tartuffe is in turn both strict and casuistic.

Today as then, the bigot is considered both a fanatic and a hypocrite. This dual stigma did not seem contradictory to the

[73] Ibid., I, 5.

[74] *Lettre sur la comédie de L'Imposteur* (Molière, éd. des Grands Écrivains, Vol. IV, p. 551.)

audience, which had no trouble at all imagining violent austerity and egoism in the same person. Only a false logic wil
raise the dilemma of sincerity and artifice. Molière undoubtedly believes in this distinction, but he himself destroys it by
instinctively denying true sincerity to anything immoderate
by identifying excess with deceit,[75] and finally by denouncing
in every case the right that the devout man arrogates to himself to admonish and govern his neighbor. Indeed it is when
pious zeal becomes indiscreet that one no longer distinguishes
between sincere fervor and hypocrisy. The "truly devout,"
those to whom Molière claims to pay homage, are those who
do not try to force themselves on others—

> They never boast of their virtue,
> One never sees in them that insufferable display,
> And their devotion is human, manageable.
> They do not find fault with our every act. . . .[76]

Tartuffe is a critic of other people's morals and he is considered a hypocrite to the extent that he interferes with the
lives of others. This is clearly the meaning of the family's
revolt, as it is expressed from the first act by the maidservant
Now undeniably it is not very edifying to accuse of every
vice someone who makes a business of censuring moral failings in others. From this point of view the whole story of
Tartuffe is clearly that of a skirmish between worldly philosophy and the Christian "moral order."

That Molière believed his play was compatible with true
religion, and that many of his contemporaries shared his
opinion, does not necessarily prove that there was nothing
subversive in *Tartuffe*; on the contrary it would tend to
prove that there was something subversive in everyone
The very existence of a "devout party," the efforts expended
in organizing the tyranny of dogma and of Christian morality
are an indisputable sign. The only justification for a "moral
order" is the threat of disorder. The alienation from religious

[75] See particularly in the same Scene 5 of Act I, Cléante's remarks, above all in line 339 ff.

[76] Same scene.

ethics had been growing for more than a century. The imminent revolt against Christian coercion was budding in society. The Church, alarmed at the quiet battle waged against it by culture, with its pleasures and its knowledge, was already reacting violently, without much success. It is significant that the *cabale* was a *cabale,* that it had to act in secret; the authorities opposed it. Louis XIV persistently defended the author of the *École des femmes, Don Juan,* and *Tartuffe* against his pious enemies. And not simply for extraneous reasons, because the pious had displeased the young king or censured his love affairs, but for deeper reasons, because the monarchy, especially in good times, was party to a broadening of life, at least in the upper classes. It is an authority that wants to be rich and makes its riches pour back over that part of society that surrounds it; it is an authority that wants to be comfortable in a certain sense and that, in its better aspects, tries to please in order to govern. The eighteenth century was to develop the idea of this enlightened monarchy that coordinates progress and natural developments as reason coordinates desires without opposing them. The ethics of reason, of reason in harmony with things, which is Molière's ethics, evolved in a parallel direction with the progress of the monarchy. Before being broadened into a doctrine of the state and the world, openly opposing the spirit of restraint and religion, it already existed at the time of Louis XIV under the more modest guise of a theory of personal and civic wisdom.

Molière's naturalism, then, consists less in exposing the presence of natural instinct under its idealized disguises, as Pascal or Nicole would do, than in exposing strictness itself (which is the conclusion of the analysis of Pascal and Nicole) as a disguise for aggressiveness and egoism. The irresistible power of nature engenders an irresistible indulgence that spreads, at least through laughter, to all forms of desire, even the least beautiful. Laughter envelops all in one and the same movement. The line of demarcation between the base and the sublime is obliterated, dispelling anxiety or scrupulousness, releasing a higher skepticism untouched by any shadow of sadness. This kind of skepticism is found again in a certain way of displaying one's "quality," whose prerogatives scarcely try to justify themselves, free of all illusions as to moral worth. They are the butt of a broad type of humor, tolerated by people of rank themselves, and in any case well-received by the audience at Versailles. For example, in the Prologue to *Amphitryon,* we have Mercury's answer to Night, who has scruples about serving the passions of Jupiter–

> Such a task is base
> Only among people of no account;
> When one is fortunate enough to be of noble station,
> Everything he does is always fine and good;
> And according to one's station,
> Things are called by different names.

Molière has a gift for the comical confrontation and the natural reconciliation of values that men sophistically keep in isolation from one another; and his greatness appears most luminous when his questioning of and disrespect for the established values go beyond, or seem to go beyond mere playfulness. It is this ring of freedom, this relaxed view, that place him among the great authors. Then the opposition of valet and master, and of maidservant and mistress, calls for secret acts of revenge that may not have been foreseen. The graft of Scapin, the deceit of Mascarille, the jealousy or cynicism of Gros-René or Alain, even the faint-heartedness of Sosie or of any bourgeois who trembles at the sight of a sword, no longer seem ignoble, but seem to be the freely acknowledged truth of human nature. All this unmasked humanity has its own poetry, as irresistible as truth, quick-moving, marvelous for destroying illusions and proprieties. The *honnête homme* needs to be completed and in some way dealt with ironically by the accompaniment of this more human counterpart, his valet; Dorine and her kind play the same role alongside of timid and proud young girls whom they teach, without circumlocution, the high roads of life and of the heart. It is not easy for the convention of feminine modesty to emerge unscathed from this confrontation with truth, coming from a lower social plane. Through the intervention of all these characters, unhindered instinct measures itself against *honnêteté* and raises doubts that the latter can withstand the attack. Everywhere amusement makes high station an object of derision, as in the Prologue to *Amphitryon,* where Jupiter's metamorphoses into animals in love inspire these truly admirable reflections in Mercury–

> Let fault-finders say what they will:
> Such transformations have a charm
> That goes beyond their understanding.
> This god knows what he is doing, here as well as elsewhere;
> And in the impulses of their tender ardor
> The beasts are not as foolish as we might think.

To leap without scruples from god to beast, the easy and leveling law of love, the dissolution of every hierarchy in the universe, the boundless playfulness of a desire free of all anguish, the ready mingling of values, such lessons of wisdom, which spring from every line of Molière's text, are more than mere banter. In the society for which he wrote they are the sign of an indisputable moral freedom.

The skepticism of the aristocrats of the court, however, has another side. Its daring was accompanied by the habit of obeying, of conforming with what is too hastily called necessity. The philosophy of pleasure led by its easygoing ways to the acceptance of the established order. At that time, and for a long time after, up to the Revolution and beyond, there was a widely accepted political axiom to the effect that privation is the price of freedom and docility the price of pleasure. Maxims of this type inherited from antiquity had been confirmed by the experience of a magnificent despotism. The same laughter that in Molière promoted pleasure is the enemy of all emancipatory idealism and is just as apt to play the game of prejudice as that of progress. In Molière's plays, common sense is often only the sense of conformity to the prevailing customs–

> We must always adapt ourselves to the majority
> And never draw attention to ourselves.
> . . . I hold that it is wrong, for whatever reason,
> To obstinately shun what everyone else accepts,
> And that it is better to be among the many foolish
> Than to see oneself on the side of wisdom alone
> against all.[77]

Far from being an instrument of subversion, reason itself is often only a resignation to a kind of natural necessity that mocks us and our pretensions. The joking in the *Femmes savantes* on the laws of equilibrium, the knowledge of which does not prevent us from falling, reveals for all its beauty a general tendency to place the force of facts–or translated into human terms, the force of habits and customs–above conscience. Together with idealism, the restless quest for a better morality is condemned. Molière, conforming to the prejudices that governed society in spite of everything, admits that a bourgeois is forever a bourgeois, a woman forever a woman. Everything else is fancy, a proper butt of a humor in tune with tradition. We need not say what use has been made of this conservative skepticism for a hundred years, distorting its nature, making it bourgeois, and inordinately magnifying its importance in Molière's work as a whole. "It is not generally through humor that we are misled," writes Saint-Marc Girardin with respect to *George Dandin;* "sentimentality corrupts us more than mirth, even when mirth strays from morality. . . . Since sophism has insinuated itself into emotion I mistrust tears more than laughter."[78] Here Molière is used against Rousseau, and justifiably, since Rousseau repeatedly stressed the differences between himself and Molière. The antithesis of laughter and sentiment, in which in this instance we can easily recognize the opposition of conform-

[77] *L'École des maris,* I, 1.

[78] Saint-Marc Girardin, *Cours de littérature dramatique,* Vol. V, Chapter XXXIII.

ism and revolt, accounts for the basic point of the polemics provoked by the *Misanthrope,* which was disputed at greater length and with more passion than any of Molière's other comedies, with the exception of *Tartuffe.* With good reason *Tartuffe* and the *Misanthrope* can pass for the two pillars on which Molière's works rest. If one defines his genius as a mixture of daring and conformity, these two plays are at the poles of his theater. Even more, *Tartuffe* marks the point at which freedom to live comes into open conflict with religious tradition, and the *Misanthrope* marks the point at which prudence turns into docility. Naturally the sharpest disagreements have occurred around these two extreme positions.

Alceste embodies and refutes a reforming idealism, which Molière portrayed in him in the most uncomplimentary way by connecting it with an unbalanced temperament, at once importunate and easily offended, selfish and unhappy, confused and yet violent. It is a fact that every revolt presupposes a profound failure to adjust to the state of things, and that every failure to adjust to reality, since it is connected with some painful dissatisfaction, must, with inevitable troubles and weaknesses, pay the price of its intellectual fruitfulness. Society, such as it is constituted in any period, is so crushing a weight that it is difficult to tip the scales against it. In a sense the best-balanced man is the one who by himself unhesitatingly takes a place in the ordering of the existing society, however inhuman it might be. The grip of a social system is so strong that it must cease to exist before it can become the object of a quiet condemnation. If we go into the psychology of individuals and not merely the comparison of values, nine times out of ten we find restlessness at the root of rebellion, and restlessness always has its liabilities—emotional impediments, unreasonable aggressiveness, and poor self-control. But if these people, who in certain respects are prevented from living a normal life by their sensitivity, their dissatisfaction, or their pride, are not pulverized by the social dynamo, they often discern its vices more clearly than others, detest and denounce them more strongly, and are able to make their own weakness a strength for mankind, so that their peculiar imbalance becomes the basis of a new general equilibrium. Obviously this is not the point of view of conservative philosophy, which spends its time turning to good advantage the coincidences it establishes between defects of character and the spirit of revolt. One must certainly acknowledge that in the case of Alceste, Molière proceeded in just this way.

Nothing can be added to or altered in Rousseau's famous criticism of the *Misanthrope* in his *Lettre à d'Alembert.* It is quite true that while giving his character the speech of ideal virtue, Molière made him inordinately sensitive to his personal troubles, confused in the application of his principles, and absurdly violent in trifling affairs. He changed a general dispute, from which society could have emerged in a sad state, into a closed debate in which only the individual concerned bears the brunt of ridicule. "The misanthrope and the hot-headed man," said Rousseau, "are two different characters; this was the occasion to distinguish between them." Molière thoroughly confused the virtuous misanthrope, who according to Rousseau was to convict society of infamy, with the weak and hot-headed man whose temperament simply makes him inferior to social life. "It is not that man is not always man," admits Rousseau, who himself—and with more fairness and penetration than is usually acknowledged—describes the often deplorable emotional circumstances of even virtuous misanthropy. But all in all it is a question of emphasis, and the problem is whether we are to lay stress on the value of general aspirations or on the presence of inner conflicts. Rousseau saw clearly that Molière put the seeming misanthrope into perspective by exposing the secret misanthrope and his weaknesses. The way in which he fashioned his Alceste is by itself an actual argument against exacting and reforming virtue.[79]

The moral illness of Alceste and the character defects that

[79] It is difficult to understand why those who congratulated Molière on his moderate and conformist notion of virtue dispute the validity of Rousseau's criticisms and claim that he did not understand Molière. He understood him very well indeed, but as a result of having fought him. One can reproach Rousseau for his ethical system but not for his lack of acumen.

are the root of his passion for virtue appear most clearly in his amorous behavior. Here again love is the mirror of all of life. Alceste fits into the category of moralizing, jealous men, of whom Molière's theater contains so many portrayals. The scenes that set him in conflict with Célimène are reminiscent up to a certain point of those in which a coquette scoffs at a ludicrous stuffy old man. Right from the first scene the misanthrope sees himself compared by Philinte to Sganarelle in the *École des maris,* to whom one could liken him in his refusal to follow custom, his nostalgia for the past, his hatred of *bel-esprit,* and finally his rude and offensive jealousy. Unaware of the least precautions of *galanterie,* he makes an audience that is accustomed to the attentions and the surrenders of *bel-amour* laugh in spite of himself—

> Yes, I wish that no one would find you lovable,
> That you were reduced to an abject state,
> That heaven, at birth, had given you nothing,
> That you had neither station, nor birth, nor wealth,
> So that the splendid sacrifice of my heart
> Could make amends for such injustices,
> And that I might have the joy and the glory this day
> Of seeing you receive everything from my love.[80]

This language is very close to that of Arnolphe. But the deep truth of Alceste, as selfish as he is, lies in his weakness, in the childish sincerity of his grief. He is a tyrant completely without weapons, defeated before he starts, and we would search in vain for the least trace of that self-sufficiency in him that is so deep-rooted in the *barbons.* Consequently, while the *barbons* tranquilly represent conservative principles, while they constantly preach the maintenance of traditional restraints, Alceste brandishes the subversive demand for justice and truth like the habitual and avenging weapon of the weak. But if his uprightness and his weakness make him likable, that uprightness nonetheless suffers in our eyes for being nothing more than the cure and the complement of his weakness. He did not choose Célimène by chance; anxious to move and

[80] *Le Misanthrope,* IV, 3.

to capture a heart, and secretly convinced that he could not succeed in doing so, he chose precisely the woman best suited to make him conscious of his failure and to justify the moralizing anger by which he tries to compensate for his failure. This psychological device, at once touching and ineffectual, is exactly the same one that guides him in his social life. Ill-prepared to withstand the struggle for life, weak, fretful, too just and not just enough, he purposely seeks out mortifying situations in order to feed his anger and his nostalgia for goodness—

> Twenty thousand francs it will cost me,
> But for twenty thousand francs I will have the right
> to curse
> The iniquity of human nature
> And to nourish an undying hatred of it.[81]

Molière made a point of highlighting everything in Alceste that could minimize the justice of his revolt by making him ridiculous. His puerile and confused egocentrism, his constant withdrawal into sulkiness, his desire for loneliness which ill-conceals the pain of being too much alone, his immoderate speech which betrays more spite than virtue, the constant explosions of his wrath which discredit him even when he is in the right—all these things make Alceste very much the entertaining character Molière's contemporaries saw in him.[82]

It is hard to imagine a more absurd interpretation of the *Misanthrope* than the Romantic interpretation, according to which Alceste's torments, in themselves sublime, were conceived as such by Molière.[83] This interpretation has been attacked so often that it is useless to go into the discussion in

[81] Ibid., V, 1.

[82] See Visé, *Lettre écrite sur la comédie du Misanthrope* (1667).

[83] It is important to note that this is not at all the interpretation of Rousseau, who undoubtedly admired an ideal misanthrope, but accused Molière of having misunderstood and made a caricature of this imaginary figure in Alceste. Rousseau perhaps originates certain Romantic ideas but he does not attribute them to Molière. On the contrary (and very legitimately from his point of view) he includes Molière among those worldly philosophers he abhors.

detail: Alceste, obviously, was a rude and extravagant figure, touching in his misfortunes and his sincerity but always laughable in his excesses and in his failures. If we remember that Alceste is the enemy of all that exists, that he is in revolt against human nature and social necessity, in short that he has taken up arms against the way things are, we will understand to what point he can contradict Molière's usual philosophy. If the word naturalism fits this philosophy it is because it expresses the superiority of the all-powerful *fact* of human pretension. Molière's whole morality consists in knowing how to yield to a certain number of facts. For him the force of custom defies justice as much as the force of desire defies propriety. It is in this sense that he is amoral. Faguet, observing that Molière "substituted the ethics of ridicule for the ethics of honor,"[84] simply discerns in him the supremacy of fact over law, whose universal weapon is laughter. The same author is right to speak of the effect achieved by Molière as "demoralizing," in the literal sense of the word; at the very least he reduced morality to the most unobtrusive accompaniment of life possible. Flexibility in morals is as it were a tribute that well-being pays to the order of things, which it makes good use of, and on the social plane to the reigning powers, to whom it must adapt itself in order to be happy.

It is difficult indeed to separate Molière's ethics from the conditions of life at court, and more broadly, from monarchical society. All through the *Misanthrope* the contrast between Alceste and the court is pronounced—

> Heaven, when it gave me life, never gave me
> A soul compatible with the atmosphere of the court;
> I do not find in myself any of the necessary virtues
> To make out well and accomplish my ends there.
> My greatest talent is being frank and sincere;
> I do not know at all how to trick men as I speak to them;
> And one who does not have the gift of concealing
>   what he thinks
> Should spend very little time there.[85]

[84] E. Faguet, *En lisant Molière,* p. 137.
[85] *Le Misanthrope,* III, 5.

Alceste belongs to another age, an age in which the servitude and pliability of the court at Versailles did not yet exist. He speaks the language of the old times, of the old freedom; he curses the reign of pleasure, of ease, and of submissiveness.

Discussions on the spirit of the court are not unusual in the *ancien régime,* even before Versailles. And the corruption of the court is always held to be something new, which one implicitly contrasts with the rude and straightforward virtue of times gone by. For example, Balzac says in his *Discours sur la Gloire,* "It is only too true that this wretched self-interest . . . is now the God of the court, and the object and end of the courtier." To blame the maxims of selfishness and pliability in this period was invariably to question the movement of high society toward material ease and moral submissiveness. The court was merely the most striking symbol of a new state of affairs; it was there above all that the aristocracy, which had as a rule been entrusted with the old virtues, learned to enjoy themselves and to obey. To condemn the brilliant amorality of the court was to go against the times, to cling to a past that was simpler and freer than the present.[86] That is why Alceste seems to be in constant conflict with his times rather than with humanity in general; that is why Philinte, in order to convert him, thinks it necessary to condemn

> That great inflexibility of the virtues of olden times.[87]

Eliante herself, who judges him favorably, sees him as a sort of Don Quixote, a belated knight-errant in the midst of moderns.[88]

[86] Alceste's taste in literature, his aversion for scintillating poetry and *bel-esprit,* are only one aspect, rich in comic effects, of his opposition to the ruling customs and the spirit of fashionable society.

[87] *Le Misanthrope,* I, 1. In this scene, which defines the terms of the debate at the same time that it initiates the action, it is constantly a question of a difference in periods (the "vices of the times," the "customs of the present," "our age," etc.)

[88] Ibid., IV, 1.

The opposition to the court betrays a more profound though perhaps less conscious opposition to despotism. To yield to the customs of the times and to yield to force were all the same. Philinte is undoubtedly preaching conformism in very broad terms–

> One must bow to the times without obstinacy,
> And it is a foolishness second to none
> To make it one's business to change the world.[89]

But the theater of the monarchical period offers us, in more than one place, analogous passages on the inanity of all resistance to the force of events, invested with a more explicit political significance–

> Then let us not examine the justice of causes,
> Let us yield to the torrent that sweeps everything along,

says King Ptolémée in the *Mort de Pompée* as he prepares to sacrifice his guest to the victorious César.[90] Putting the philosophy of nature still more clearly at the service of the amoral politics of despotism, Voltaire's César will preach to Brutus a meek and submissive philosophy that, allowing for differences in tone and situation, is in essence no different from that of Philinte–

> Change the way you feel, I implore you.
> Do not force your soul to overcome nature.[91]

The drama of Alceste, then, is not simply that of a character pitted against the world; the misanthrope with pretensions to virtue is the enemy of docile and shrewd morals, and those morals are both the result and the support of absolute power.

Victor Cousin, denying the legend that made the Duc de Montausier the model for Alceste, cites the fact that Montausier was a convinced absolutist. Although he does not ex-

[89] Ibid., I, 1.
[90] *Pompée,* I, 1.
[91] Voltaire, *La mort de César,* III, 4.

plain too clearly why Cousin rightfully seems to think that this position is incompatible with Alceste's temperament.[92] The profound meaning of Alceste in the history of French society is attested to by the interest devoted to him under the *ancien régime* by some moralists especially wont to tie moral discussions to political discussions. It is not by chance that Fénelon, an aristocratic enemy of despotism, and another champion of the old times and frugal ways, took Alceste's side against Molière.[93] The controversy sketched out in the *Misanthrope* was to go on for more than a hundred years. The opposition of these two attitudes, one of which could be defined by its preference for a life of ease and submission, and the other by a spirit of justice with a nostalgia for a simple way of life, filled the *ancien régime* to the very end. In this conflict each of the adversaries has its prestige, each its flaws–docility on one side, aversion for progress on the other. Alceste was already the caricature of the second side, as seen by a man belonging to the first. This spontaneous portrayal is of even greater value for having preceded the explicit discussions of the following century. If it was possible for Rousseau to avenge Alceste more successfully than Fénelon had done, it was because the denunciation of the court and of the regime it symbolized had in Rousseau's times acquired a new social significance. It had ceased to be simply the expression of the ill-humor of some noblemen in the face of innovations. Nostalgia for the past and the maxims of simple life, acquiring a broader sweep, expressed the hopes of all those who felt they were victims of the "train of events." In defending Molière's cranky gentleman, Rousseau was defending his own completely plebeian revolt against society; and the French Revolution staged Alceste's rehabilitation against Philinte.[94] In addition to its permanent value, to which we can amply testify three hundred years later, the symbol Molière created was endowed on the historical plane with such

[92] V. Cousin, *La Société française d'après le Grand Cyrus,* Ch. IX.

[93] Fénelon, *Lettre à l'Académie,* VII.

[94] In the *Suite du Misanthrope,* of Fabre d'Énglantine (1790).

meaningful force that it accompanied to the very end the society from which it had sprung.

If one seeks to define, in all the wealth of Molière's work, the essence of his moral attitude, he is repeatedly struck by the contrast between a widening of the human range toward pleasure and optimism, and a concomitant narrowing of ambitions, the effect of a skeptical complacency before events. These traits are found not only in Molière but in his times and in the following century. They define the final form of the civilization of the *ancien régime*. And the two contrasting terms find their common denominator in their acquiescence to an irresistible order; the natural law of pleasure and the rule of social adaptation have the same sovereign authority, and it is enough to accept both at the same time to discover the equilibrium of wisdom. The original thought of that whole period was to view as compatible, indeed inseparable, a full flowering of the human being according to nature and the spirit of acquiescence to social norms.

The dispute over man's greatness and wretchedness that constantly asserts itself in Corneille, Pascal, and even Racine here receives its calmest and at the same time its most evasive solution, that which consists in avoiding man's wretchedness by disavowing his ambition to greatness, by reducing it at least to a game in which all anguish melts away. The misgivings man feels as a result of his limitations is considered an evil to cure or to contemplate, and not a sign of nobility. The very idea of nobility or of baseness tends to melt away in the leveling of all things, and the concern with *values* loses everything won by the sense of conformity to reality. Nobility now lies only in the most tasteful harmony of man with his station. All poetry, all success, all value, reside in this harmony. The anxious obsession with fate that is at the root of all idealistic affirmations of heroism vanishes in the idea of a concordance of desire and of things, in which things are perhaps less demanding but above all where desire is less strained. What is left of poetic prestige in this accord is the only remnant of heroic grandeur, adapted to a new use. It is an indefinable something that denies wretchedness even as it recognizes it, an easygoing charm that has taken the place of the *élan* of glorious conquest.

The characteristic feature of this idea is that by granting man everything he can desire (since his condition is no longer considered humiliating) it forces him to renounce the belief that he is of greater value than anything else in the universe, that he is more than a fact, or a nature like others. The paths that lead in that direction, to that emancipation of life in the leveling of values, broadened still further in the eighteenth century, in the course of which they finally led to a vast and varied panorama of humanity. This is not the place to define the progress of this form of thought nor to try to understand how it finally destroyed the order in which it originated. What cannot be disputed is that in Molière we already find its two essential qualities–the boldness of rehabilitated natural desire and the skeptical disintegration of conscience.

Reflections on Classical Humanism

The study of the thought of a past age has real meaning and value only in relation to the present and the future. It might seem strange to find this statement at the end of a work that has tried to explain ideas of the past through transitory social conditions that have since been forgotten. But how can one possibly think that ideas have meaning only in this historical relationship? The condition of society, along with the psychology of the human groups that compose it, determine the formation and the direction of currents of moral thought; but this is so only because society first needs thought, or in other words because social man needs to conduct himself by something much broader than his immediate interests. Consequently social psychology is always more than a psychology. In this field a way of living and feeling is always a way of thinking, and of thinking about values. Social man by definition is an ideologist, because every society is necessarily an organization, and a debatable organization that lives only by justifying itself. It follows that ideas cannot be simply reflections of social conditions. To reduce ideas to this rather worthless function is at the same time to make them inexplicable and to strip them of all interest. Ideas are the effective means by which a group orients thought in the direction of its needs and ultimately guides the behavior of its members. The relation of thought to life was once perfectly expressed by a word used to designate ideas by their active element, by the element in them that justifies and animates a certain behavior. The word "maxims" accurately conveyed the useful, tendential aspect and at the same time the pretension to universality proper to all moral thought. One could say that any system of ideas is a set of maxims whose origin, and even destination, is illuminated by social conditions.

Yet we cannot be satisfied with this statement. It is of the utmost importance that the suggestions of the social environment be offered in the form of general imperatives whose expression goes far beyond the cause that provoked them. It is important that what arises from a passing state of affairs professes to be the expression of an eternal need. In every idea there is a transposition of this order. One could argue that this is a hoax, and make this hoax the very definition of the spiritual life, if the creations of the mind did not in turn go beyond the social system in which they originated. Social man is searching for norms superior to his individual existence, and doubtless a social class or society as a whole (that is to say, in the last resort, the ruling class) inspires his quest and directs it to its own ends. But man's faculty of forming general ideas on life and the good, and of legislating on values, has a double meaning. As valuable as it is to society, by definition it claims to function above society and calls society before its tribunal. Most often, certainly, this is to justify it, with the result that the powers of reality continue to dominate those of thought to which they surrender only an illusory superiority. But this does not prevent man from being able to imagine more justice, happiness, truth, and greatness than he has before his eyes. These fancies correspond to needs that are undoubtedly eminently social, but which are also agents that transform real society and that can, when circumstances are propitious, support new social forces and overthrow the established order. As a matter of fact, every ethical system is an attempt at compromise between social necessity and less limited yearnings, between the values that the state of society approves and others, more undisputed although more unreal, which support them while transcending them. How would it be possible to stress this divergence instead of hiding it, to expose the hypocrisy of the prevailing morality—an attitude so frequently adopted and so favorable to progress—if there were not at all times a divorce between what man can conceive and that to which he adapts himself?

That is what makes it so difficult to speak of creations of the mind without passing judgment on them, to set them in the social landscape in which they originated and developed, without at the same time evoking a desire greater than that which animated them but was unable to free itself from them entirely for lack of a real, yet sufficiently broad, horizon. Thus some old values, checked as soon as they were conceived, worn out by time or by failure, may after a long eclipse yield an unexpected legacy, come to life again and grow under more propitious circumstances. The interest we feel for the history of thought almost always springs from the desire to make some new use of it, and this desire is the very expression of the perfectibility of mankind.

If today we still consider the classical centuries great, it is because in those centuries a moral philosophy developed that gave humanity a true sense of its own value. Modern humanism first based itself on the authority of the traditions of antiquity and claimed to find in the Greeks and Romans already perfected models of its own ideal. Nonetheless it had its own roots in the modern European world. It would be unfair to disregard at the very heart of the Middle Ages the perennial presence of a certain understanding and a certain cult of the human. Classical humanism never really lost the memory of chivalry. Furthermore, as it developed it soon revealed its completely modern character. Under the dress of antiquity there appeared a new power, nourished by widespread progress in life and in social relations that owed nothing to the heritage of antiquity.

The development of this modern humanism, with all the daring it called for in the conquest of lucidity and happiness, ultimately endangered the sum of traditional ideas and beliefs according to which European society continued to live. To be sure this humanism, understood as an overturning of values and of moral life, reached its highest point on the eve of the Revolution. But the eighteenth century simply carries on a work that was undertaken before it, and to which, in spite of superficial appearances, its predecessor contributed no small share. It would be wrong to allow ourselves to be deceived by the reacquisition, indeed the reinforcement of the power of the Church and the monarchy in the course of this century. Without even approaching it from the side that makes it the clear harbinger of the following century, without searching in the last decades of the Great Century for the first open affirmations of the critical spirit, of disrespect and moral naturalism, and limiting ourselves to viewing it in its own period of originality, where the arguments stay within prescribed limits, we will see that even kept within the limits of pure ethics, this century is an important stage in the conquest of the human. Heroism, *galanterie,* beauty, *honnêteté,* or pleasure in that century originate in nature, owe their charm to nature, and transmit their value to nature. It is clearly a mistake to contrast this century with the following one as if they were enemies, the one building on the ruins of the other. From one point of view, Descartes, Corneille, Molière, Voltaire, Diderot, and even Rousseau belong to the same lineage. It is only after the French Revolution, in a period in which the main concern is to arm oneself against new dangers of subversion, that people applied themselves to contrasting the two centuries. One had to dishonor everything that had inspired the Revolution without repudiating altogether a humanistic tradition that was inseparable from monarchic civilization itself. Under the influence of this need they ended up attributing an exaggerated importance to the differences that separated the reign of Louis XIV from those following. The Encyclopedists would have been quite astonished if they had been told that they were essentially different from the *honnêtes gens* of the preceding century. They thought they were more enlightened, more open to truth and to humanity, but of the same breed. In the nineteenth century Taine was the only one to assert the continuity of the classical and the encyclopedic spirit, and he did so with hostile intent. And what is more, his motives are very questionable. It is not so much the cult of abstract reason that links these two centuries, as he claims; rather it is the value that they both attribute, on the whole, to the quality of man, to the balance of lucidity and instinct; it is the way in which both combine the beautiful and the natural, with which they outline the character and the needs of an authentic humanity. Nevertheless, it became a literary postulate that an absolutely new era began with the *Lettres persanes.* With some subordinate views obscuring the general unity of the historical direction, the two centuries finally stood opposing one another like two contrary symbols, one the symbol of order and discipline, the other the symbol of subversion and utopia. The chief victim of this distortion was obviously the earlier of the two centuries, in which only those principles opposed to man remained visible. We have seen in several places at what cost this was done, considering the false judgments passed on its greatest writers.

In reality the *grand siècle* evidenced a general strengthening of certain properly human moral values which, considering the limitations and the precautions the period imposes, acquired permanent rights of citizenship. Jansenism itself, taken in its broadest sense as an intensification of Christian rigor, merely underscored, by a short-lived reaction, the triumph of a new climate that was well-disposed to natural man and henceforth inseparable from the moral civilization of France. In a sense one might say that Christian pessimism itself was assimilated by humanism. The seventeenth century had a certain lucid way of scrutinizing the defects of nature and a serene acceptance of the least flattering view of man that owe more to philosophy than to religion. Anguish and loathing play less of a role in this period than a thirst for truth, pride in attaining it even at our own expense, and concern for an unpretentious wisdom.[1]

In the preceding century everything had been challenged, in a confused seething of innovations, of violence, and of varied crises. Under Louis XIII and Louis XIV, everything is meditated upon and stabilized; there is a clearer awareness of both aspirations and obstacles. The opposition is defined, daring sets its own limits, prudence becomes the law and as it were the natural style of humanism. But the seventeenth century, by the very sobriety of its thought, by its predilection for debates on pure ethics, both limited in their content and

[1] Seen from this angle, La Rochefoucauld is following in Montaigne's footsteps much more than going along with Port-Royal. In this connection see, in the *Lettres de M. le Chevalier de Méré,* 1682 (in–12°, Vol. I, pp. 83–91) the letter to Madame la Duchesse de X . . . , on a conversation he had with La Rochefoucauld. See also Maxim 182.

universal in their application, makes it possible to grasp with uncommon clarity the nature of that humanistic ethics that characterizes a long period before and after it in the history of thought.

Since every moral system gravitates around the two ideas of pleasure and greatness, a study of the French seventeenth century reveals that the moral orders elaborated continuously from the Renaissance to the Revolution can be defined by three interrelated elements–the triumph of pleasure, the toning-down of the contradiction between the pleasant and the great, and the reconciliation of the idea of greatness with humanity. This was clearly the work of the three great centuries. First of all they weakened the guilt feelings attached to the satisfaction of desires, and more generally man's loathing for his nature. Voltaire asks Pascal, "Why do you make us repulsive to ourselves?" But what Voltaire says openly, without fear of running counter to a formidable tradition, is to be found in a vague way in the thought of almost all of the secular seventeenth century, and it permeates the life and works of the period. The primacy attributed to pleasure as the criterion of the beautiful is only the form, transposed on the esthetic plane, of a moral philosophy whose ultimate law is gratification, contentment, and honor paid to nature. It is not by chance, then, that Christian antinaturalism repeats its anathemas against all dramatic literature, and even poetry. The fact is that all poetry and theater of the period are filled with the charm of nature, of pleasure, and of glory. The hardening of the Christian position that we so frequently observe in the seventeenth century (Jansenism is the most drastic form) failed to make people see as sinful that all-powerful pleasure, which remains the most important characteristic of the beautiful in ethics as in poetry, and which is the law of heroes, of *honnêtes gens,* and of poets.

This fundamental rehabilitation of human desire made it possible to respond in a different way to death and misfortune and to conceive, as a result, a steadier and more serene idea of greatness. The dilemma of pleasure and greatness tended to disappear. There is nothing more striking about the seventeenth century than the constant fusion of greatness and pleasure, of that which exalts and that which beguiles. Not that the contrast of the two terms did not persist; their perfect reconciliation could only be conceived as a border-line notion, more consonant with the condition of the gods than that of men. But the tendency is beyond question. The whole of seventeenth-century literature could be characterized by it. Its notion of the hero never presupposes the crushing of instinct, the deadly silence of nature. Everything we said about Corneille amounts to saying that in his works heroism is all one with a yearning for life. There is no possibility that in the quest for greatness the hero will be mesmerized by death, feel its attractiveness or vertigo, experience hatred or disgust for life. This possibility is ignored, cast into the shade, or more precisely dissolved in the impulse of the ego toward glory. Furthermore, if it is true that one perceives the courtier at the hero's side, if one imagines separately nobility and enjoyment, valor and relaxation, they are nonetheless fused as often as they are separate. From *Le Cid* to *Nicomède,* to *La Princesse d'Élide,* even to *Amphitryon,* there is never an absolute contradiction nor an explicit denial. Not to be aware of this hidden kinship is to be deaf to the fundamental tonality of the age. Nowhere, not even in Corneille, who nonetheless went as far as possible in the direction of the difficult and the rare —nowhere does greatness rule out a certain ease[2] that is the mark of the wellborn. The whole concept of the sublime in Corneille, as we have tried to demonstrate, rests ultimately on what is sublime in human nature. And in the mind of the

[2] That for some years now this word has been used only in a pejorative sense is overwhelming evidence that the future will not hesitate to use against us. Nothing could be more certain, as remote as this may seem. *Facilité,* or ease, is mistakenly confused with cowardice and condemned along with it. One thus avoids the main question, which relates to the end, not the means; improvement of the human condition can only consist in the difficult conquest of greater *facilités* in every sense of the word. For a thousand reasons our age prefers to repeat incessantly the pompous defense of its helplessness, transformed with great difficulty into its glory.

seventeenth century as a whole, lofty wisdom and natural wisdom are almost always blended, as are magnanimity and happiness, despite the fact that one may predominate in the works of Descartes and Corneille, and the other in the works of Méré and Molière. On a wider plane, in the following century the philosophy of pleasure and civic morality will blend as often as they conflict with one another. It is this blending of the two moral principles, pleasure and greatness (which every form of barbarism and wretchedness tends to oppose) that was in the France of old the true mark of a lofty civilization.[3]

The blend of pleasure and greatness could not exist if greatness and humanity were not joined together. Less repulsed by his nature, when he experiences its failings he thinks he will be able to find the remedy as he finds the ill. The attenuation of human weakness, the triumph over death, that victory that is always at the heart of the idea of greatness, no longer seems to him to depend on a power outside of him, on a providence in relation to which he is nothing. Instead of denying himself in order to escape from his wretchedness, he relies on himself, tends to imagine nothing greater than his own nature, to which he gives back, since it originated there, the very desire he still feels to transcend it. Once the interdict that broods over nature is lifted, the sense of greatness rejoins the sense of the human. The vogue of stoic ethics from the beginning of modern times; the enduring fortune of this morality in the seventeenth century, interpreted as an ethics of purely human greatness, and its open conflict with religion; the broadening of the idea of ethical beauty in the following century, in which the human being is the source and the end of all enthusiasms–these are the signs and the stages of that

[3] This is the source of extreme difficulty to those who claim to base a doctrine of pure reaction on the intellectual traditions of early France. If we wish to look closely, these apologists are reduced to admiring the social relations of this period more than the works of its writers or, in these works, principally that which may betray social relations. From their viewpoint an authentic anthology of the seventeenth century would be an anthology of dedicatory epistles.

return of greatness to its true source that is the accomplishment of the classical centuries and the ultimate reason for their prestige. Whether we like it or not, that natural strength, that clarity, and that permanent value of the figures they traced and the thoughts they conceived are all due to the fact that they gave mankind back to itself.

One could not overemphasize the fact that this re-evaluation of human potential coincided with a general progress in the material order. Man appreciates his own worth from the time he sees that he is able to make inroads against poverty. He tends to forget, along with his material distress, the humiliating ethics by which he condemned life, making a virtue of necessity. The first rudiments of a humanist ethics are already developing in the Middle Ages among the richest court circles in moments of peace and relative prosperity. The growth and the triumph of these seeds was possible in the modern age only through the vast progress achieved in human industry, riches, and enjoyment. The awareness of a fuller and easier life and the natural rejection of anguish closely and almost consciously accompany the thought of the great centuries. Poverty, on the contrary, leaves the mind no other refuge but humility, the repudiation of nature. If one does not accept this, how can he avoid the temptation and the vertigo of violence, which is the only means of satisfying oneself when everything is scarce, and a satisfaction itself for want of anything better? For one who wishes to assert his greatness, there is no other way out of poverty and wretchedness than force and dominion. Human glory thus conceived, the poetry of the sword, were sustained by too powerful a tradition not to have left a vivid impression on the thought of the modern age. We have pointed out more than once these reminiscences, very vivid in the notion of the hero or the great soul, still perceptible in the idea of pleasure, which is very often hard to distinguish from *bon plaisir*. But the prestige of power declined even more in thought than in custom with the lessening of widespread poverty. Consequently glory, becoming more humane, seeking the least unfeeling and also the least disquieting way out, chose to assume an attitude of generous concession, of benevolence, and of justice. Corneille's heroes, though completely permeated with a fierce pride, know how to be magnanimous and just; these are even their supreme virtues. The ideas of nobility in love, of justice, or of clemency, are almost inseparable from glory as Corneille sees it, as brutal as that glory may be in other respects. And there where greatness tends to give way to pleasure, in poetry, entertainments, comedy, or even in the happy moments in tragedy, what is left of majesty derives from a semblance of benevolence, both noble and easygoing, that is inseparable from the expression of happiness. We cannot read a stanza of *galante* poetry of that period, one of Molière's *divertissements,* or a final scene from Corneille, without experiencing this peculiar tonality. To the extent that life became less difficult, barbarous self-assertion gave way to the general reestablishment of the dignity of man. Satisfaction, reclaiming the prestige that had been usurped by violence, suggested the idea of a mankind reconciled with itself and rediscovering its worth in each of its members. The disparagement of brutality, by changing the notion of greatness, makes greatness coincide with respect for human nature, in other words with justice. The very name humanity indicates not only the dignity of man but also the view that disposes one to respect this dignity wherever it is found.

Such teachings, passed on when the paths of happiness and knowledge were beginning to open up before man, have lost none of their value in an age like ours, in which the very meaning of the human is endangered at the same time that the paths of progress are blocked, in which the narrowing of life breeds a contempt for man and a worship of nothingness. The *grand siècle,* too often admired or opposed merely for its powers of restraint, gives early witness to a notion of civilized man that has continued to gain strength and breadth ever since. Our age would try in vain to reject it. A future that is perhaps closer than we think will have the task of rescuing and deepening it still further.

Index